Discover The Joy of Painting™

with

Bob Ross

by Annette Kowalski

WEBER
martin

The Artist's
MAGAZINE

JOY OF PAINTING: The Collection

TO THE ARTIST

In truth, there are absolutely no good reasons why you shouldn't begin painting. Many people imagine there are strict barriers to overcome before becoming an artist, but they soon *discover* that "The Joy of Painting" removes every obstacle. They say painting is hard, I say "wet-on-wet" to that.

"They say" mixing colors properly is very difficult and can stop a beginner from proceeding with a favorite painting. This is not true! With the Bob Ross Wet-On-Wet Technique™ there is no painstaking measuring and mixing of paint portions on the palette. Your brush or knife does all the blending on the canvas which is the real key to beautiful paintings.

"They say" you need quite a few tools to paint landscapes, including mahl stick, sketching instrument, ruler, or even a large variety of brushes and colors. However, some of the most fantastic paintings I've ever seen have been completed with just one brush and three oil colors. The special technique I use in this book allows you to do so much with just a little.

"They say" it takes too long before you get to the truly enjoyable part of painting, that you must plan your course of action first before the brush meets the canvas. With the wet-on-wet method you begin making decisions and expressing your creativity on canvas immediately on the first day, while learning important lessons too.

Through the years I have found that painting is many things to many people. It can be a tough uphill battle, or it can be easy, fun and fulfilling for the artist. "I say" everyone should experience the joy of painting.

This book is specially designed to help you get started without delay. Begin by carefully reading the introduction section and studying the basic how-to photographs and try to become familiar with the equipment, its use and care. Understand the paints and mediums and what to expect from each.

Read through the instructions of your painting before beginning to paint to develop a preconceived understanding of the steps involved to complete the project. Study the photos to familiarize yourself with the various techniques in each painting.

These paintings are presented to you as guides and ideas. As you become familiar with the technique and its tools, make your own changes and create individual masterpieces. In a very short period of time you will be amazed at the amount of progress you have made since your first painting.

Happy Painting,

1994

To the world's devoted Bob Ross certified instructors,
may you continue to experience the special joy of teaching others
that Bob has blessed you with.

INTRODUCTION

There are no great mysteries to painting. You need only the desire, a few basic techniques and a little practice. If you are new to this technique, I strongly suggest that you read the entire Introduction prior to starting your first painting. Devote some time to studying the instructions, looking carefully at the "how-to" pictures and at the finished paintings. Use each painting as a learning experience, add your own ideas, and your confidence as well as your ability will increase at an unbelievable rate. For the more advanced painter, the progressional "how-to" photographs may be sufficient to paint the picture.

PAINTS

This fantastic technique of painting is dependent upon a special firm oil paint for the base colors. Colors that are used primarily for highlights (Yellows) are manufactured to a thinner consistency for easier mixing and application. All of the paintings in this book were painted with the Bob Ross Paint Products. The use of proper equipment helps assure the best possible results.

The Bob Ross technique is a wet-on-wet method, so normally our first step is to make the canvas wet. For this, apply a thin, even coat of one of the special base paints (Liquid White, Liquid Black or Liquid Clear) using the 2" brush. Long horizontal and vertical strokes, assure an even distribution of paint. The Liquid White/Black/Clear allows us to actually blend and mix colors right on the canvas rather than working ourselves to death on the palette.

The Liquid White/Black/Clear can also be used to thin other colors for application over thicker paints much like odorless thinner or Copal Medium. The idea that a thin paint will stick to a thick paint is the basis for this entire technique. This principle is one of our Golden Rules and should be remembered at all times. The best examples of this rule are the beautiful highlights on trees and bushes. Your Liquid White/Black/Clear is a smooth, slow-drying paint which should always be mixed thoroughly before using.

Liquid Clear is a particularly exciting ingredient for wet-on-wet painting. Like Liquid White/Black, it creates the necessary smooth and slippery surface. Additionally, Liquid Clear has the advantage of not diluting the intensity of other colors especially the darks which are so important in painting seascapes. Remember to apply Liquid Clear *very* sparingly! The tendency is to apply larger amounts than necessary because it is so difficult to see.

Should your Liquid White/Black/Clear become thickened, thin it with Ross Odorless Thinner (not turpentine or other substances).

I have used only 13 colors to paint the pictures in this book. With these 13 colors the number of new colors you can make is almost limitless. By using a limited number of colors, you will quickly learn the characteristics of each color and how to use it more effectively. This also helps keep your initial cost as low as possible. The colors we use are:

*Alizarin Crimson	*Sap Green
Bright Red	*Phthalo (Phthalocyanine) Blue
*Dark Sienna	*Phthalo (Phthalocyanine) Green
Cadmium Yellow	Titanium White
*Indian Yellow	*Van Dyke Brown
*Midnight Black	Yellow Ochre
*Prussian Blue	

(*Indicates transparent or semi-transparent colors, which may be used as underpaints where transparence is required.)

MIXING COLORS

The mixing of colors can be one of the most rewarding and fun parts of painting, but may also be one of the most feared procedures. Devote some time to mixing various color combinations and become familiar with the basic color mixtures. Study the colors in nature and practice duplicating the colors you see around you each day. Within a very short time you will be so comfortable mixing colors that you will look forward to each painting as a new challenge.

Avoid overmixing your paints and strive more for a marbled appearance. This will help keep your colors "alive" and "vibrant." I try to brush mix a lot of the colors, sometimes loading several layers of color in a single brush. This double and triple loading of brushes creates effects you could never achieve by mixing color on the palette. Pay very close attention to the way colors are loaded into the brushes or onto the knife.

THE PAINTER'S GLOVE

To solve the problem of removing paint from hands after completing a painting project, try using a liquid hand protector called THE PAINTER'S GLOVE, which I developed. This conditioning lotion is applied to the hands *before* you begin painting. Then, simply wash with warm, soapy water.

PALETTE

To me, my palette is one of the most important pieces of equipment I own. I spent a lot of time designing the palette I use, making it both functional and comfortable. It is large enough to provide ample working space for the large brushes and knives, yet lightweight. I recommend that your palette be made from a smooth, nonporous material such as clear acrylic plastic. Avoid wooden palettes which have not been varnished, or fiberboard or paper palettes. Wood palettes are rarely smooth and, unless well sealed, will absorb the oil from your paint as will fiberboard and paper. These types of palettes can cause your paint to become dry and chalky causing numerous problems. My palette is clear, so it will not distort color, is extremely smooth for easy brush or knife loading, and the plastic will not absorb oil and is easy to clean.

Form the habit of placing your paints in the same location

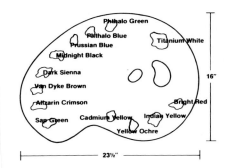

on your palette each time you paint. You can spend an unbelievable amount of time looking for a color on an unorganized palette. The illustration gives the dimensions and color layout of my palette as used on the TV series.

Unused colors may be saved for several days if covered with plastic wrap or foil; for longer periods, cover and freeze. To clean your palette, scrape off excess paint and wipe clean with the thinner. Do not allow paint to dry on your palette. A smooth, clean surface is much easier to work on.

BRUSHES

The brushes you use should be of the finest quality available. Several of the brushes I paint with look very similar to housepainting brushes, but are specifically designed for this method of painting. They are manufactured from all-natural bristles and come in four basic shapes: 2", 1", 1" round and 1" oval. Be careful not to confuse natural bristle with manmade bristles such as nylon, polyester or other synthetic bristles. AVOID WASHING THE BRUSHES IN SOAP AND WATER. Clean your brushes with odorless thinner.

The four large brushes will normally be your most used pieces of equipment. They are used to apply the Liquid White/Black/Clear, paint clouds, skies, water, mountains, trees, bushes and numerous other effects with surprising detail. The 2" brush is small enough that it will create all the effects the 1" brush is used for, yet large enough to cover large areas very rapidly. Another member of the large-brush family is the 1" round brush. This brush will create numerous fantastic effects such as clouds, foothills, trees and bushes. Using several of each brush, one for dark colors and one for light colors, will save you brush-washing time and lessen the amount of paint used.

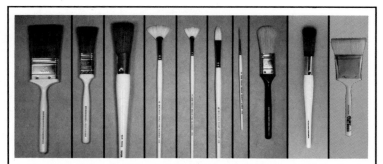

Left to right: 2" Brush, 1" Brush, 1" Round Brush, #6 Fan Brush, #3 Fan Brush, #6 Filbert Brush, Liner Brush, 1" Oval Brush, Half-Sized Round Brush, and 2" Blender Brush.

A #6 Filbert Bristle Brush is used mostly for the seascapes and can also be used for tree trunks and other small detail work. The 1" Oval Brush is primarily used for making evergreen trees and foothills and for highlighting trees and bushes. The small Half-Sized Round Brush will create beautifully shaped trees, bushes and foliage.

Two other brushes that I use a great deal are the #6 and #3 bristle fan brushes. Your fan brush may be used to make clouds, mountains, tree trunks, foothills, boats, soft grassy areas and many other beautiful effects. Devote some practice time to these brushes and you will not believe the effects you can achieve.

A #2 script liner brush is used for painting fine detail. This brush has long bristles so it holds a large volume of paint. Normally, the paint is thinned to a water consistency with a thin oil (such as linseed or Copal oil) or odorless thinner. Turn the brush in the thin paint to load it and bring the bristles to a fine point. This brush is also used to complete one of the most important parts of the painting, your signature.

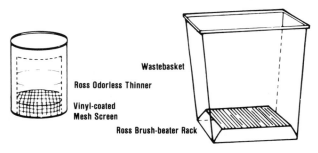

Wastebasket

Ross Odorless Thinner

Vinyl-coated Mesh Screen

Ross Brush-beater Rack

The 2" Blender Brush makes it possible now, as never before, to achieve all of those soft, delicate, subtle areas so often found in landscapes and seascapes: skies with soft, wispy clouds, the misty areas at the base of mountains, background trees and waterfalls. In seascapes, the 2" Blender is especially effective for blending the transparency or "eye" of the large wave.

CLEANING THE BRUSHES

Cleaning the brushes can be one of the most fun parts of painting. It's an excellent way to take out your hostilities and frustrations without doing any damage. I use an old coffee can that has a ¼" mesh screen in the bottom. The screen stands about 1" high and the Ross Odorless Thinner is approximately ¾" above that. To clean your brush, scrub the bristles firmly against the mesh screen to remove the paint. (Be sure to use a screen with vinyl coating to avoid damage to your brush bristles.) Shake out the excess thinner then beat the bristles firmly against a solid object to dry the brush. Learn to contain this procedure or you will notice your popularity declining at a very rapid rate. One of the simplest and most effective ways of cleaning and drying your brushes is illustrated below (left).

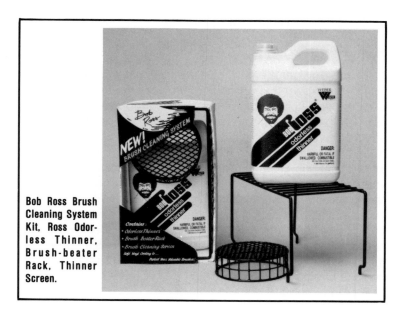

Bob Ross Brush Cleaning System Kit, Ross Odorless Thinner, Brush-beater Rack, Thinner Screen.

The brush is shaken inside the wastebasket to remove excess thinner, then the bristles are firmly beaten against the Ross Brush-beater Rack. (The rack size is 10¾" L x 5¼"W x 5¾"H.)

Odorless thinner never wears out. Allow it to settle for a few days, then reuse. Smaller brushes are cleaned with the thinner and wiped dry on a paper towel or rag.

After cleaning, your brushes can be treated and preserved with THE PAINTER'S GLOVE lotion before storing. Take care of your brushes and they will serve you for many years.

PALETTE KNIFE

The palette knives I use are very different from traditional painting knives. They are larger and firmer. Practice is required to make these knives into close friends, so spend some time learning to create different effects.

I use two different knives, a large one as well as a smaller knife. The smaller knife is excellent for areas that are difficult to paint with the standard-size knife. The knives have straight edges, so loading is very easy and simple.

The palette knives are used to make mountains, trees, fences, rocks, stones, paths, buildings, etc. Entire paintings can be done by using only knives. The more you use the knives the more your confidence will increase and very soon you will not believe the many effects you can create.

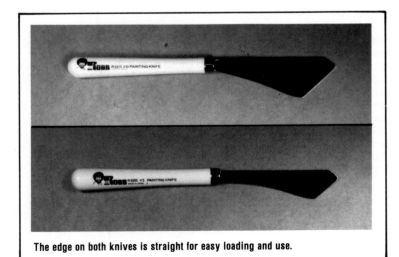

The edge on both knives is straight for easy loading and use.

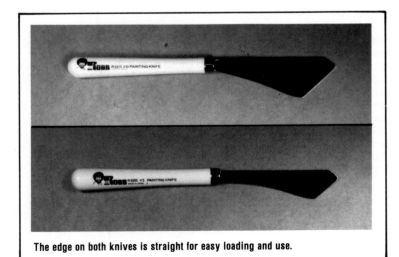

GESSO CANVAS PRIMERS

Available in White, Black and Gray colors, gesso is a flat acrylic liquid primer used in a variety of projects requiring a dry pre-coated canvas. This water-based paint should be applied very thinly with a foam applicator (NOT A BRUSH) and allowed to dry completely before starting your painting. Clean the foam applicator with water.

EASEL

A sturdy easel that securely holds the canvas is very important when painting with large brushes. I made the easel I use for mounting on a platform ladder. Any type of step ladder also works well for this type of easel.

CANVAS

The canvas you paint on is also very important. You need a good quality canvas that will not absorb your Liquid White/Black/Clear and leave you with a dry surface.

For this reason, I do not recommend canvas boards or single-primed canvases. I use only very smooth, pre-stretched, double-primed, canvases that are covered with a Gray primer. (The Gray-primed canvas allows you to see at a glance if your Liquid White is properly applied.) You may prefer a canvas with a little tooth, particularly when your painting involves a great deal of work with the knife. Whether the canvas is ultra-smooth or has a little tooth is a matter of individual choice.

All of my original paintings in this book and on the TV series were painted on 18" x 24" canvases. The size of your paintings is totally up to you.

Basic "How To" Photographs: Learn and master these procedures as they are used repeatedly to complete the paintings.

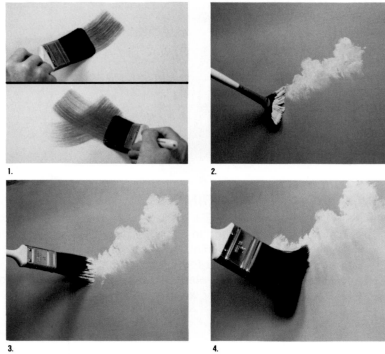

1.

6.

7.

3.

4.

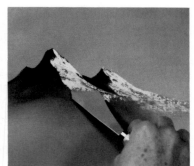

8.

9.

SKIES

Load the 2" brush with a very small amount of paint, tapping the bristles firmly against the palette to ensure an even distribution of paint throughout the bristles. Use criss-cross strokes to begin painting the sky, starting at the top of the canvas and working down towards the horizon. (Photo 1.) Add cloud shapes by making tiny, circular strokes with the fan brush (Photo 2) the 1" brush (Photo 3) or you can use the 2" brush, the 1" round brush or the oval brush. Blend the base of the clouds with circular strokes using just the top corner of a clean, dry 2" brush. (Photo 4.)

MOUNTAINS

Load the long edge of the knife with a small roll of paint and use firm pressure to shape just the top edge of the mountain. (Photo 6.) Remove the excess paint with a clean knife (Photo 7) and then use the 2" brush to pull the paint down, completing the entire mountain shape. (Photo 8.) With a small roll of paint on the long edge of the knife, apply highlights and shadows (paying close attention to angles) using so little pressure that the paint "breaks." (Photo 9.) Use a clean, very dry 2" brush to tap and diffuse the base of the mountain, creating the illusion of mist. (Photo 10.)

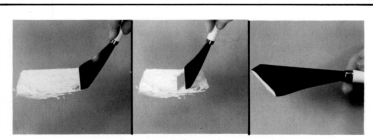

5. Pull the paint out flat on your palette—then cut across to load the long edge of the knife with a small roll of paint.

10.

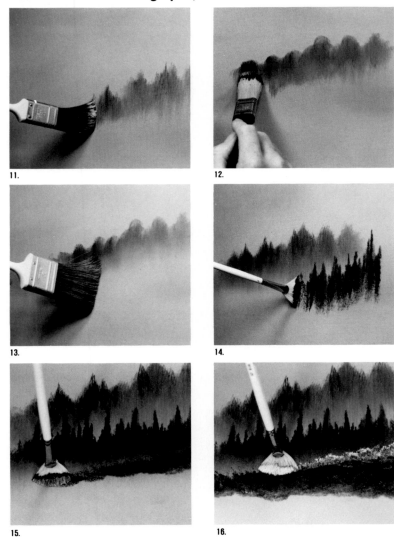

11.

12.

13.

14.

15.

16.

FOOTHILLS
Foothills are made by holding the 1" brush vertically (Photo 11) or the oval brush (Photo 12) and tapping downward. Use just the top corner of the 2" brush to firmly tap the base of the hills, to create the illusion of mist. (Photo 13.) Indicate tiny evergreens by tapping downward with the fan brush. (Photo 14.) The grassy area at the base of the hills is added with the fan brush (Photo 15) and then highlighted, forcing the bristles to bend upward. (Photo 16.)

17.

18.

19.

REFLECTIONS
Use the 2" brush to pull the color straight down (Photo 17) and then lightly brush across to give the reflections a watery appearance. Load the long edge of the knife with a small roll of Liquid White (Photo 18) and then use firm pressure to cut-in the water lines. (Photo 19.) Make sure the lines are perfectly straight, you don't want the water to run off the canvas.

20.

21.

WATERFALLS
Use single, uninterrupted strokes with the fan brush to pull the water over the falls (Photo 20) then use push-up strokes to "bubble" the water at the base of the falls. (Photo 21.)

22. 23.

24. 25.

26. 27.

28. 29.

30. 31.

32. 33.

LEAF TREES AND BUSHES
Pull the 1″ brush in one direction through the paint mixture (Photo 22) to round one corner.
(Photo 23.) With the rounded corner up, force the bristles to bend upward (Photo 24) to shape
small trees and bushes. (Photo 25.) You can also just tap downward with the 2″ brush (Photo
26) or the round brush. (Photo 27.)

HIGHLIGHTING LEAF TREES AND BUSHES
Load the 1″ brush to round one corner. (Photo 28.) With the rounded corner up, lightly touch
the canvas, forcing the bristles to bend upward. (Photo 29.) You can also tap to highlight
using the corner of the 1″ brush or 2″ brush (Photo 30) the round brush (Photo 31) or the oval
brush. (Photo 32.) Use just the point of the knife to scratch in tiny trunks, sticks and twigs.
(Photo 33.)

34.   35.   36.

37.   38.   39.

EVERGREENS

"Wiggle" both sides of the 1″ brush through the paint mixture (Photo 34) to bring the bristles to a chiseled edge. (Photo 35.) Starting at the top of the tree, use more pressure as you near the base, allowing the branches to become larger. (Photo 36.) You can also make evergreens using just one corner of the fan brush (Photo 37) or the oval brush (Photo 38.) The trunk is added with the knife. (Photo 39.)

40.   41.   42.

LARGE EVERGREEN TREES

Hold the fan brush vertically and tap downward to create the "fuzzy" bark (Photo 40.) Use thinned paint on the liner brush to add the limbs and branches then push up with just the corner of the fan brush (Photo 41) to add the foliage (Photo 42.)

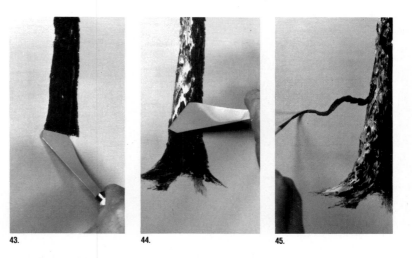

43.   44.   45.

LARGE TREE TRUNKS

Load the long edge of the knife with paint and starting at the top of the tree, just pull down. (Photo 43.) Apply highlights, using so little pressure that the paint "breaks." (Photo 44.) With a very thin paint on the liner brush, add the limbs and branches. (Photo 45.)

MOUNTAIN WATERFALL

A high mountain overlooks a beautiful little waterfall. An excellent painting to allow you to practice with all the tools.

MATERIALS

2″ Brush	Cadmium Yellow
1″ Brush	Bright Red
Large Knife	Prussian Blue
Liquid White	Sap Green
18 × 24 Canvas	Phthalo Blue
#6 Fan Brush	Phthalo Green
#2 Script Liner Brush	Titanium White
Alizarin Crimson	Van Dyke Brown
Dark Sienna	

Cover the entire canvas with a thin, even coat of Liquid White using the 2″ brush. Work the paint back and forth, up and down, in long horizontal and vertical strokes to cover the canvas evenly. Do not allow the Liquid White to dry before you begin.

SKY AND WATER

The large brush loaded with Phthalo Blue and Van Dyke Brown is used to make the sky. Work all the way across the top of the canvas, using criss-cross strokes completing the sky in downward layers. Without cleaning the brush, add more Phthalo Blue and a little Phthalo Green to create the water. With the brush flat, pull toward the center in horizontal strokes, leaving an area open for the reflection. You can use Alizarin Crimson on the large brush to create pink highlights in the sky and water if desired. Hypnotize the entire canvas and blend to your satisfaction.

MOUNTAINS

The base color of the mountain is a mixture of Prussian Blue, Van Dyke Brown and Alizarin Crimson. With a roll of paint on the edge of the knife, lay in your basic mountain shape using a very firm pressure. Use the knife to scrape off all excess paint then blend downward with the large brush. The highlights are Titanium White with a touch of Bright Red applied with the knife. Load a small roll of paint on the long edge of the knife and lay in your highlights using as little pressure as possible, allowing the paint to break. Pay very close attention to the angles in your highlights and think where light would strike. The shadows are Titanium White and Prussian Blue applied the same way in the opposite direction. Hold the large brush vertically and gently tap the bottom of the mountain to create mist. Use the brush flat and pull upward to remove the tap marks and blend.

Foothills are made with the 2″ brush loaded with Prussian Blue, Van Dyke Brown and Sap Green. Hold the brush horizontally and tap downward on the canvas. Leave an area of mist between the mountains and foothills to create distance. A short, gentle upward stroke with a clean brush will give the impression of distant trees. Complete the most distant foothills first and allow them to get darker in color as they get closer. With the large brush held horizontally, pull just the very bottom of the foothills down to create reflections. Light, horizontal strokes will give the reflections a watery look. Use Liquid White on the edge of the knife to cut in your waterlines. Distant trees are made with the fan brush loaded with Prussian Blue, Van Dyke Brown and Sap Green. Hold the brush vertically and tap downward.

WATERFALL

Load Prussian Blue and Van Dyke Brown on the large brush and pull straight down where you want the waterfall to be. Cover the entire bottom of the canvas, under the waterfall, with the same color. With the fan brush loaded with Liquid White and Titanium White, paint the highlights in the waterfall. Hold the brush horizontally, making a short horizontal stroke then straight down. Start with the most distant part of the waterfall and work forward. You will need to wipe or clean your brush between each stroke. The foam under the waterfall and in the stream is made with Liquid White and Titanium White on the fan brush. Hold the brush horizontally, push into the canvas moving slightly upward. The foam is created by the bristles bending upward and touching the canvas.

CLIFFS AND ROCKS

The basic shapes are made with a roll of Van Dyke Brown on the long edge of the knife. Your cliffs should be higher than the waterfall. Highlights on the cliffs and rocks are a mixture of Van Dyke Brown, Burnt Umber and Cadmium Yellow applied with the knife using very little pressure. Allow the paint to break and pay particular attention to angles to create the needed effects. Keep the shadows on the rocks very dark, using just a touch of Van Dyke Brown and Titanium White.

TREES AND BUSHES

The 2½" brush loaded with Van Dyke Brown, Burnt Umber and Sap Green is used to make the basic tree and bush shapes. Load the brush so one corner is rounded, place the rounded corner up and push slightly upward. Trunks are Van Dyke Brown loaded on the knife and pulled sideways. Highlight the trunks with Van Dyke Brown, Titanium White and a touch of Prussian Blue. Highlights on the trees and bushes are varying mixtures of Magic White, Cadmium Yellow, Sap Green and Permanent Red. Load the 1" brush to round one corner and with the rounded corner up, lay in your highlights.

FINISHING TOUCHES

Sticks and twigs may be cut in with the point of the knife. Small trees and limbs are made with the liner brush filled with Van Dyke Brown thinned with a light oil. A clean fan brush can be used to pull roots over the edge of the cliffs. Your masterpiece should now be completed and ready for a signature.

1. The basic mountain shape is made with the knife.

2. Tap the bottom of the mountain with the large brush to create mist.

3. Foothills are made with the 2" brush.

4. Completed foothills.

5. Indications of evergreens are made with the fan brush.

6. Larger evergreens are made with the fan brush.

7. Pull downward with the large brush to create reflections.

8. Background completed.

9. Laying in the base color for the waterfall.

10. Waterfall base completed.

11. Start with a short horizontal stroke, using the fan brush . . .

. . . then pull straight down to make the waterfall.

12. Completed waterfall.

13. A roll of paint is used . . .

. . . to make and highlight cliffs and rocks.

14. Loading the 1" brush . . .

. . . to make and highlight trees and bushes.

AUTUMN DAYS

MATERIALS

2" Brush
1" Brush
Painting Knife
Liquid White
18 x 24 Canvas
#6 Fan Brush
#2 Script Liner Brush
Black Gesso
Alizarin Crimson
Dark Sienna

Cadmium Yellow
Indian Yellow
Bright Red
Prussian Blue
Phthalo Blue
Phthalo Green
Sap Green
Titanium White
Van Dyke Brown
Yellow Ochre

Start with a canvas that has been painted with Black Gesso and allow to dry completely. Using the 2" brush, cover some areas of the canvas with Alizarin Crimson; without cleaning the brush repeat with Phthalo Blue and then Prussian Blue. Make sure the entire canvas is covered with a thin layer of paint, using long horizontal and vertical strokes to blend. Do not allow the paint to dry before you begin.

SKY

To make the sky, use Liquid White on the 2" brush and begin by making criss-cross strokes at the horizon, working all the way across the canvas and upward in layers. The sky should automatically get darker as you near the top of the canvas. With a clean, dry 2" brush, blend the entire sky area.

BACKGROUND

The basic shapes for the background trees and bushes are made by loading the 2" brush with Alizarin Crimson, Sap Green, Dark Sienna and Van Dyke Brown. This mixture should be quite dark and just brush mixed. Holding the brush vertically, and always tapping towards the center of the tree, lay in the trees and bushes along the horizon. Highlight the background trees and bushes by just tapping with one corner of the 2" brush using various mixtures of Sap Green, Indian Yellow, Cadmium Yellow, Yellow Ochre, and Bright Red. Using the same highlight colors

and the 2" brush held horizontally, tap in the grassy areas. Pay close attention to the lay of the land as you work forward in the painting.

Background tree trunks are made using the liner brush and Van Dyke Brown which has been thinned with paint thinner.

WATER

Use Liquid White on the 2" brush to make the water in this painting. Use firm pressure, holding the brush horizontally, pull in the water with long vertical strokes. Gently brush across with a clean, dry 2" brush.

The land area around the water is laid in with Van Dyke Brown loaded on the long edge of the knife. Highlight these banks with a mixture of Yellow Ochre, Bright Red and Dark Sienna, using the knife with so little pressure that the paint is allowed to "break".

The grassy areas around the water's edge are made with the fan brush using mixtures of Sap Green, Yellow Ochre, Indian Yellow and Cadmium Yellow. Holding the brush horizontally, push it straight into the canvas, causing the bristles to bend. Again, be sure to follow the lay of the land.

The water lines are cut in using Liquid White with a little Phthalo Blue and Van Dyke Brown loaded on the long edge of the knife. Be sure these lines are perfectly straight, parallel with the bottom edge of the canvas.

LARGE TREES

Mix a small amount of Black using equal amounts of Phthalo Green and Alizarin Crimson. Load the fan brush with this mixture and holding it vertically, touch the canvas and pull in long tree trunks. The tree branches are also made with the fan brush. Highlight the tree trunks by loading the fan brush with Titanium White and Yellow Ochre. Using the brush vertically, just tap along the side of the tree trunk where the light would strike. The leaves are made with the 2" brush using various mixtures of all the Yellows. Still using the large brush, tap in grass at the base of these trees.

FINISHING TOUCHES

Using the point of the knife, cut in additional sticks and twigs. With the liner brush and paint that has been thinned to the consistency of water, sign your painting.

Autumn Days

1. Use criss-cross strokes to make the sky.

2. Sky completed.

3. The 2" brush is used . . .

4. . . . to paint the background trees.

5. Highlights are applied with the corner of the large brush.

6. Sticks and twigs made with the liner brush.

7. With the 2" brush . . .

8. . . . lay in the soft, grassy areas . . .

9. . . . paying particular attention to angles.

Autumn Days

10. Top corner of the large brush used to highlight trees.

11. Reflections are made with the 2" brush.

12. Land areas are layed in with the knife.

13. Push upward with the fan brush to make grass.

14. Cut in waterlines with the edge of the knife.

15. The fan brush is used to make . . .

16. . . . and high-light the large tree trunks.

17. Use the corner of the large brush . . .

18. . . . to paint leaves on the trees.

19. Sign your painting with the liner brush.

EVERGREENS AT SUNSET

MATERIALS

2" Brush	Titanium White
#6 Fan Brush	Midnight Black
#3 Fan Brush	Alizarin Crimson
Liner Brush	Sap Green
18 x 24 Canvas	Cadmium Yellow
Flat Yellow Acrylic	Indian Yellow
Liquid Black	Bright Red

Cover the canvas with a flat Yellow acrylic (water base) paint and allow to dry completely.

Make the sun in this painting by cutting a 4" circle from adhesive-backed paper (masking tape works very well). Adhere the sun to the canvas, over the dry, Yellow paint, before you begin.

Note that the entire painting is done on a dry canvas.

SKY

Using Liquid Black on the 2" brush, paint some dark diagonal areas into the sky portion of the dry canvas, pulling some of the dark paint across the taped sun. With a clean, dry brush, add some Alizarin Crimson to the sky, allowing it to mix and blend with the Liquid Black. Without cleaning the brush, add some Indian Yellow into the sky and then some Cadmium Yellow into the area nearest the sun. With the same brush, go into a little Titanium White and add a few highlights and clouds. Now, blend the entire sky with gently horizontal strokes.

When the sky has been blended to your satisfaction, use the point of the knife and peel the taped sun from the sky. With a clean, dry fan brush begin pulling a little of the sky colors across the sun—just to soften the harsh edges. Be very careful not to lose your entire sun. Blend, ever so lightly.

DISTANT TREES

Load the fan brush with Midnight Black, hold the brush vertically and tap downward to indicate the distant trees. Use a clean dry 2" brush and firmly tap the base of the trees to create a misty effect. While the color from these trees is still in the 2" brush, begin pulling in the "lay-of-the-land" and lifting upward with short strokes for a grassy effect. Be careful not to cover the entire canvas, allowing the small patches of light to show through.

Larger more distinct trees are made with the fan brush loaded with Midnight Black. Hold the brush vertically, go straight into the canvas and just touch to create a center line. Begin making the top branches using just the corner of the fan brush and pushing upward. As you work down the tree use a larger area of the brush and more pressure creating larger branches. At this time you can also push in a few grassy areas at the base of the trees using the same brush and paint.

Using the 2" brush, blend out the base of these trees and grassy areas using scrubbing and lifting strokes, again creating the "lay-of-the-land". Work in layers, still allowing the canvas to create the light areas.

FOREGROUND TREES

The large trees are made by filling the fan brush with Midnight Black, touching the canvas and firmly tapping downward. This motion will give the bark a very rough appearance. Still using the fan brush and the Midnight Black paint, pull in the ground area at the base of the trees.

Limbs and branches are made with Liquid Black which has been thinned, using the liner brush.

For leaves on the large trees, load the #3 fan brush with Midnight Black, go straight into the canvas bending the bristles upward. Without cleaning the brush, add some Sap Green and use the same technique to highlight the leaves and foreground.

FINISHING TOUCHES

Use the liner brush to pull up some long grasses, sticks and twigs.

Sign your painting, then stand back and experience the Joy of Painting!

Evergreens at Sunset

1. Use tape to make a circle on a dry canvas.

2. With the 2" brush . . .

3. . . . and Liquid Black . . .

4. . . . paint in the dark areas of the sky.

5. Titanium White, on the large brush . . .

6. . . . is used to create highlights in the sky.

7. Remove the tape . . .

8. . . . to expose the basic sun shape.

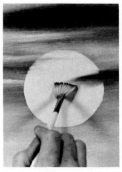

9. Use the fan brush to bring clouds over the sun . . .

10. . . . and to soften any harsh edges.

11. The indication of distant trees made with the fan brush.

Evergreens at Sunset

12. Tap the bottom of the trees with the 2" brush . . .

13. . . . to create the soft, grassy areas.

14. Push upward with the fan brush to make evergreens.

15. Work in layers, completing the most distant areas first.

16. Tap firmly with the fan brush . . .

17. . . . to make the large evergreen trunks.

18. Use the liner brush with a thin paint . . .

19. . . . to make tree limbs on the large evergreens.

20. Push upward with the fan brush to make leaves.

21. The liner brush, with a thin paint, is used to sign the painting.

BOB ROSS OIL COLORS

1.25 fl. oz.

GREY WINTER

MATERIALS

2" Brush	18 x 24 Canvas
1" Brush	Liquid White
1" Round Brush	Titanium White
#6 Fan Brush	Midnight Black
#2 Script Liner Brush	Alizarin Crimson
Large Knife	

Start by covering the entire canvas with a thin, even coat of Liquid White, using the 2" brush. Use long horizontal and vertical strokes, working back and forth to assure an even distribution of paint on the canvas. Do not allow the Liquid White to dry before you begin.

SKY

Load the 2" brush with a little Alizarin Crimson, tapping the brush firmly against the palette for an even distribution of paint throughout the bristles.

Begin by making Pink criss-cross strokes in the lower, right portion of just the sky area. Without cleaning the brush, add some Midnight Black. Cover the remainder of the sky with circular cloud shapes. With a clean, dry brush, blend the entire sky using circular and criss-cross strokes. The Black will mix with the Liquid White and automatically become several different shades of Grey. Add Midnight Black to the brush and just lay in some dark shadow color across the base of the canvas.

Clouds are made using Titanium White on the 1" round brush. Move the brush through the sky using small circular motions.

Use the top corner of a clean, dry 2" brush to blend out the base of the cloud shapes. Gently lift and fluff. Blend the entire sky.

BACKGROUND

Small hills in the background are made by loading the round brush with a mixture of Midnight Black and Titanium White. Tap the brush to the canvas and pull downward to create hill shapes. Mist the bottom of the hills by tapping with a clean, dry 2" brush and lightly lift upward. The second range of hills is made darker by adding more Midnight Black to the round brush. Again use the 2" brush to tap, mist and lift upward.

Load the fan brush with Titanium White and begin laying snow on the ground at the base of the distant hills. Carefully watch your angles—this is where you can create the "lay-of-the-land".

Larger trees and bushes are made using the round brush and Midnight Black. Simply tap in tree shapes. Again, use Titanium White on the fan brush to form the contours of the ground, pulling some of the dark tree color to create shadows and valleys.

Complete the background in layers, finishing one area before moving forward.

The large evergreen is made using the 2" brush with Midnight Black and a small amount of Titanium White. Pull both sides of the brush through the paint to form a chisel edge. Touch the canvas to create a center line and then begin making branches by using just one corner of the brush. As you work down the tree, more pressure on the brush will cause the lower branches to get larger. Continue adding little bush and grassy areas with the 2" brush. Load the edge of the knife with Midnight Black and just lay in a trunk indication. Highlight the tree with a little Titanium White on the fan brush.

The water is made by pulling down some dark color using the 2" brush. With a clean, dry brush, again pull down and gently brush across. With a mixture of Liquid White and Titanium White on the fan brush, lay in some snow-covered edges around the water. Use a small roll of Liquid White on the long edge of the knife to cut in the water lines.

FOREGROUND

The large evergreen in the foreground is made using the 2" brush loaded with Midnight Black. The tree trunk is

Midnight Black loaded on the long edge of the knife. Highlight the trunk using a mixture of Midnight Black and Titanium White. Highlight the tree with the 2″ brush and Titanium White.

Pull the 2″ brush through the Midnight Black paint in one direction to round one corner. With the rounded corner up, push in some bush shapes and ground area at the base of the large foreground tree. Highlights are made using the 1″ brush and a mixture of Liquid White and Titanium White. Turn the brush horizontally to create grassy areas. Use the large brush and Titanium White to lay in land areas.

FINISHING TOUCHES

Cut in sticks and twigs with the point of the knife. Now, sign your completed work of art!

Grey Winter

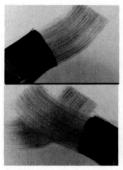

1. Use criss-cross strokes to paint the sky.

2. With the top corner of the 2″ brush . . .

3. . . . swirl in very basic cloud shape, then blend with a clean brush.

4. Highlights for clouds are applied with the round brush . . .

5. . . . then blended with the top corner of the 2″ brush in small circular strokes.

6. Lift upward with a large circular stroke . . .

7. . . . then blend with long horizontal strokes.

8. Distant tree indications are made by tapping downward with the round brush.

9. With the 2″ brush, tap the bottom of the distant trees . . .

10. . . . to create a misty area.

11. Retain the misty area between each layer for separation.

12. The indication of snow is layed in with the fan brush.

13. With a chisel edge on the 2″ brush, paint the evergreen tree.

14. Small amounts of the tree/bush color . . .

Grey Winter

15. . . . may be pulled out to create the illusion of shadows in the snow.

16. Pull downward, then across to create reflections.

17. The fan brush is used to make . . .

18. . . . individual highlights in the snow.

19. The point of the knife is used to scratch in twigs and sticks.

20. The fan brush is used to highlight . . .

21. . . . the large evergreen in the background.

22. Start the large evergreen with a chisel edge, then . . .

23. . . . with the corner of the brush . . .

24. . . . work down the tree.

25. Push upward with the large brush . . .

26. . . . to paint in the basic bush shapes in the foreground.

27. Trunks made with the knife.

28. Highlight the large tree with the 2" brush.

29. Push upward with the 1" brush to highlight individual bushes.

30. Back and forth strokes with the 2" brush . . .

31. . . . will create a path in the painting.

QUIET MOUNTAIN RIVER

MATERIALS

2" Brush	Prussian Blue
1" Brush	Midnight Black
#6 Fan Brush	Dark Sienna
#2 Script Liner Brush	Van Dyke Brown
Large Knife	Alizarin Crimson
Small Knife	Sap Green
18 x 24 Canvas	Cadmium Yellow
Liquid White	Yellow Ochre
Titanium White	Indian Yellow
Phthalo Blue	Bright Red

Start by covering the entire canvas with a thin, even coat of Liquid White using the 2" brush. With long horizontal and vertical strokes, work back and forth to ensure an even distribution of paint on the canvas. Do NOT allow the Liquid White to dry before you begin.

SKY

With Alizarin Crimson on the 2" brush, use criss-cross strokes to make Pink areas randomly throughout the sky. The remaining areas of the sky are then covered with a Lavender (made by adding Phthalo Blue to the Alizarin Crimson already in the brush) still using criss-cross strokes. Use Phthalo Blue and long, horizontal strokes to underpaint the water on the lower portion of the canvas. With a clean, dry 2" brush use long, horizontal strokes to blend the entire canvas.

Load the 1" brush with Titanium White and a very small amount of Bright Red. Use tiny, circular strokes to add the cloud shapes. Lightly diffuse the bottoms of the clouds with just the corner of a clean, dry 2" brush and then use sweeping, upward strokes to "fluff" the clouds. Very lightly blend the entire sky.

MOUNTAIN

The mountain is made with Midnight Black, Phthalo Blue and Alizarin Crimson. load the long edge of the knife with a small roll of paint by pulling the mixture out flat on your palette and just cutting across. Use the knife to push the paint firmly into the canvas as you shape just the top edge of the mountain. With a clean, dry 2" brush, pull the paint down towards the base of the mountain, thereby completing the entire mountain shape.

Highlight the mountain by again loading the long edge of the knife with a small roll of Titanium White to which you have added a small amount of Bright Red. Hold the knife vertically, and starting at the top of each peak, use so little pressure that the paint "breaks" as you glide the knife down the sunny (right) side of each peak. You can also use the small knife for the small, hard-to-reach areas of the mountain. The snow on the shadow (left) sides of the peaks is made with a mixture of Titanium White and Phthalo Blue, applied by pulling the paint in the opposing direction.

Carefully following the angles, use a clean, dry 2" brush to tap and diffuse the base of the mountain. Use the brush to gently lift upward, creating the illusion of mist.

BACKGROUND

Use the knife with the same mountain mixture of Midnight Black, Phthalo Blue and Alizarin Crimson to shape the foothills at the base of the mountain. With a circular motion, really scrub-in the paint at the base of the foothills, creating the misty area.

Load the 2" brush with a mixture of Van Dyke Brown, Dark Sienna and Alizarin Crimson. Moving forward in the painting, hold the brush horizontally and tap downward to underpaint the distant, rolling hills. Don't just tap at random, this is where you begin creating the lay-of-the-land, at the same time being very careful not to extend the paint into the area which will be used for the water. Use various mixtures of all the Yellows and Bright Red on the 2" brush to highlight the hills, still tapping downward.

Use a Liquid White-Titanium White mixture on the fan brush and short horizontal strokes to add the edges and other small details to the water.

Load the fan brush with a mixture of Sap Green, Van Dyke Brown, Alizarin Crimson and Midnight Black. Add the indication of tiny trees to the tops of the distant hills by holding the brush horizontally, pushing it straight into the canvas, forcing the bristles to bend upward.

FOREGROUND

Underpaint the large trees and bushes in the foreground with a mixture of Midnight Black, Van Dyke Brown, Dark Sienna, Sap Green, Alizarin Crimson and Prussian Blue. Load the 2" brush by pulling it in one direction through the paint, to round one corner. With the rounded corner UP, touch the canvas and force the bristles to spread and bend upward as you underpaint the large trees and bushes in the foreground.

With a mixture of Titanium White and Dark Sienna on the long edge of the knife, hold the knife vertically to add the tree trunks. Use the point of the knife to just scratch-in the indication of tiny trunks and branches.

Paying close attention to angles, use Van Dyke Brown and Dark Sienna on the knife to add the land area under the trees. Highlight this area with a mixture of Titanium White and Dark Sienna, using so little pressure on the knife that the paint "breaks".

Use the 1" brush to highlight the foreground trees. Dip the brush in Liquid White (to thin the paint) and then pull it in one direction through various mixtures of Midnight Black and all the Yellows (to make Green) to round one corner. With the rounded corner up, use very little pressure as you apply the highlights. As you work in layers, you can create individual tree and bush shapes if you are very careful not to "kill" all of the dark underpaint. The highlight mixtures should be quite thin (you need a thin paint to stick to a thick paint); you can also use paint thinner to thin the highlight colors. Turn the brush horizontally and force the bristles to bend upward as you add little grassy areas beneath the trees.

Use the dark mixture (Midnight Black, Van Dyke Brown, Alizarin Crimson, Sap Green and Prussian Blue) loaded on the fan brush to add the small evergreens. Holding the brush vertically, touch the canvas to create the center line of the tree. Starting at the top of the tree, use one corner of the brush to just touch the canvas to form the top branches. Working from side to side (forcing the bristles to bend downward) use more pressure as you work down the tree, allowing the branches to become larger as you near the base of the tree.

FINISHING TOUCHES

Use horizontal strokes with Van Dyke Brown on the fan brush to add the path in the foreground and then highlight with Titanium White on the fan brush. Now, the painting will be complete with only the addition of your signature.

Quiet Mountain River

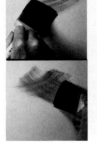

1. Use criss-cross strokes to make the sky.

2. Add clouds with the 1" brush and circular strokes . . .

3. . . . and then blend with the top corner of the 2" brush . . .

4. . . . to complete the sky.

5. Use the knife and firm pressure to shape the mountain . . .

6. . . . and then highlight with no pressure.

7. Tap to mist the base of the mountain with the 2" brush.

Quiet Mountain River

8. Use the knife . . .

9. . . . to add the foothills.

10. Tap downward with 2" brush to paint soft grassy areas.

11. Use horizontal strokes with the fan brush . . .

12. . . . to add the river.

13. Push up with the 2" brush to underpaint leaf trees . . .

14. . . . and evergreen trees.

15. Use the knife to add tree trunks . . .

16. . . . and the path.

17. Apply highlights with the 1" brush . . .

18. . . . and the fan brush.

19. The liner brush is used . . .

20. . . . to add the final tree.

DISTANT MOUNTAINS

MATERIALS

2" Brush	Midnight Black
1" Brush	Dark Sienna
#6 Fan Brush	Van Dyke Brown
#2 Script Liner Brush	Alizarin Crimson
Large Knife	Sap Green
Liquid White	Cadmium Yellow
Titanium White	Yellow Ochre
Phthalo Green	Indian Yellow
Phthalo Blue	Bright Red
Prussian Blue	

Start by covering the entire canvas with a thin, even coat of Liquid White, using the 2" brush. Use long horizontal and vertical strokes to ensure an even distribution of paint on the canvas. Do NOT allow the Liquid White to dry before you begin.

SKY AND WATER

Load the 2" brush with a small amount of Phthalo Blue, tapping the bristles firmly against the palette to ensure an even distribution of paint. Use criss-cross strokes to apply the color to the sky. (Photo 1.) By starting at the top of the canvas, the color will automatically become lighter as you work down towards the horizon.

Without cleaning the brush, pick up a little more Phthalo Blue and a very small amount of Phthalo Green. Use long horizontal strokes to add the water, holding the brush flat and pulling from the outside edges of the canvas in towards the center. Allow that center area of the canvas to remain quite light, to create the illusion of shimmering light across the water. Use a clean, dry 2" brush to blend the entire canvas. (Photo 2.)

Load the fan brush with Titanium White. With just one corner of the brush use tiny circular strokes to form the cloud shapes. (Photo 3.) Blend the base of the clouds with just the top corner of a clean, dry 2" brush. Again, use small circular strokes (Photo 4), then gently lift upward to "fluff" (Photo 5).

MOUNTAIN

The mountains are made with a mixture of Prussian Blue, Midnight Black, Van Dyke Brown and Alizarin Crimson, loaded on the long edge of the knife. Using very firm pressure, push the paint into the canvas forming the top edge of the basic mountain shape. (Photo 6.) Use the knife to remove any excess paint from the canvas. With the 2" brush, pull the color down towards the base of the mountain to complete the entire shape. (Photo 7.) Your mountain should be more distinct at the top than at the bottom. To highlight the mountain, load the long edge of the knife with a small roll of Titanium White by pulling the paint out very flat on your palette and just cutting across. Starting at the top of the mountain (and paying close attention to angles) glide the knife down the right sides of the peaks, using so little pressure that the paint "breaks". (Photo 8.)

The shadows on the left sides of the peaks are made with a mixture of Titanium White and Phthalo Blue. With the 2" brush, tap to diffuse the base of the mountain, paying close attention to angles. (Photo 9.) Gently lift upward with the brush to create a misty effect. (Photo 10.)

BACKGROUND

Load the fan brush with the mountain mixture and a small amount of Sap Green. Hold the brush vertically and tap downward to indicate the small evergreens at the base of the mountain. (Photo 11.) Extend this dark color into the water for reflections. With a clean, dry 2" brush, gently pull down the reflections (Photo 12), then brush across—giving the appearance of water (Photo 13). Use various mixtures of all the Yellows and Sap Green on the fan brush to create the grassy areas at the base of the small trees.

Pull some Liquid White out flat on your palette and just "cut" across to load the long edge of the knife. Push the knife straight into the canvas and use firm pressure to "cut-in" the water lines and ripples. (Photo 14.) Make sure the lines are horizontal to the top and bottom of the canvas. (Photo 15.)

LARGE EVERGREEN TREES

Load the fan brush with the Prussian Blue-Midnight Black-Van Dyke Brown-Alizarin Crimson mixture. To make each evergreen, hold the brush vertically and touch the canvas to form the center line of the tree. Turn the brush horizontally and starting at the top of the tree, use one corner of the brush and just touch the canvas to begin adding the small top branches. (Photo 16.) Working from side to side, as you move down the tree, use more pressure on the brush (forcing the bristles to bend downward) and automatically the branches will become larger as you near the base of each tree.

Touch a few highlights to the branches using a mixture of Sap Green and Cadmium Yellow, still keeping these trees quite dark for contrast.

FOREGROUND

The large leaf trees and bushes are underpainted with the same dark mixture (Midnight Black, Van Dyke Brown, Alizarin Crimson and Prussian Blue). Use the 2" brush to just block in the very basic tree and bush shapes (Photo 17) in the foreground (Photo 18).

Highlight the trees and bushes with various mixtures of all the Yellows, Sap Green and Bright Red. Dip the 1" brush into Liquid White, then pull the brush in one direction through the various mixtures, to round one corner. With the rounded corner up, shape the small trees and bushes by gently touch-ing the canvas forcing the bristles to bend upward. (Photo 19.) Try not to just hit at random, this is where you create distinct, individual tree and bush shapes. Working in layers, be careful not to "kill" all the dark base color.

PATH

To make the path in the foreground, load the knife with a small roll of Van Dyke Brown and use short horizontal strokes to shape the path. Watch your perspective, the path should get wider as it comes forward in the painting. (Photo 20.) Highlights are the same horizontal strokes, using a mixture of Dark Sienna, Phthalo Blue and Titanium White. Use so little pressure on the knife that the paint to "breaks". (Photo 21.)

FINISHING TOUCHES

Add small bushes and grasses over the edges of the path and then use the point of the knife to scratch in additional sticks and twigs.

You can also add final details (small tree trunks, etc.) with the liner brush. (Photo 22.) Thin the paint with either paint thinner, Liquid Clear or Copal Oil. Slowly turn the liner brush as you pull it through the mixture, forcing the bristles to come to a sharp point. Then, using very little pressure (adding more paint to the brush when necessary) add the final details, especially your signature! Stand back and admire your finished painting.

Distant Mountains

1. Use criss-cross strokes to paint the sky . . .

2. . . . and horizontal strokes to paint the water.

3. Clouds are made with the fan brush . . .

4. . . . then blended with the 2" brush . . .

5. . . . to complete the sky.

Distant Mountains

6. Shape the mountain top with the knife . . .

7. . . . then pull down with the 2" brush to complete the shape.

8. Highlight the mountain . . .

9. . . . tap to mist the base . . .

10. . . . and the mountain is complete.

11. Add small evergreens with the fan brush.

12. Use the 2" brush to pull down reflections . . .

13. . . . then lightly brush across.

14. Cut in water lines with the knife . . .

15. . . . to complete the background.

16. Add evergreens with the fan brush . . .

17. . . . and leafy trees and bushes with the 2" brush . . .

18. . . . to block in the foreground.

19. Highlights are made with the 1" brush.

20. Use the knife to shape . . .

21. . . . and highlight the path.

22. Add final details with the liner brush . . .

23. . . . to complete your painting.

MEADOW BROOK SURPRISE

MATERIALS

2" Brush	Dark Sienna
#6 Fan Brush	Van Dyke Brown
#2 Script Liner Brush	Alizarin Crimson
Large Knife	Sap Green
Liquid White	Cadmium Yellow
Titanium White	Yellow Ochre
Phthalo Blue	Indian Yellow
Prussian Blue	Bright Red
Midnight Black	

Start by covering the entire canvas with a thin, even coat of Liquid White, using the 2" brush. Use long horizontal and vertical strokes, work back and forth to ensure an even distribution of paint on the canvas. Do NOT allow the Liquid White to dry before you begin. Clean and dry the 2" brush.

SKY

Load the 2" brush with a Lavender mixture of Phthalo Blue and Alizarin Crimson. Starting at the top of the canvas, use criss-cross strokes to "dance-in" your sky, allowing the colors to vary a bit. (Photo 1.) Be sure to leave open, unpainted areas for the indication of clouds. Use a clean, dry 2" brush and criss-cross strokes to blend the sky together, then lightly brush across to soften. (Photo 2.)

BACKGROUND

Load the 2" brush with the same mixture of Alizarin Crimson and Phthalo Blue. Use the top corner of the brush and tap downward to shape the misty trees in the background. (Photo 3.) Diffuse the bottoms of the trees by tapping firmly with a clean, dry 2" brush (Photo 4), then lightly lift upward to complete the soft, misty effect (Photo 5).

With Titanium White, Alizarin Crimson and Phthalo Blue, use one corner of the fan brush (Photo 6) to add small branches to the more distinct evergreens (Photo 7). Complete the background in layers, adding a small amount of Van Dyke Brown to darken the Lavender mixture as you work forward. Tap downward with the fan brush to just indicate small evergreens (Photo 8) and again, tap to diffuse and mist the base of the trees (Photo 9). The small leafy trees are made with one corner of the 2" brush. (Photo 10.)

MIDDLEGROUND

Load the 2" brush with the same dark mixture of Phthalo Blue, Alizarin Crimson and Van Dyke Brown. Hold the brush horizontally and tap downward to underpaint the grassy areas. (Photo 11.) Work in layers and pay close attention to the "lay-of-the-land", leaving an unpainted area in the center of the stream. (Photo 12.) To highlight the grassy area, add various mixtures Sap Green and all of the Yellows to the same brush; again just tap downward. (Photo 13.)

EVERGREENS

The evergreens on the right side of the painting are made with the fan brush and a mixture of Midnight Black, Prussian Blue, Van Dyke Brown and Alizarin Crimson. Holding the brush vertically, and starting at the top of each tree, begin tapping in the large tree trunks, making fuzzy, bark-like edges.

Hold the brush horizontally and use one corner to begin adding the small top branches. Working from side to side and forcing the bristles to bend downward, use more pressure as you near the base of the tree allowing the lower branches to become quite large. (Photo 14.) Use the 2" brush to tap in the grassy highlights at the base of the trees, pulling in the dark tree mixture to create the shadow areas. (Photo 15.)

STREAM

Load the small knife with a roll of Van Dyke Brown. Scrub the paint firmly into the canvas to underpaint the stream bed. (Photo 16.) Highlight with a mixture of Titanium White, Dark Sienna, Van Dyke Brown and Midnight Black on the knife, using so little pressure that the paint "breaks". Push in grassy areas along the edges of the stream bed with the fan brush using various mixtures of all the Yellows. (Photo 17.)

To add the water to the stream, load a clean fan brush with a mixture of Liquid White, Titanium White, and a touch of Phthalo Blue. Hold the brush horizontally and pull straight down as you spill the water over the rocks and crevices along the stream. *(Photo 18.)* Use push-up strokes to create little splashes at the base of the small trickling falls and short, horizontal strokes to add ripples and movement to the water. *(Photo 19.)*

Moving forward in the painting, don't forget to use the fan brush to add the large evergreen on the left. *(Photos 20 & 21.)*

FOREGROUND

The two large trees in the foreground are made by loading the fan brush with a mixture of Midnight Black and Van Dyke Brown. Starting at the top of the canvas, hold the brush vertically and tap firmly downward, perhaps several times for the desired width of each tree trunk. Add the highlights to the right sides of the tree trunks with a mixture of Titanium White and Phthalo Blue on the fan brush, gently tapping and blending into the dark. *(Photo 22.)* The branches are made with thinned Van Dyke Brown on the liner brush. *(Photo 23.)*

FINISHING TOUCHES

Sign your painting, then stand back and admire! *(Photo 24.)*

Meadow Brook Surprise

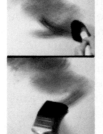

1. Use the 2" brush and criss-cross strokes . . .

2. . . . to paint the sky.

3. Use the large brush to shape the background trees . . .

4. . . . then tap downward . . .

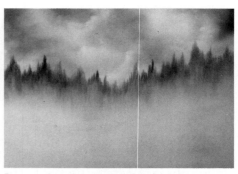

5. . . . to create the mist at the base of the trees.

6. Use the fan brush . . .

7. . . . to add small evergreens to the background.

8. Tap down with the fan brush . . .

9. . . . mist with the 2" brush . . .

10. . . . and the background trees are complete.

Meadow Brook Surprise

11. Tap downward with the 2" brush . . .

12. . . . to underpaint . . .

13. . . . and highlight the grassy areas.

14. Use the fan brush . . .

15. . . . to add the large evergreens.

16. Use the knife to scrub in . . .

17. . . . and highlight the stream bed.

18. Use the fan brush . . .

19. . . . to add the "Meadow Brook".

20. Pull down the tree trunk . . .

21. . . . then add branches with the fan brush.

22. Make the large tree trunks with the fan brush . . .

23. . . . the limbs and branches with the liner brush.

24. . . . and your painting is complete.

SNOWY SOLITUDE

MATERIALS

2" Brush	Phthalo Blue
1" Brush	Midnight Black
#6 Fan Brush	Dark Sienna
#2 Script Liner Brush	Van Dyke Brown
Liquid White	Alizarin Crimson
Titanium White	Yellow Ochre

Start by covering the entire canvas with a thin, even coat of Liquid White, using the 2" brush. Use long horizontal and vertical strokes, working back and forth to ensure an even distribution of paint on the canvas. Do NOT allow the Liquid White to dry before you begin. Now, clean and dry your 2" brush.

SKY

Load the 2" brush by tapping the bristles firmly into a mixture of Midnight Black and Phthalo Blue. Make sure the paint is evenly distributed throughout the bristles. Starting at the top of the canvas, paint the sky using criss-cross strokes. (Photo 1.) To create just the illusion of clouds, leave some areas in the sky open and unpainted, as you work down towards the horizon. With the same mixture and long horizontal strokes, underpaint the lower portion of the canvas. Use small criss-cross strokes to blend the sky and then long horizontal strokes to blend the entire canvas. (Photo 2.)

BACKGROUND

The small foothills along the horizon are made by loading the 2" brush with a mixture of Van Dyke Brown, Midnight Black and Phthalo Blue. Use the corner of the brush and just tap downward to indicate the distant foothills. (Photo 3.) Clean and dry the brush.

With Titanium White on the 2" brush, pull long horizontal strokes across the base of the foothills for the snow-covered ground. (Photo 4.) Allow the White to pick up some of the Blue already on the canvas, automatically creating shadows in the snow. Use blending strokes and pay close attention to the lay-of-the-land. (Photo 5.)

FOREGROUND

Use various mixtures of Van Dyke Brown, Dark Sienna, Midnight Black, Phthalo Blue and Alizarin Crimson to underpaint the trees and bushes. With just the corner of the 2" brush, tap in the basic tree and bush shapes. (Photo 6.) By starting at the base of the trees and working upward, automatically your trees will become lighter as you near their tops. (Photo 7.) You can even add a small amount of Yellow Ochre to the mixture to help lighten the tree tops. Watch your composition, following the lay-of-the-land and the inward curve of the tree limbs. (Photos 8 & 9.)

Small tree trunks, branches and twigs are made with thinned Van Dyke Brown on the liner brush. (Photo 10.) Use the fan brush with Van Dyke Brown for the larger tree trunks by holding the brush vertically, starting at the top of each tree and just pulling down. (Photos 11 & 12.)

Again, with a mixture of Titanium White and a small amount of Alizarin Crimson on the 2" brush use horizontal strokes to add snow to the base of the trees and bushes and to the remainder of the lower portion of the canvas. (Photo 13.) Pay close attention to the lay-of-the-land and allow the brush to pull some of the dark tree color into the snow for shadows. (Photo 14.)

To highlight the tree and bush shapes, dip the 1" brush into Liquid White and then tap the bristle tips firmly into a mixture of Titanium White with a very small amount of Alizarin Crimson. Highlight the trees, thinking about the form and shape. Don't just hit at random, create individual limbs and branches, being very careful not to "kill" all of the dark under-color. (Photo 15.)

Use a Titanium White-Phthalo Blue mixture on the fan brush and short, sweeping, horizontal strokes to create the indication of a path in the snow. (Photos 16 & 17.)

WATER

With Phthalo Blue and Van Dyke Brown on the 2" brush, use straight downward strokes to add the pond. (Photo 18.)

Lightly brush across to create the appearance of water. Add the snow-covered edges to the pond with Titanium White on the fan brush. *(Photo 19.)* With Van Dyke Brown on the fan brush, "tuck in" some stone indications underneath the snowy edges. *(Photos 20 & 21.)* The small fence is made with thinned Van Dyke Brown on the liner brush and highlighted with Titanium White. *(Photo 22.)*

FINAL TOUCHES

Use thinned Van Dyke Brown on the liner brush to add long grasses, sticks, twigs and other final details. *(Photo 23.)* You can also use thinned paint on the liner brush to add a bird or two, but most important, don't forget to sign your painting! *(Photo 24.)*

Snowy Solitude

1. Use criss-cross strokes to paint the sky . . .

2. . . . and long horizontal strokes to add the water.

3. Tap downward with the 2" brush for the distant hill.

4. Use the 2" brush . . .

5. . . . to add snow to the base of the hill.

6. Tap downward with the 2" brush . . .

7. . . . to underpaint all of the trees . . .

8. . . . and bushes . . .

9. . . . in the painting.

10. Add small trunks with the liner brush . . .

Snowy Solitude

11. . . . the larger trunks with the fan brush . . .

12. . . . and your painting is ready for highlights.

13. Use the 2" brush . . .

14. . . . for the snow-covered ground areas.

15. Highlight the trees and bushes with the 1" brush.

16. Use the fan brush and short strokes . . .

17. . . . to indicate the path in the painting.

18. Pull down with the 2" brush to add the water.

19. Use the fan brush to add the snow-covered edges . . .

20. . . . and tiny rocks . . .

21. . . . to the water.

22. Use the liner brush to add fence posts . . .

23. . . . to the finished painting.

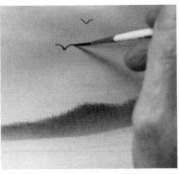

24. You can also add a bird or two.

PEACEFUL REFLECTIONS

MATERIALS

2″ Brush	Midnight Black
1″ Brush	Dark Sienna
#6 Fan Brush	Van Dyke Brown
#2 Script Liner Brush	Alizarin Crimson
Large Knife	Sap Green
Liquid White	Cadmium Yellow
Titanium White	Yellow Ochre
Phthalo Green	Indian Yellow
Phthalo Blue	Bright Red
Prussian Blue	

Start by covering the entire canvas with a thin, even coat of Liquid White, using the 2″ brush. With long, horizontal and vertical strokes, work back and forth to ensure an even distribution of paint on the canvas. Do NOT allow the Liquid White to dry before you begin.

SKY AND WATER

Load the 2″ brush with a small amount of Indian Yellow, tapping the bristles firmly against the palette to ensure an even distribution of paint throughout the bristles. Using criss-cross strokes, add the Indian Yellow areas of the sky (Photo 1) and then use horizontal strokes to reflect the Yellow into the water area of the canvas. Without cleaning the brush, pick up a very small amount of Alizarin Crimson and again use criss-cross strokes to add this color above and below the Yellow in the sky and horizontal strokes to reflect the same color into the water. With a small amount of Phthalo Blue on the same brush, use criss-cross strokes to add the Blue color to the sky. Use horizontal strokes to add a mixture of Phthalo Blue and Phthalo Green to the bottom and sides of the water, pulling from the outside edges of the canvas in towards the center. Now, with a clean, dry 2″ brush, use criss-cross strokes to blend the sky and horizontal strokes to blend the water. (Photo 2.)

MOUNTAIN

The mountain is made with a mixture of Prussian Blue, Midnight Black, Alizarin Crimson and Van Dyke Brown. Load the long edge of the knife with a small roll of paint and use firm pressure to shape just the top edge of the mountain. (Photo 3.) With the 2″ brush, pull the paint down to the base of the mountain to complete the entire mountain shape. (Photo 4.)

To highlight the mountain, load the long edge of the knife with a small roll of a mixture of Titanium White and a touch of Alizarin Crimson. In this painting, the light is coming from the right. So, starting at the top of the mountain, glide the knife down the right side of each peak, using so little pressure that the paint "breaks". (Photo 5.) Add the shadows to the left sides of the peaks with a mixture of Phthalo Blue and Titanium White on the knife. With a clean, dry 2″ brush, carefully following the angles of the mountain, tap to diffuse the base of the mountain (Photo 6) and then gently lift upward to create the illusion of mist (Photo 7).

BACKGROUND

The tiny background trees at the base of the mountain are made with the fan brush and a dark mixture of Midnight Black, Prussian Blue, Phthalo Green, Alizarin Crimson and Van Dyke Brown. Load the fan brush full of paint, hold it vertically and tap downward. (Photo 8.)

For the more distinct evergreens, load the fan brush full of the dark mixture and then holding the brush vertically, just touch the canvas to form the center line of the tree. Turn the brush horizontally and use one corner of the brush to begin adding the small top branches. Working from side to side, as you move down the tree, use more pressure on the brush (forcing the bristles to bend downward) and automatically the branches will become larger as you near the base of the tree. (Photo 9.)

Holding the 2″ brush flat against the canvas, pull some of the dark tree color straight down into the water to create reflections (Photo 10), then lightly brush across to give the reflections a watery appearance. Load the long edge of the knife with a mixture of Liquid White and Phthalo Blue to cut in the water lines and ripples in the background water. *(Photos 11 & 12.)*

MIDDLEGROUND

Moving forward in the painting, use the same dark mixture (Midnight Black, Prussian Blue, Phthalo Green, Alizarin Crimson and Van Dyke Brown) on the fan brush to add the larger evergreens. *(Photo 13.)* You can add the grassy land projection at the base of the trees by holding the fan brush horizontally and forcing the bristles to bend upward. *(Photo 14.)* Pull this dark color straight down into the water, using a clean, dry 2″ brush and then lightly brush across to create reflections. Highlight the grassy area by adding Cadmium Yellow to the same dark fan brush and again, force the bristles to bend upward. Use a small roll of Liquid White on the long edge of the knife to cut in the water lines.

Create just the indication of the evergreen tree trunks using a mixture of Dark Sienna and Titanium White on the long edge of the knife. Add Cadmium Yellow to the dark mixture on the fan brush and very lightly highlight the right sides of the evergreen branches where the light would strike.

FOREGROUND

Use the dark paint mixture on the 2″ brush to underpaint just the basic shape of the large bushes and trees at the base of the evergreens. *(Photo 15.)* Reverse the brush to reflect the bushes and trees into the water. Pull straight down with a clean, dry 2″ brush and then lightly brush across for reflections. *(Photos 16 & 17.)* Add the tree trunks with a mixture of Dark Sienna and Titanium White on the knife. *(Photo 18.)*

Highlight the trees and bushes using various mixtures of Liquid White, Sap Green and all the Yellows and Bright Red. Load the 1″ brush to round one corner and lightly force the bristles to bend upward (don't let the brush slide) as you shape and highlight each tree and bush. *(Photo 19.)* Don't just hit at random, work in layers and be very careful not to "kill" all of your dark base color. Reverse the brush and reflect the highlight colors into the water. Very, very lightly, use a clean, dry 2″ brush to pull down and brush across, giving the reflections a watery appearance. *(Photo 20.)*

You can also shape a small stone in the foreground using Van Dyke Brown on the knife and then highlight with a mixture of Dark Sienna and Titanium White. *(Photo 21.)* Also, use Van Dyke Brown on the knife to add the banks along the water's edge and then highlight with a mixture of Van Dyke Brown and Titanium White. *(Photo 22.)* Use a small roll of Liquid White on the long edge of the knife to cut-in the water lines and ripples. *(Photo 23.)*

FINISHING TOUCHES

Use the point of the knife to scratch in small sticks and twigs and a mixture of paint thinner and Van Dyke Brown on the liner brush for additional small details *(Photo 24 & 25)* and the last LARGE detail, your signature!

Peaceful Reflections

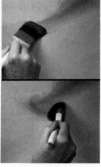     

1. Use criss-cross strokes to paint the sky . . .

2. . . . and horizontal strokes to add the water.

3. Shape the mountain top with the knife . . .

4. . . . and then pull the paint down with the 2″ brush.

5. Apply the highlights with the knife . . .

6. . . . then tap with the 2″ brush . . .

Peaceful Reflections

7. . . . to mist the base of the mountain.

8. The indication of small evergreens . . .

9. . . . and more distinct trees are made with the fan brush.

10. Pull down reflections with the 2" brush . . .

11. . . . then cut in the water lines with the knife . . .

12. . . . to complete the background.

13. Use the corner of the fan brush . . .

14. . . . to add the large evergreen trees.

15. Push up with the brush to underpaint the foliage . . .

16. . . . then pull down the reflections . . .

17. . . . in the foreground.

18. Add tree trunks with the knife . . .

19. . . . highlights with the 1" brush . . .

20. . . . then use the 2" brush to pull down the reflections.

21. Use the knife to shape the stones . . .

22. . . . and the banks . . .

23. . . . and water lines.

24. Add tiny details . . .

25. . . . to your finished painting.

FOREST DAWN OVAL

MATERIALS

2" Brush	Phthalo Blue
1" Brush	Midnight Black
#6 Fan Brush	Dark Sienna
#3 Fan Brush	Van Dyke Brown
#2 Script Liner Brush	Alizarin Crimson
Large Knife	Sap Green
Adhesive-Backed Plastic	Cadmium Yellow
Black Gesso	Yellow Ochre
Liquid White	Indian Yellow
Titanium White	Bright Red

Start by covering the entire canvas with adhesive-backed plastic (such as Con-Tact Paper) from which you have removed a 14x20 center oval. Then, cover the exposed oval area of the canvas with a thin, even coat of Black Gesso and allow it to DRY COMPLETELY before you begin painting.

Use the 2" brush to cover the Black oval area of the canvas with very thin coat of a mixture of Alizarin Crimson and Phthalo Blue; allowing the center to be quite light by using less Phthalo Blue in that area. Because this mixture is made with transparent colors, the canvas should still look quite dark. DO NOT allow the canvas to dry before you begin! *(Photo 1.)*

SKY

Using the 2" brush with Liquid White, decide where the lightest area of your sky is and begin making criss-cross strokes, blending from the lightest area outward. *(Photo 2.)* Notice how the sky "comes alive" as the Liquid White picks up the transparent colors already on the canvas. This step can be repeated as many times as necessary to achieve the desired amount of lightness in the sky, but be sure to clean and dry the brush before each application! Gently blend the entire sky with long, horizontal strokes. *(Photo 3.)*

BACKGROUND

Use the 2" brush and the same Alizarin Crimson-Phthalo Blue mixture to block in the general background tree and bush shapes. Hold the brush horizontally and, starting at the base of the trees and working upward, tap downward with just the corner of the brush, paying close attention to form and shape. *(Photo 4.)* These shapes should be very soft and quiet, this will help create the illusion of distance in your painting. Be careful not to "kill" the bright center area of the sky. Working in layers, add more Phthalo Blue to darken the paint mixture as you move further away from the light area.

Use the liner brush for the tree trunks, limbs and branches. Add paint thinner to the Alizarin Crimson-Phthalo Blue mixture (to an ink-like consistency) then slowly turn the handle of the brush as you pull the bristles through the mixture, forcing them to a sharp point. Use very little pressure on the fully-loaded brush as you paint the individual tree trunks. *(Photo 5.)*

For leaf clusters and foliage on the background tree and bush shapes, use the 1" brush and various "not too bright" mixtures of Alizarin Crimson and Phthalo Blue with a small amount of Titanium White. Hold the brush horizontally and, using just one corner, tap in the individual shapes. *(Photo 6.)* Try not to just hit at random, this is where you create *individual* tree and bush shapes. Work in layers, keeping the most distant trees and bushes quite dark; add a small amount of Phthalo Blue to the mixture as you move further away from the light area. *(Photo 7.)*

FOREGROUND

The soft grassy highlights are made with the 2" brush and various mixtures of Alizarin Crimson, Phthalo Blue, all the Yellows, Sap Green and a small amount of Bright Red. Load the brush by holding it at a 45-degree angle and tapping the bristles into the various paint mixtures. Allow the brush to "slide" slightly forward in the paint each time you tap (this assures that the very tips of the bristles are fully loaded with paint).

Begin at the base of the most distant trees and work forward in layers, carefully creating the lay-of-the-land. By holding the brush horizontally and gently tapping downward

(Photo 8) you can create grassy highlights that look almost like velvet *(Photo 9)*. Add a small amount of Titanium White to the brush for the brightest areas in the grass. But again, don't "kill" all of the dark base color.

With a mixture of Van Dyke Brown and Dark Sienna on the fan brush, use horizontal, sweeping strokes for the wandering path. Watch your perspective, allow the path to get wider as it comes forward. *(Photo 10.)* Without cleaning the brush, use Titanium White to lightly "graze" over the path for highlights. Use a clean fan brush with the Yellow-Green mixtures to complete the grassy areas along the edges of the path. *(Photo 11.)*

For the larger tree trunks, use the small fan brush and Midnight Black. Holding the brush vertically, and starting at the top of each tree, just pull down. *(Photo 12.)* Use more pressure on the brush as you near the base of each tree and automatically the trunk will become wider.

Using the 1" brush with a mixture of Midnight Black and Phthalo Blue, "pop in" the indication of a few bushes at the base of the trees. Hold the brush vertically, touch the canvas and gently force the bristles to bend upward. *(Photo 13.)* Highlight the bushes by dipping the 1" brush into Liquid White, then pulling it in one direction (to round one corner) through various mixtures of Cadmium Yellow and Sap Green. With the rounded corner up, shape each bush using

gentle pressure, again allowing the bristles to bend upward. Remember, be very careful not to cover all of your dark base color. *(Photo 14.)*

Highlight the bright side of the tree trunks (the light source is in the center of the painting) with Titanium White, Dark Sienna and a small amount of Bright Red on the knife, gently "touching and tapping" the highlights for a muted effect. *(Photo 15.)* Use a mixture of Phthalo Blue and Titanium White for the shadow side.

The limbs and branches are made with a mixture of Midnight Black and paint thinner on the liner brush. Bring the bristles to a sharp point and use very little pressure on the brush. *(Photo 16.)*

Add the foliage to the branches with the 1" brush and a mixture of Alizarin Crimson and Midnight Black. Use one corner of the brush and tap downward. *(Photo 17.)* If the paint doesn't want to stick to the canvas, add a little paint thinner to the mixture; remember, a thin paint will stick to a thick paint.

FINISHING TOUCHES

When you are satisfied with your painting *(Photo 18)*, remove the adhesive-backed plastic from the canvas *(Photo 19)* to expose your masterpiece *(Photo 20)!* Don't forget to add the most important part, your signature!

Forest Dawn Oval

1. Cover the exposed area of the canvas with Black Gesso.

2. Use criss-cross strokes . . .

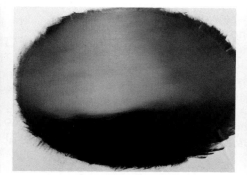

3. . . . to paint the sky.

4. Block in the shapes . . .

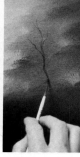

5. . . . then add trunks . . .

6. . . . and leaf clusters . . .

Forest Dawn Oval

   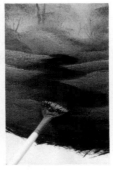 

7. . . . to complete the background trees.

8. Use the 2" brush . . .

9. . . . to tap in the "velvet" grassy areas.

10. Use the fan brush . . .

11. . . . to add the path to the center of the painting.

    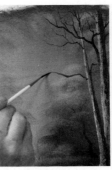 

12. Pull down the trunks . . .

13. . . . and then add small bushes . . .

14. . . . to the base of the trees.

15. Highlight the trunks . . .

16. . . . then add branches . . .

17. . . . and leaves . . .

18. . . . to your finished painting.

19. Remove the adhesive-backed plastic . . .

20. . . . to expose your completed masterpiece!

PATHWAY TO AUTUMN

MATERIALS

2″ Brush	Midnight Black
1″ Brush	Dark Sienna
#6 Fan Brush	Van Dyke Brown
#2 Script Liner Brush	Alizarin Crimson
Large Knife	Sap Green
Liquid White	Cadmium Yellow
Titanium White	Yellow Ochre
Phthalo Blue	Indian Yellow
Prussian Blue	Bright Red

Start by covering the entire canvas with a thin, even coat of Liquid White using the 2″ brush. With long, horizontal and vertical strokes, work back and forth to ensure an even distribution of paint on the canvas. Do NOT allow the Liquid White to dry before you begin.

SKY

Load the 2″ brush with a very small amount of Phthalo Blue, tapping the bristles firmly against the palette to ensure an even distribution of paint throughout the bristles. Starting at the top of the canvas, paint the sky using criss-cross strokes. *(Photo 1.)* To create just the illusion of clouds, leave some areas open and unpainted, as you work down towards the horizon. With the same brush, use long horizontal strokes to blend the entire sky. *(Photo 2.)*

BACKGROUND

Load the same 2″ brush with various mixtures of Midnight Black, Van Dyke Brown and Dark Sienna. Use the corner of the brush to tap in the basic tree and bush shapes across the horizon. *(Photo 3.)* By starting at the base of the trees and working upward the color will automatically get lighter near the tree tops, the dark shadow area will remain at the bottoms of the trees. At this time, you can also underpaint the lower portion of the canvas, using the same dark mixtures. *(Photos 4 & 5.)* Make trunk indications using the liner brush and a thinned mixture of Dark Sienna and Van Dyke Brown.

Use thinned Titanium White for the lighter trunks, sticks and twigs. *(Photo 6.)*

To highlight the trees and bushes, use the 1″ brush and various mixtures of Dark Sienna and all the Yellows and Bright Red. Use just the corner of the brush to tap in leaf-cluster shapes on your trees. *(Photo 7.)* Think of each tree and bush as individual, don't just hit at random. *(Photo 8.)*

Load a clean 2″ brush by tapping the bristles into various mixtures of all the Yellows, Bright Red, Alizarin Crimson and Sap Green. Highlight the grass-covered ground area by holding the brush horizontally and tapping downward. *(Photo 9.)* Starting at the base of the background trees, work in layers as you move forward, creating the lay-of-the-land. Be very careful not to destroy all of the dark base color already on the canvas. *(Photo 10.)*

BARN

Use a clean knife to remove paint from the canvas in the basic shape of the barn. Load the long edge of the knife with a small roll of a mixture of Dark Sienna and Van Dyke Brown by pulling the paint out very flat on your palette and just cutting across. Paying close attention to angles, paint the front of the roof and then the back edge of the roof. Pull down to add the side and front of the barn.

Use a mixture of Bright Red and Dark Sienna to "bounce" highlights onto the roof and then "sparkle" the edges of the roof by touching with a mixture of Titanium White and Prussian Blue. Very lightly highlight the front of the barn with a mixture of Dark Sienna, Yellow Ochre and Titanium White on the knife, using so little pressure that the paint "breaks". Add Van Dyke Brown to the mixture to highlight the side of the barn and then use Van Dyke Brown on the knife to add the door. Use the knife to remove excess paint from the base of the barn. Create the indication of boards using Van Dyke Brown on the long edge of the knife. *(Photo 11.)* With the grassy highlight mixture on the 2″ brush, add grass to the base of the barn. *(Photo 12.)*

FOREGROUND

Tap the bristles of the 2″ brush into the various highlight mixtures (all the Yellows, Alizarin Crimson and Bright Red) to continue adding the grassy area in the foreground, working in layers. The path is made with short, horizontal "scrubbing" strokes using the fan brush and a mixture of Dark Sienna and Van Dyke Brown. *(Photo 13.)* Use the highlight mixture on a clean fan brush to "pop in" additional grassy areas along the edges of the path. *(Photo 14.)*

The large trees in the foreground are made with Van Dyke Brown on the fan brush. Hold the brush vertically and, starting at the very top of the canvas, pull down allowing the trunk to become wider as you near the base. *(Photo 15.)*

Highlight the trunks with Titanium White and Dark Sienna on the knife; hold the knife vertically, touch just the right edge of the trunk and give a little sideways pull. *(Photo 16.)* Add the indication of limbs and branches using thinned Van Dyke Brown on the liner brush. *(Photo 17.)* Use Cadmium Yellow on the 1″ brush to "drop in" some leaf clusters on the trees. Again, just tap downward. *(Photo 18.)*

FINAL TOUCHES

Use the point of the knife to scratch in tiny sticks, twigs and other small details and your new masterpiece is ready for a signature! *(Photo 19.)*

Pathway To Autumn

 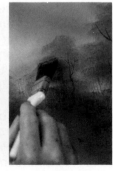   

1. Use criss-cross strokes . . .

2. . . . to paint the sky.

3. Underpaint the trees . . .

4. . . . and then add the dark mixture . . .

5. . . . to the lower portion of the canvas.

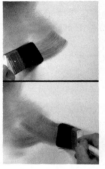    

6. Add tree trunks . . .

7. . . . and highlights . . .

8. . . . to the background trees.

9. Tap down with the 2″ brush . . .

10. . . . to add the grassy highlights.

Pathway To Autumn

11. Progressional steps used to paint the barn.

12. The background is complete.

13. Use the fan brush . . .

14. . . . to extend the path into the foreground.

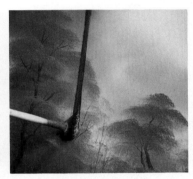

15. Pull down trunks with the fan brush . . .

16. . . . add highlights with the knife . . .

17. . . . limbs and branches with the liner brush . . .

18. . . . leaf clusters with the 1" brush . . .

19. . . . and your painting is complete.

PEAKS OF MAJESTY

MATERIALS

2″ Brush	Prussian Blue
1″ Brush	Midnight Black
#6 Fan Brush	Dark Sienna
#2 Script Liner Brush	Van Dyke Brown
Large Knife	Alizarin Crimson
Small Knife	Sap Green
Liquid White	Cadmium Yellow
Titanium White	Yellow Ochre
Phthalo Blue	Indian Yellow

Start by covering the entire canvas with a thin, even coat of Liquid White using the 2″ brush. With long, horizontal and vertical strokes, work back and forth to ensure an even distribution of paint on the canvas. Do NOT allow the Liquid White to dry before you begin.

SKY AND WATER

Load the 2″ brush by tapping the bristles firmly into a very small amount of Alizarin Crimson. Create the Pink area in the sky by making criss-cross strokes just above the horizon. *(Photo 1.)* Allow some of the color to extend up towards the top of the canvas. Make a Lavender mixture with Alizarin Crimson and Phthalo Blue on the 2″ brush. Still using criss-cross strokes, cover the remainder of the sky.

Use horizontal strokes (with the 2″ brush) to reflect the Pink into the center of the canvas, add Phthalo Blue to the remainder of the water. Blend the entire canvas with a clean, dry 2″ brush.

For the clouds, load the 1″ brush with Titanium White and tap in the diagonal cloud shapes using just one corner of the brush. *(Photo 2.)* Lightly blend with a clean, dry 2″ brush. *(Photo 3.)* Be very careful not to overblend. *(Photo 4.)*

MOUNTAIN

Make a mixture of Midnight Black, Prussian Blue, Van Dyke Brown and Alizarin Crimson on your palette. Load the long edge of the knife with a small roll of paint, by pulling the mixture out flat on your palette and just cutting across. Use firm pressure to shape just the top edge of the mountain. *(Photo 5.)* Still using the knife, remove any excess mountain paint from the canvas and then, with the 2″ brush, pull the paint down to the base of the mountain, to complete the entire shape. *(Photo 6.)*

To highlight the mountain, load the long edge of the small knife with a small roll of a mixture of Dark Sienna and Titanium White. In this painting, the light is coming from the right. So, starting at the top of the mountain, glide the knife down the right side of each peak, using so little pressure that the paint "breaks". *(Photo 7.)* Add the shadows to the left sides of the peaks with various mixtures of Prussian Blue, Van Dyke Brown, Midnight Black and Titanium White on the knife, pulling the paint in the opposite direction. With a clean, dry 2″ brush, carefully following the angles, tap to diffuse the base of the mountain, creating the illusion of mist. *(Photo 8.)*

BACKGROUND

Carefully following the angles of the mountain, hold the 2″ brush horizontally and just tap downward with various mixtures of Cadmium Yellow, Yellow Ochre, Dark Sienna and Sap Green to add the grassy areas at the base of the mountain. *(Photo 9.)* Working forward in layers, and paying close attention to the lay-of-the-land, vary the color by allowing the brush to pick up the mountain mixtures already on the canvas. Again, with a clean, dry 2″ brush, tap the base of the mountain to mist.

When you are satisfied with the grassy areas, load the 2″ brush with the dark mountain mixture. Holding the brush horizontally and again working in layers, tap downward to shape the foothills at the base of the mountain *(Photo 10)*, then use short upward strokes to indicate tiny trees on the hill tops. Reflect the hills into the water by pulling the color straight down with the same 2″ brush. *(Photo 11.)* Lightly brush across to give the reflections a watery appearance.

Cut in the water lines and ripples with a small roll of Liquid White on the long edge of the knife *(Photo 12)* and the background is complete *(Photo 13)*.

MIDDLEGROUND

The small evergreens on the right side of the painting are made with a mixture of Midnight Black, Prussian Blue, Van Dyke Brown, Alizarin Crimson and Sap Green. Load the fan brush full of paint and then holding the brush vertically, tap downward to just indicate the smaller evergreens. *(Photo 14.)* Create the grassy land projection by turning the fan brush horizontally and forcing the bristles to bend upward. For the more distinct trees, touch the canvas to form the center line of the tree. Turn the brush horizontally and with one corner of the brush lightly touch the canvas to begin adding the top branches. Working from side to side, as you move down the tree, use more pressure on the brush (forcing the bristles to bend downward) and automatically the branches will become larger as you near the base of each tree. *(Photo 15.)*

Reverse the brush to reflect the small evergreens into the water, pull down again with a clean, dry 2" brush and lightly brush across to give the reflections a watery appearance. *(Photo 16.)* Use a bit of Cadmium Yellow, Yellow Ochre, Indian Yellow and Sap Green on the fan brush to highlight the grassy areas, holding the brush horizontally and forcing the bristles to bend upward. *(Photo 17.)*

Rub-in the banks along the water's edge with Van Dyke Brown on the long edge of the knife. *(Photo 18.)* Highlight with a mixture of Dark Sienna and Titanium White *(Photo 19)*, then use a small roll of Liquid White on the knife to add the water lines and ripples.

FOREGROUND

Add the large evergreen trees in the foreground with the Midnight Black, Prussian Blue, Van Dyke Brown, Alizarin Crimson and Sap Green mixture on the fan brush. Use Dark Sienna and Titanium White on the knife for tree trunks, then add Cadmium Yellow to the dark fan brush and lightly highlight the branches of the evergreens. Be very careful not to "kill" the dark base color of the trees.

Underpaint the ground area with the dark tree color on the 2" brush. Highlight the grassy area with various mixtures of all the Yellows and Sap Green on the 2" brush. Load the brush by holding it at a 45-degree angle and tapping the bristles into the various paint mixtures. Allow the brush to "slide" slightly forward in the paint each time you tap (this assures that the very tips of the bristles are fully loaded with paint). Carefully creating the lay-of-the-land, by holding the brush horizontally and gently tapping downward, you can create grassy highlights that look almost like velvet.

FINISHING TOUCHES

Use a thinned paint on the liner brush to sign your new masterpiece. *(Photo 20.)*

Peaks of Majesty

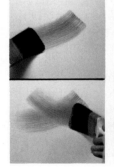

1. Use criss-cross strokes to paint the sky.

2. Tap in clouds with the 1" brush...

3. ...then blend with the 2" brush...

4. ... to complete the sky.

5. Shape the mountain with the knife...

Peaks of Majesty

6. . . . then pull the paint down with the 2″ brush.

7. Apply highlights and shadows . . .

8. . . . then tap to diffuse.

9. Use the 2″ brush to add the growth . . .

10. . . . and foothills.

11. Pull down reflections . . .

12. . . . and cut in water lines . . .

13. . . . to create the water at the base of the mountain.

14. Use the fan brush to make small . . .

15. . . . and large evergreens.

16. Reflect the evergreens . . .

17. . . . then highlight the grassy areas at the base of the trees.

18. Add the banks . . .

19. . . . and highlights to the water's edge.

20. Add the foreground to finish the painting.

MATERIALS

2" Brush	Midnight Black
1" Brush	Dark Sienna
#6 Fan Brush	Van Dyke Brown
#2 Script Liner Brush	Alizarin Crimson
Large Knife	Sap Green
Small Knife	Cadmium Yellow
Black Gesso	Yellow Ochre
Liquid White	Indian Yellow
Titanium White	Bright Red
Phthalo Blue	

Use a foam applicator to cover your canvas with a thin coat of the Black Gesso, allowing an irregular-shaped area to remain unpainted just above the horizon. (Photo 1.) Allow the Black Gesso to dry completely before you begin your painting.

With the 2" brush, cover the dry Black Gesso with a thin coat of a mixture of Van Dyke Brown, Phthalo Blue and Sap Green. Cover the White, unpainted area in the sky with a thin coat of Liquid White. Do NOT allow these colors to dry before you begin. (Photo 2.)

SKY

Load the 2" brush with Cadmium Yellow. Starting in the lightest area of the sky, begin making criss-cross strokes just above the horizon. (Photo 3.) Without cleaning the brush, add Yellow Ochre above the Cadmium Yellow and then Bright Red. (The Red will look Orange because of the Yellows already on the brush.) Starting at the top of the canvas, make criss-cross strokes with Phthalo Blue on the brush, allowing the color to extend downward and blend with the Bright Red. With a clean, dry 2" brush, blend the entire sky-areas of the canvas.

BACKGROUND

Highlight the grassy areas with the 2" brush and various mixtures of Midnight Black and all of the Yellows (to make Green). Load the brush by holding it at a 45-degree angle and tapping the bristles into the various paint mixtures. Allow the brush to "slide" slightly forward in the paint each time you tap (this assures that the very tips of the bristles are fully loaded with paint). Hold the brush horizontally and gently tap downward, carefully creating the lay-of-the-land. (Photo 4.) If you are also careful not to destroy all of the dark color already on the canvas, you can create grassy highlights that look almost like velvet. (Photo 5.)

Using the same mixtures, tap downward with just the top corner of the brush (Photo 6) to lightly highlight the small background trees (Photo 7).

CABIN

The cabin is made with the knife and Van Dyke Brown. Pull the paint out very flat on your palette and just cut across to load the long edge of the knife with a small roll of paint. Begin with the back edge of the roof and then pull down the front of the roof. Add the side and front of the cabin. "Bounce" the highlights on the roof with a mixture of Titanium White, Midnight Black and Van Dyke Brown.

Use the small knife to highlight the front of the cabin with a mixture of Titanium White, Dark Sienna and Van Dyke Brown, using so little pressure that the paint "breaks." Add more Van Dyke Brown to the mixture for the darker highlights on the side of the cabin. The door is made with Van Dyke Brown and the window with a mixture of Titanium White and Phthalo Blue. Touch additional highlights to all of the edges with a very small amount of Titanium White on the knife and your cabin is complete. (Photo 8.)

Remove any excess paint from the base of the cabin and then add additional small trees and grassy highlights. (Photo 9.) The path is made with short horizontal strokes using Van Dyke Brown on the long edge of the knife. Watch your perspective here, the path should be wider as it moves forward and nears the bottom of the canvas. (Photo 10.)

LARGE TREES

The tree trunks are made with a very thin mixture of paint thinner, Titanium White and Van Dyke Brown. Start at the top of the canvas and pull downward. *(Photo 11.)* You can give your trunks (and branches) a gnarled appearance by continually turning the brush as you pull downward. *(Photo 12.)*

Add foliage to the trees by tapping the bristles of the 1″ brush into various mixtures of Midnight Black and all of the Yellows. Just tap downward with the brush *(Photo 13)* to create the leaf clusters. Don't be in too much of a hurry here, you want individual limbs and branches. You can create form and shape in your tree if you are very careful not to "kill" all of the dark color already on the canvas. *(Photo 14.)*

FOREGROUND

Working in layers and still creating the lay-of-the-land *(Photo 15)* extend the grassy highlights into the foreground *(Photo 16)*. Highlight the path with short, horizontal strokes using Titanium White on the fan brush. *(Photo 17.)*

FINISHING TOUCHES

Add small rocks and stones to the edges of the path with Titanium White and Van Dyke Brown on the fan brush *(Photo 18)* and your painting is finished and ready for a signature *(Photo 19)*.

Nestled Cabin

1. Paint the canvas with Black Gesso shapes . . .

2. . . . then add various transparent paints over the Black Gesso.

3. Create the light sky with criss-cross strokes.

4. Use the 2″ brush . . .

5. . . . to tap in the grassy areas . . .

6. . . . in the background.

7. With the top corner of the 2″ brush . . .

8. . . . highlight the background trees.

Nestled Cabin

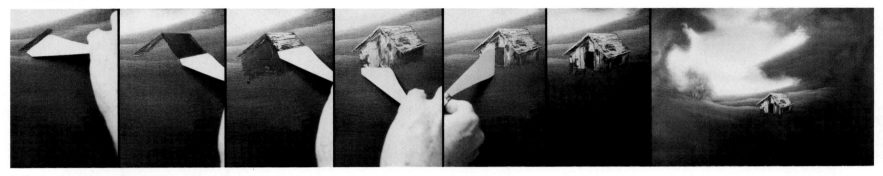

9. Progressional steps used to paint the cabin.

10. Add the grassy area to the base of the cabin . . .

11. . . . then use the knife for the path.

12. With very thin paint on the liner brush . . .

13. . . . add the large tree trunks.

14. Use the 1″ brush to tap the foliage . . .

15. . . . on the larger trees.

16. Continue adding grass.

17. Use the fan brush to highlight the path, . . .

18. . . . add small stones . . .

19. . . . and the painting is ready for a signature.

MATERIALS

2″ Brush	Midnight Black
1″ Brush	Dark Sienna
#6 Fan Brush	Van Dyke Brown
#2 Script Liner Brush	Alizarin Crimson
Large Knife	Sap Green
Adhesive-Backed Plastic	Cadmium Yellow
Black Gesso	Yellow Ochre
Liquid White	Indian Yellow
Titanium White	Bright Red
Phthalo Blue	

Start by covering the entire canvas with adhesive-backed plastic (such as Con-Tact Paper) from which you have removed a center oval.

Use a foam applicator to cover the exposed area of the canvas with a thin, even coat of Black Gesso, and allow to DRY COMPLETELY. (Photo 1.)

With the 2″ brush, apply a very thin, even coat of Alizarin Crimson to the Black canvas. Do NOT allow this paint to dry before you begin.

SKY

Load the 2″ brush with Cadmium Yellow and a small amount of Titanium White. Begin by making criss-cross strokes in the center of the lightest area of the sky, just above the horizon. (Photo 2.) The color will become darker as you work outward towards the edges of the canvas. Repeat this process as many times as necessary to achieve the desired amount of lightness, always starting with a clean, dry brush. Blend the entire sky. (Photo 3.)

BACKGROUND

Load the 2″ brush by tapping the bristles into Alizarin Crimson with a very small amount of Phthalo Blue. Use just the corner of the brush to tap downward to add the small trees and bushes along the horizon. As you work forward, underpaint the larger tree and bush shapes in the background. (Photo 4.)

Thin the Alizarin Crimson-Phthalo Blue mixture with paint thinner and use the liner brush to add the tree trunks, limbs and branches. (Photo 5.) Try to give the trunks a gnarled appearance by turning and wiggling the brush as you apply the paint. (Photo 6.)

Add Titanium White to the same mixture to highlight the trees. Again, use just one corner of the 2″ brush and tap downward, concentrating on individual limbs and branches—don't just hit at random. (Photo 7.) Working forward in layers, be careful not to completely cover all of the dark undercolor; allow it to separate the individual tree and bush shapes. (Photo 8.)

To highlight the soft grassy areas, load the 2″ brush by holding it at a 45-degree angle and tapping the bristles into the various mixtures of Midnight Black with all of the Yellows, Sap Green and Bright Red. Allow the brush to "slide" slightly forward in the paint each time you tap (this assures that the very tips of the bristles are fully loaded with paint).

Starting at the base of the background trees, hold the brush horizontally and gently tap downward. Work in layers, carefully creating the lay-of-the-land. If you are also careful not to destroy all of the dark color already on the canvas, you can create grassy highlights that look almost like velvet. (Photo 9.)

STREAM

Starting in the background and working forward, use a mixture of Van Dyke Brown and Dark Sienna on the knife and short, horizontal strokes to underpaint the stream. (Photo 10.) (To load the knife, pull the mixture out very flat on your palette and holding the knife upright, just cut across to load the long edge of the knife with a small roll of paint.) Watch your perspective here, allow the stream to become wider as it nears the foreground. Add highlights to this rocky land area by adding Titanium White to the mixture on the knife, using so little pressure that the paint "breaks". (Photo 11.)

Use a mixture of Liquid White and Titanium White with a very small amount of Phthalo Blue on the fan brush to add the water. Starting in the distance, use short, horizontal strokes to begin adding the stream. As you work forward, pull straight down for the waterfalls *(Photo 12)*, then use tiny push-up strokes *(Photo 13)* for the foaming action at the base of the falls *(Photo 14)*.

FOREGROUND

To add the water in the foreground, use Titanium White on the 2″ brush, pull straight down *(Photo 15)*, then lightly brush across. Continue highlighting the grassy areas along the water's edge *(Photo 16)* still using the 2″ brush.

Underpaint the foreground grassy area with the Alizarin Crimson-Phthalo Blue mixture on the 2″ brush *(Photo 17)*, then highlight by re-loading the brush with the Yellow highlight mixtures *(Photo 18)*.

Underpaint the foreground bushes with the Alizarin Crimson-Phthalo Blue mixture on the 1″ brush. To highlight the bushes, dip the 1″ brush into Liquid White and then pull the brush several times in one direction through the Yellow highlight mixtures (to round one corner). With the rounded corner up, force the bristles to bend upward to shape individual bushes *(Photo 19)* along the water's edge *(Photo 20)*.

At this point, carefully remove the Con-Tact Paper from the canvas *(Photo 21)* to expose your painted oval *(Photo 22)*.

LARGE TREES

Use a small roll of Van Dyke Brown on the long edge of the knife to add the tree trunks. Hold the knife vertically and starting at the base of the tree, use a series of short, sideways strokes, allowing the top of one tree to extend outside of the oval. *(Photo 23.)*

Highlight the left sides of the trunks with Titanium White on the knife, using slightly rounded strokes and so little pressure that the paint "breaks". *(Photo 24.)*

Use a very thin mixture of Van Dyke Brown on the liner brush to add the limbs and branches. *(Photo 25.)* (To load the liner brush, thin the paint to an ink-like consistency by first dipping the liner brush into paint thinner. Slowly turn the brush as you pull the bristles through the mixture, forcing them to a sharp point.) Apply very little pressure to the brush as you shape the limbs and branches. If you have trouble making the paint flow, be sure that the brush is FULLY loaded with a THIN mixture.

FINISHING TOUCHES

To sign your masterpiece, again use a thinned mixture on the liner brush. Hopefully, you have again experienced the true joy of painting! *(Photo 26.)*

Crimson Oval

1. Cover the oval with Black Gesso.

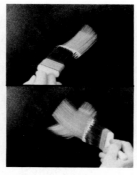

2. Use criss-cross strokes . . .

3. . . . to paint the sky.

4. Tap down tree shapes with the 2″ brush.

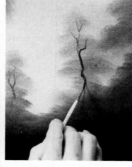

5. Use the liner brush . . .

6. . . . to add trunks to the background trees.

Crimson Oval

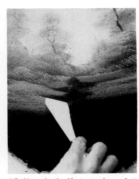
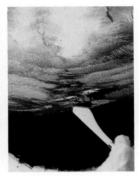

7. Use the corner of the 2" brush . . .

8. . . . to highlight the trees.

9. Tap in soft grassy areas with the 2" brush.

10. Use the knife to underpaint the stream . . .

11. . . . then apply the highlights.

12. Pull down with the fan brush for waterfalls . . .

13. . . . push up for water splashes . . .

14. . . . as the stream moves forward.

15. Pull down with the 2" brush . . .

16. . . . to add the still water at the base of the falls.

17. Use the 2" brush to underpaint . . .

18. . . . and highlight the foreground grassy areas.

19. Use the 1" brush . . .

20. . . . to highlight fore-ground bushes.

21. Carefully remove the Con-Tact Paper . . .

22. . . . before continuing.

23. Use the knife to paint . . .

24. . . . and highlight the large trunk.

25. After adding limbs and branches . . .

26. . . . your painting is complete.

RIPPLING WATERS

MATERIALS

2″ Brush	Dark Sienna
#6 Filbert Brush	Van Dyke Brown
#6 Fan Brush	Alizarin Crimson
#2 Script Liner Brush	Sap Green
Liquid White	Cadmium Yellow
Liquid Black	Yellow Ochre
Titanium White	Indian Yellow
Phthalo Blue	Bright Red
Midnight Black	

Use the 2″ brush to cover the upper ¾ of the canvas with a thin, even coat of Liquid White. With long horizontal and vertical strokes, work back and forth to ensure an even distribution of paint on the canvas. With a clean, dry 2″ brush, cover the lower ¼ of the canvas with Liquid Black, diffusing the harsh edge between the two colors. With the Liquid Black still on the brush, tap in just the basic indication of tree shapes along the horizon. Do NOT allow the Liquid White and Liquid Black to dry before you begin.

SKY

Load a clean, dry 2″ brush with a small amount of Yellow Ochre, tapping the bristles firmly against the palette to ensure an even distribution of paint throughout the bristles. Use criss-cross strokes *(Photo 1)* to paint a circular area in the sky where you would like your sun to be. (Slightly off-center.)

Clean the brush and re-load it by tapping the bristles into Alizarin Crimson. Still using criss-cross strokes, paint an area around the Yellow Ochre. Continuing to work out from the center to the edges of the canvas, use a mixture of Alizarin Crimson and Phthalo Blue on the brush. Use a clean, dry 2″ brush to blend the entire sky.

With Titanium White on a clean, dry 2″ brush, again, starting in the center and working out towards the edges of the canvas, make criss-cross strokes *(Photo 2)* to lighten the sky. Blend with a clean, dry 2″ brush. *(Photo 3.)* Use Titanium White on your finger tip to add the sun *(Photo 4)* then, lightly blend.

BACKGROUND

Use long horizontal strokes to underpaint the lower portion of the canvas (over the Liquid Black) with a Lavender mixture of Alizarin Crimson and Phthalo Blue on the 2″ brush. Use the same mixture on the same brush to tap in the more distinct, background tree shapes. *(Photo 5.)*

Add the background tree trunks *(Photo 6)* using the Lavender mixture and the liner brush. (To load the liner brush, thin the Lavender mixture to an ink-like consistency by first dipping the liner brush into paint thinner. Slowly turn the brush as you pull the bristles through the mixture, forcing them to a sharp point.) Apply very little pressure to the brush, as you shape the trunks. By turning and wiggling the brush, you can give your trunks a gnarled appearance. *(Photo 7.)*

Load the 2″ brush by tapping the bristles into various mixtures of all of the Yellows, Bright Red, Sap Green and Van Dyke Brown. Highlight the trees by just tapping downward with one corner of the brush. *(Photo 8.)* Don't just hit at random, this is where you begin to shape separate, individual trees. *(Photo 9.)*

Use the same mixtures to highlight the soft grassy area at the base of the trees. Load the 2″ brush by holding it at a 45-degree angle and tapping the bristles into the various paint mixtures. Allow the brush to "slide" slightly forward in the paint each time you tap (this assures that the very tips of the bristles are fully loaded with paint). Hold the brush horizontally and gently tap downward. *(Photo 10.)* Work in layers, carefully creating the lay-of-the-land. If you are also careful not to destroy all of the dark color already on the canvas, you can create grassy highlights that look almost like velvet. *(Photo 11.)*

STREAM

Load the fan brush with a mixture of Liquid White and Titanium White with a very small amount of Phthalo Blue. Starting in the distance, use short, horizontal strokes to begin adding the stream. (Watch your perspective here, the stream is very narrow in the distance and becomes quite wide near the foreground.) As you work forward, pull straight down for the waterfalls *(Photo 12),* then use tiny push-up strokes *(Photo 13)* for the foaming action at the base of the falls.

As you continue to move the water forward, add the rocks and stones with the filbert brush. Load both sides of the bristles with Van Dyke Brown, then pull one side of the bristles through a mixture of the Liquid White and Dark Sienna (to double-load the brush). By always keeping the light side of the brush facing upward *(Photo 14)* you can shape and highlight the stones in single strokes *(Photo 15).*

FOREGROUND

Use a mixture of Midnight Black, Alizarin Crimson and Van Dyke Brown on the 2″ brush to underpaint the large bushes in the foreground, along the water's edge. *(Photo 16.)* Highlight the bushes with various mixtures of all of the Yellows, Midnight Black, Sap Green, and Bright Red on the 2″ brush. With just one corner of the brush, tap downward to shape each individual bush.

Use the point of the knife to scratch in stems, sticks and twigs. With the Titanium White mixture on the fan brush, "swirl" in water at the base of the foreground bushes.

LARGE TREES

Still using the Midnight Black-Alizarin Crimson-Van Dyke Brown mixture on the 2″ brush, hold the brush horizontally and tap downward *(Photo 17)* to underpaint the foliage on the tall trees. (Be careful not to lose your sun!)

Use a mixture of paint thinner and Van Dyke Brown on the liner brush to add trunks, limbs and branches to the trees. *(Photo 18.)* Again, try to give your trunks a gnarled appearance. We don't want telephone poles.

Highlight the foliage with various mixtures of all of the Yellows, Midnight Black, and Sap Green on the same brush. Use just the corner of the brush to tap downward, shaping the individual leaf clusters. *(Photo 19.)* Be very careful not to completely cover all of the dark undercolor. You need this dark in order to show the bright highlights.

FINISHING TOUCHES

Use thinned mixtures on the liner brush to add final, small details (sticks, twigs, branches, etc.), not the least of which is your signature. Sign with pride and your painting is complete! *(Photo 20.)*

Rippling Waters

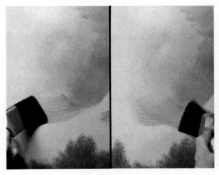

1. Use criss-cross strokes to begin painting the sky . . .

2. . . . then add the light area around the sun.

3. After tapping in background tree shapes . . .

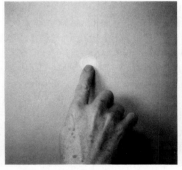

4. . . . use White paint on your finger tip . . .

5. . . . to add the sun to the sky.

Rippling Waters

6. Use thinned paint on the liner brush . . .

7. . . . to add the background tree trunks.

8. Tap downward with the 2" brush . . .

9. . . . to highlight the background trees.

10. Also tap down with the 2" brush . . .

11. . . . to highlight the soft grassy areas.

12. Pull down waterfalls with the fan brush . . .

13. . . . then push up at the base of the falls.

14. Use single strokes with the filbert brush . . .

15. . . . to paint and highlight the rocks and stones . . .

16. . . . along the water's edge.

17. Underpaint large trees with the 2" brush . . .

18. . . . then add trunks with the liner brush . . .

19. . . . and highlights with the 2" brush . . .

20. . . . and your painting is ready for a signature!

QUIET MOUNTAIN LAKE

MATERIALS

2" Brush	Prussian Blue
1" Brush	Midnight Black
#6 Fan Brush	Dark Sienna
#2 Script Liner Brush	Van Dyke Brown
Large Knife	Alizarin Crimson
Black Gesso	Sap Green
Liquid White	Cadmium Yellow
Liquid Clear	Yellow Ochre
Titanium White	Indian Yellow
Phthalo Blue	Bright Red

Prepare the canvas by pre-painting the dark shapes with Black Gesso. Be sure to include the small rock and stone shapes in the foreground. Allow the Black Gesso to DRY COMPLETELY. (Photo 1.)

Use the 2" brush to cover the dry Black Gesso-areas with a VERY, VERY THIN coat of Liquid Clear. Do NOT allow the Liquid Clear to dry. Over the wet Liquid Clear, apply a mixture of Sap Green, Phthalo Blue and Van Dyke Brown, to the dark areas of the canvas.

The light areas (above the horizon) are covered with a very thin, even coat of Liquid White. Do NOT allow these paints to dry before you begin.

SKY

With Prussian Blue, use the corner of the fan brush and circular strokes to form the cloud shapes. (Photo 2.) Actually, you are not painting "cloud" shapes, but shaping the Blue-sky area behind the clouds. Use a 1" brush and criss-cross strokes to carefully blend the sky. (Photo 3.) The portions of the canvas which remain White will be the clouds, so try not to drag the Blue into the White shapes as you blend.

Use Titanium White on the fan brush and tiny, circular strokes with the corner to highlight just the edges of the cloud-shapes. (Photo 4.) Still using circular strokes, blend with the corner of a clean, dry 2" brush. (Photo 5.) Use upward sweeping strokes to "fluff". (Photo 6.)

MOUNTAIN

The mountain is painted with the knife and a mixture of Van Dyke Brown and Midnight Black. Pull the mixture out very flat on your palette, hold the knife straight up and "cut" across the mixture to load the long edge of the blade with a small roll of paint. (Holding the knife straight up will force the small roll of paint to the very edge of the blade.) With firm pressure, shape just the top edge of the mountain. (Photo 7.) When you are satisfied with the basic shape of the mountain top, use the knife to remove any excess paint. Then, with the 2" brush, blend the paint down to the base of the mountain (Photo 8) to complete the entire mountain shape.

Highlight the mountain with various mixtures of Titanium White, Dark Sienna and a small amount of Bright Red and Van Dyke Brown. Again, load the long edge of the knife with a small roll of paint. Starting at the top (and paying close attention to angles) glide the knife down the right side of each peak, using so little pressure that the paint "breaks". You can vary the color by using mixtures of Titanium White and Midnight Black. (Photo 9.) Use the original, dark, mountain-mixture, applied in the opposing direction, for the shadow sides of the peaks. Again, use so little pressure that the paint "breaks".

Diffuse the base of the mountain by tapping with a clean, dry 2" brush (carefully following the angles) then gently lift upward to create the illusion of mist. (Photo 10.)

BACKGROUND

Load the fan brush with a mixture of Sap Green, Midnight Black, Van Dyke Brown and Prussian Blue. Holding the brush vertically, just tap downward to indicate the small trees at the base of the mountain. (Photo 11.) Extend the color into the water and then pull the color straight down with the 2" brush for reflections. Lightly brush across to give the reflections a "watery" appearance. Shimmer the water by pulling down with a very small amount of Titanium White on the 2" brush (Photo 12) and again, lightly brush across.

Add the land at the base of the small trees with the same dark tree mixture, using "push-up" strokes with the fan brush. To indicate the tiny tree trunks, use Titanium White on a clean fan brush. Hold the brush horizontally and starting at the base of the trees, make a series of very short, upward strokes. *(Photo 13.)*

With a mixture of Cadmium Yellow and Midnight Black (to make a very dark Green) on the fan brush, lightly highlight the ground area at the base of the trees, again using small "push-up" strokes. *(Photo 14.)*

Use a mixture of Liquid White and Dark Sienna on the long edge of the knife *(Photo 15)* to "cut" in the water lines and ripples *(Photo 16)*.

TREES

Add the subtle indication of trunks to the dark, under-painted tree shapes with a mixture of Van Dyke Brown, Dark Sienna and Titanium White on the fan brush. Hold the brush vertically and starting at the top of the trees, just pull down. *(Photo 17.)*

To highlight the foliage on the large trees, load the 2" brush by holding it at a 45-degree angle and tapping the bristles into the various mixtures of Midnight Black, all of the Yellows and a small amount of Bright Red. Allow the brush to "slide" slightly forward in the paint mixtures each time you tap (this assures that the very tips of the bristles are fully loaded with paint).

Hold the brush horizontally and use just one corner of the brush to gently tap downward *(Photo 18)* carefully creating layers of individual leaf-clusters. Don't just hit at random. *(Photo 19.)*

With Van Dyke Brown on the fan brush, hold the brush vertically and tap in the larger, closer tree trunks. Use Titanium White on the fan brush and tap highlights to the right sides of the trunks. *(Photo 20.)* Add limbs and branches to these trunks with thinned Van Dyke Brown on the liner brush. *(Photo 21.)* Again, use the corner of the 2" brush to highlight the lighter, brighter foliage on the closer trees. *(Photo 22.)* Carefully shape individual leaf clusters and then small bushes at the base of the trees. *(Photo 23.)* At the same time, be very careful not to completely destroy the dark under-color.

Use the same highlight mixtures on the 2" brush to add the soft grassy area in the foreground. Again, after fully loading the tips of the bristles, hold the brush horizontally and gently tap downward. *(Photo 24.)* Work in layers, carefully creating the lay-of-the-land. If you are again careful not to destroy all of the dark color already on the canvas, you can create grassy highlights that look almost like velvet. *(Photo 25.)*

FINISHING TOUCHES

Load the liner brush with thinned paint to add small sticks and twigs and other final details, not the least of which is your signature!

Quiet Mountain Lake

1. Under-paint the dark areas with Black Gesso.

2. Shape the sky-area with the corner of the fan brush . . .

3. . . . then blend with the 1" brush.

4. Highlight the clouds with White on the fan brush.

5. Use the top corner of the 2" brush . . .

6. . . . to blend the clouds.

Quiet Mountain Lake

7. Shape the mountain-top with the knife . . .

8. . . . then blend down to the base with the 2″ brush.

9. Use a small roll of paint on the edges of the knife . . .

10. . . . to apply highlights and shadows to the mountain.

11. Tap down with the fan brush to paint distant evergreens.

12. Pull straight down with the 2″ brush to paint the water.

13. Tiny trunks are made with short, upward strokes . . .

14. . . . and grassy highlights are push-up strokes.

15. Use a small roll of paint on the edge of the knife . . .

16. . . . to cut in water lines and ripples.

17. Tree trunks are pulled down with the fan brush.

18. Then use the 2″ brush . . .

19. . . . to add foliage to the trees.

20. Make and highlight trunks with the fan brush . . .

21. . . . then use the liner brush . . .

22. . . . to add the limbs and branches.

23. Use the 2″ brush to highlight small brushes . . .

24. . . . and grassy areas, by tapping downward . . .

25. . . . and your painting is complete.

WATERFALL IN THE WOODS

MATERIALS

2" Brush	Phthalo Blue
1" Brush	Midnight Black
#6 Fan Brush	Dark Sienna
#2 Script Liner Brush	Van Dyke Brown
Small Knife	Alizarin Crimson
Black Gesso	Sap Green
Liquid White	Cadmium Yellow
Liquid Clear	Yellow Ochre
Titanium White	Indian Yellow

Use a foam brush and Black Gesso to block in the basic dark shapes of the painting. Be sure to leave the light area, near the center of the canvas, unpainted. (Photo 1.) Allow the Black Gesso to DRY COMPLETELY before proceeding.

Use the 2" brush to cover the entire canvas with a VERY THIN coat of Liquid Clear. While the Liquid Clear is still wet, apply a thin, even coat of a Lavender mixture made with Phthalo Blue and Alizarin Crimson. Do NOT allow these colors to dry before you begin.

SKY

Load a clean, dry 2" brush with Titanium White. Begin by making criss-cross strokes in the light (un-Gessoed) area of the sky, above the waterfall. (Photo 2.) Repeat until you achieve the desired amount of lightness in the sky. (Photo 3.)

Without cleaning the brush, load it with a small amount of the Phthalo Blue-Alizarin Crimson (Lavender). Use one corner of the brush to tap in the very subtle, background tree shapes. (Photo 4.)

Add just the indication of background tree trunks using a thinned Lavender mixture on the liner brush (Photo 5) then lightly highlight the trees with a small amount of Titanium White on the 2" brush (Photo 6).

Continue highlighting the background trees with the Phthalo Blue-Alizarin Crimson Lavender mixture and Titanium White on the 2" brush. You can also use the same mixtures on the fan brush (Photo 7) to paint small, background tree shapes (Photo 8).

WATERFALL

The waterfall is made with Titanium White, and a very small amount of Phthalo Blue. Thin the mixture by first dipping the 1" brush into Liquid Clear and then pulling both sides of the bristles through the mixture, loading the brush to a chiseled edge.

To paint the waterfall, hold the brush horizontally. Starting at the top of the falls, make a short horizontal stroke and then pull straight down (to the base of the falls) with a single, long vertical stroke. (Photo 9.) Repeat this stroke as many times as necessary. Use a clean, dry 2" brush to blend the base of the falls by lightly lifting upward. (Photo 10.) Tap downward with Titanium White on the 2" brush (Photo 11) to create the mist at the base of the falls (Photo 12).

TREE

Add the larger tree trunk (at the top of the cliff on the right side) with a mixture of Dark Sienna and Titanium White on the liner brush. Use very little pressure on the brush, as you shape the trunk. By turning and wiggling the brush, you can give the trunk a gnarled appearance. (Photo 13.)

Highlight the tree with various mixtures of Sap Green, all of the Yellows and Midnight Black (to make a dark Green). Load the 2" brush by holding it at a 45-degree angle and tapping the bristles into the mixture. Allow the brush to "slide" slightly forward in the paint each time you tap (this assures that the very tips of the bristles are fully loaded with paint). Gently tap downward with one corner of the brush, shaping individual leaf clusters. (Photo 14.)

CLIFFS

Use the small knife and a mixture of Van Dyke Brown and Dark Sienna to add the cliff on the right side, starting at the base of the tree, extending this color towards the base of the falls. Very lightly highlight the top of the cliff with a mixture of Van Dyke Brown, Dark Sienna and Titanium White on the knife, using so little pressure that the paint "breaks". *(Photo 15.)* Be very careful of angles as you lightly "pull" the highlights over the edge and down the side of the cliff.

Use the Yellow-Green highlight mixtures on the 2" brush to add the soft grassy area at the top of the cliff, extending down the side of the cliff. Just tap downward with the corner of the brush, again, be very careful of angles. *(Photo 16.)* Working in layers, you can continue to use the Van Dyke Brown mixture on the small knife to add rocks and stones *(Photo 17)* near the base of the falls *(Photo 18)*. (Highlight by adding Titanium White to the mixture.)

The still water at the base of the falls is made with the 2" brush. Load the brush with Titanium White and a very small amount of Phthalo Blue. Holding the brush horizontally, start at the base of the falls, press the bristles against the canvas and pull straight down, several times. *(Photo 19.)* Lightly brush across, to blend. Notice how the White mixes with the color already on the canvas and you have beautiful, Lavender water. *(Photo 20.)*

FOREGROUND

As you work forward in the painting, the large cliff on the left is also shaped with a mixture of Van Dyke Brown and Dark Sienna on the knife. Again, highlight by adding Titanium White to the mixture, using so little pressure that the

paint is allowed to "break". *(Photo 21.)*

Still paying close attention to angles, add the soft grass on the side of the cliff with the Yellow-Green highlight mixtures on the 2" brush. *(Photo 22.)* Try not to completely cover the highlights on the cliff, but you can allow some of the grassy area to extend out over the waterfall. Pull a small amount of this Green highlight color into the water with the 2" brush and lightly brush across, for reflections. *(Photo 23.)*

Under-paint the large foreground trees with the original Phthalo Blue-Alizarin Crimson mixture on the 2" brush. Add the trunks, limbs and branches with a thinned mixture of Dark Sienna, Van Dyke Brown and Titanium White on the liner brush. Highlight the foliage with the Yellow-Green mixtures on the 2" brush. Be very careful to create individual leaf clusters, paying close attention to shape and form. *(Photo 24.)*

Underpaint the foreground grassy area with the Phthalo Blue-Alizarin Crimson on the 2" brush and highlight with the same Yellow-Green mixtures. *(Photo 25.)* Use Van Dyke Brown and Dark Sienna on the knife to shape small rocks and stones and again highlight by adding Titanium White to the mixture.

FINISHING TOUCHES

Use Liquid White on the long edge of the knife for the water lines *(Photo 26)* and your masterpiece is ready for a signature *(Photo 27)*!

Waterfall In The Woods

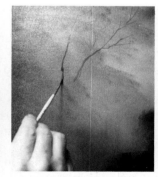

1. Under-paint the canvas with Black Gesso.

2. Use the 2" brush and criss-cross strokes . . .

3. . . . to paint the sky.

4. Paint background trees with the 2" brush . . .

5. . . . then add trunks with the liner brush . . .

6. . . . then, highlight with the large brush.

Waterfall In The Woods

7. Also use the fan brush . . .

8. . . . to paint the background trees.

9. Pull the falls down with the 1" brush . . .

10. . . . then blend up with the 2" brush.

11. Use White on the 2" brush . . .

12. . . . to tap in the mist at the base of the falls.

13. Add light trunks with the liner brush . . .

14. . . . and foliage with the 2" brush.

15. Use the small knife to paint the cliffs.

16. Foliage with the 2" brush . . .

17. . . . and rocks and stones with the knife . . .

18. . . . are added to the cliff.

19. Pull straight down to add the water . . .

20. . . . then lightly brush across.

21. Use the knife to add the cliff . . .

22. . . . and the brush to add the foliage . . .

23. . . . to the left side of the painting.

24. Use the 2" brush to tap in trees . . .

25. . . . and grassy areas.

26. Cut in water lines with Liquid White . . .

27. . . . and the painting is finished!

WINTER ELEGANCE

MATERIALS

2" Brush	Phthalo Blue
1" Round Brush	Midnight Black
#6 Filbert Brush	Dark Sienna
#6 Fan Brush	Van Dyke Brown
#2 Script Liner Brush	Alizarin Crimson
Large Knife	Cadmium Yellow
Small Knife	Yellow Ochre
Liquid White	Bright Red
Titanium White	

Start by using the 2" brush to cover the entire canvas with a thin, even coat of Liquid White. With long horizontal and vertical strokes, work back and forth to ensure an even distribution of paint on the canvas. Do NOT allow the Liquid White to dry before you begin. Clean and dry the brush.

SKY

Load the 2" brush with a small amount of Cadmium Yellow, tapping the bristles firmly against the palette to ensure an even distribution of paint throughout the bristles. Use criss-cross strokes to begin painting the center of the sky, just above the horizon. (Photo 1.)

Working outward and upward, add Yellow Ochre and then Bright Red to the same brush, continuing to use criss-cross strokes. The outside edges of the sky are painted with a mixture of Phthalo Blue and Midnight Black.

With the Phthalo Blue-Midnight Black mixture still in the brush, use long, horizontal strokes to under-paint the lower portion of the canvas.

Use a clean, dry 2" brush and criss-cross strokes to add Titanium White to the lightest area of the sky. Repeat as many times as necessary to achieve the desired lightness, always starting with a clean, dry brush and working from the center of the sky outward. (Try not to drag the dirty brush back into the light area.)

Clean and dry the brush to blend the entire sky, working from the center of the light area outward, still using criss-cross strokes. You can also add a small amount of Alizarin Crimson near the Blue area, to create the Lavender areas in the sky. Blend the entire canvas with a clean, dry 2" brush. (Photo 2.)

BACKGROUND

Load the round brush by tapping the bristles into Midnight Black. Starting at the base of the trees and working upward, tap in the basic tree shapes along the horizon. (Photo 3.)

Add the background tree trunks using thinned Midnight Black on the liner brush. (Photo 4.) To load the liner brush, thin the Midnight Black to an ink-like consistency by first dipping the liner brush into paint thinner. Slowly turn the brush as you pull the bristles through the paint, forcing them to a sharp point. Apply very little pressure to the brush as you shape the trunks. By turning and wiggling the brush, you can give your trunks a gnarled appearance. (Photo 5.)

Load the 2" brush with Titanium White and use long horizontal strokes to add snow to the base of the background trees. (Photo 6.)

WATER

Load the small knife with a small roll of a mixture of Midnight Black and Titanium White (to make Gray). To load the knife, pull the mixture out very flat on your palette, hold the knife straight up and "cut" across the mixture to load the long edge of the blade with a small roll of paint. (Holding the knife straight up will force the small roll of paint to the very edge of the blade.)

Add the banks along the water's edge, paying close attention to the lay-of-the-land. You want the banks to slope down towards the water. (Photo 7.)

Extend the Gray color into the water for reflections and then pull straight down with the 2" brush. (Photo 8.) Lightly brush across to give the reflections a "watery" appearance. Again, with Titanium White on the 2" brush, use long sweeping strokes (Photo 9) to bring the snow over the banks (Photo 10).

Working in layers, extend the banks, water and snow to the bottom of the canvas. You can add a very small amount of Phthalo Blue to your brush for additional shadows in the snow. *(Photo 11.)*

TREES

Load the fan brush with a mixture of Van Dyke Brown and Dark Sienna. Holding the brush vertically, start at the top of the trees and just pull down. Apply more pressure to the brush as you near the base of the trees to create the thicker bottom of the trunk. *(Photo 12.)*

Highlight the trunks with a small roll of a mixture of Titanium White and Dark Sienna on the long edge of the knife. Hold the knife vertically and touch the highlights to the right sides of the trunks. *(Photo 13.)*

Use a thinned mixture of Van Dyke Brown and Dark Sienna on the liner brush to add the limbs and branches *(Photo 14)* then use a small amount of Liquid White to add snowy details to the base of the trees.

STONES

Load the filbert brush with the Gray mixture (Titanium White and Midnight Black), then pull ONE side of the bristles through a thin mixture of Liquid White and Gray, to double-load the brush. With the light side of the brush up, use a series of curved, single strokes to shape the rocks and stones. *(Photo 15.)* Extend the dark color into the water for reflections, then with a small roll of Liquid White on the edge of the small knife, cut in the water lines at the base of each of the rocks and stones *(Photo 16)* to complete the water *(Photo 17)*.

LARGE FOREGROUND TREE

Again, use Van Dyke Brown on the fan brush to paint the large, foreground tree trunk *(Photo 18)* and highlight with Titanium White and Dark Sienna on the knife *(Photo 19)*. Use thinned Van Dyke Brown to add the limbs and branches. *(Photo 20.)*

With the Gray mixture on the round brush, tap in the indication of foliage on all of the trees. *(Photo 21.)*

Use a mixture of Liquid White and Titanium White on the round brush to add snow to the foliage, again just tapping downward. Form individual leaf clusters, try not to just "hit" at random and be very careful not to completely cover all of the dark under-color. *(Photo 22.)*

FINISHING TOUCHES

Add final snowy details with Liquid White on the liner brush and your "warm" winter painting is complete. *(Photo 23.)*

Don't forget to sign your name with pride using the liner brush and thinned color of your choice.

Winter Elegance

1. Paint the sky with criss-cross strokes . . .

2. . . . then blend the entire canvas.

3. Tap down with the round brush . . .

4. . . . then use the liner brush . . .

5. . . . to add trunks to the background trees.

Winter Elegance

6. Use the 2" brush to paint the snow.

7. Under-paint snow banks with the knife . . .

8. . . . then reflect them into the water.

9. Use the 2" brush . . .

10. . . . to pull snow over the banks.

11. Continue working forward in layers.

12. Add trunks with the fan brush . . .

13. . . . then highlight with the knife.

14. Limbs and branches are painted with the liner brush.

15. Paint rocks and stones with the filbert brush . . .

16. . . . add water lines with the knife . . .

17. . . . to complete the water.

18. Add the large foreground trunk . . .

19. . . . then highlight with the knife . . .

20. . . . and add limbs and branches.

21. Under-paint foliage . . .

22. . . . and highlight with the round brush . . .

23. . . . to complete the painting.

MATERIALS

2" Brush	Midnight Black
#6 Fan Brush	Dark Sienna
#2 Script Liner Brush	Van Dyke Brown
Large Knife	Alizarin Crimson
Liquid White	Yellow Ochre
Titanium White	Indian Yellow
Phthalo Blue	Bright Red

Start by covering the entire canvas with a thin, even coat of Liquid White. With long horizontal and vertical strokes, work back and forth to ensure an even distribution of paint on the canvas. Do NOT allow the Liquid White to dry before you begin.

SKY

Load the 2" brush with Indian Yellow, tapping the bristles firmly against the palette to ensure an even distribution of paint throughout the bristles. Starting in the upper right hand corner of the canvas, begin painting the sky with criss-cross strokes. (Photo 1.) Without cleaning the brush, as you work outward, add Yellow Ochre and then a small amount of Bright Red to the brush, always using criss-cross strokes. Use a Lavender mixture of Alizarin Crimson and Phthalo Blue on the brush and criss-cross strokes to complete the remainder of the sky.

You can also use long, horizontal strokes to add the Lavender mixture to the lower portion of the canvas, for later shadows in the snow.

With Titanium White on a clean 2" brush, use criss-cross strokes to further lighten the upper right hand corner of the canvas. Blend the entire sky with criss-cross strokes. (Photo 2.)

MOUNTAIN RANGE

The ridge of mountains is made with the knife and a mixture of Midnight Black, Phthalo Blue and Alizarin Crimson. (To load the knife, pull the mixture out very flat on your palette and holding the knife upright, just cut across to load the long edge of the knife with a small roll of paint.) With firm pressure, shape just the top edge of the mountains. (Photo 3.) Use the knife to remove any excess paint and then with the 2" brush, pull the paint down to the base of the mountains to mist and blend. (Photo 4.)

To highlight the ridge of mountains, use a mixture of Titanium White with a very small amount of Bright Red. Again, load the knife with a small roll of paint. In this painting, the light is coming from the right. Starting at the top of the mountain (and paying close attention to angles) apply the snowy highlights to the right sides of the peaks, using so little pressure that the paint "breaks". (Photo 5.)

The shadow areas are a mixture of Titanium White, Midnight Black and the Lavender (Alizarin Crimson-Phthalo Blue) mixture. Again, use so little pressure that the paint "breaks". Use the original mountain color for the very darkest crevices of the mountain.

Diffuse the base of the mountain by tapping with a clean, dry 2" brush (Photo 6) then lightly brush upward (Photo 7) to mist (Photo 8).

BACKGROUND

Load the fan brush with a mixture of Van Dyke Brown, Dark Sienna and Titanium White. Hold the brush vertically and just tap downward to paint the indication of small evergreens at the base of the mountain. (Photo 9.) Use the corner of the brush to add tiny branches to the more distinct evergreens. (Photo 10.) Firmly tap the base of the trees with the top corner of a clean, dry 2" brush (Photo 11) then lightly brush upward to mist (Photo 12).

EVERGREENS

Working forward in layers, use a darker mixture (by adding more Van Dyke Brown) to paint the larger evergreens. Load the fan brush to a chiseled edge. Holding the brush vertically, touch the canvas to create the center line of each tree. Use just the corner of the brush to begin adding the small top branches. Working from side to side, as you move down each tree, apply more pressure to the brush, forcing the bristles to bend downward and automatically the branches will become larger as you near the base of each tree. Again, tap the base of the trees firmly with the 2″ brush to mist.

Allowing the mist to separate the layers, continue working forward by using the Lavender mixture (Alizarin Crimson and Phthalo Blue) on the 2″ brush to underpaint the small grassy hill at the base of the evergreens. *(Photo 13.)*

Use a mixture of Titanium White and a very small amount of Bright Red on the 2″ brush to add snowy highlights to the hill. Load the brush by holding it at a 45-degree angle and tapping the bristles into the White mixture. Allow the brush to "slide" slightly forward in the paint each time you tap (this assures that the very tips of the bristles are fully loaded with paint).

To highlight the hill, hold the brush horizontally and gently tap downward. *(Photo 14.)* Work in layers, carefully creating the lay-of-the-land. Try not to destroy all of the dark undercolor on the canvas, use it for shadows in the snowy highlights. *(Photo 15.)*

Continuing to work forward, use Titanium White on the 2″ brush and long horizontal strokes to lay in the snow at the base of the trees and the hill. *(Photo 16.)* Extend this snow-covered ground area to the bottom of the canvas. *(Photo 17.)*

TREES

Load the 2″ brush by tapping the bristles into the Lavender mixture and Van Dyke Brown. Just tap downward with the corner of the brush to underpaint the basic shape of the large foreground tree on the left side of the painting. *(Photo 18.)*

Use Titanium White with a very small amount of Bright Red on the 2″ brush to add the snowy highlights to the trees by just tapping downward with one corner of the brush. Think about form and shape. Give your trees individual leaf clusters, try not to just hit at random. Be very careful not to "kill" the dark undercolor—use it to separate individual limbs and branches. *(Photo 19.)* If your paint refuses to stick, you can add a small amount of Liquid White to the mixture. Use Liquid White on the liner brush to indicate the tree trunks. *(Photo 20.)*

Use thinned Van Dyke Brown on the liner brush to paint the small leafless tree on the right. *(Photo 21.)* The grassy area at the base of the tree is added with the Lavender mixture on the fan brush. *(Photo 22.)* Use the 2″ brush to pull a small amount of this color into the snow for shadows. *(Photo 23.)*

FINISHING TOUCHES

Use Liquid White on the liner brush to add small snowy details or just scratch in sticks and twigs with the point of the knife and your masterpiece is ready for a signature. *(Photo 24.)* Sign with pride!

Pastel Winter

1. Make criss-cross strokes with the 2″ brush . . .

2. . . . to paint the sky.

3. Shape the mountain top with the knife . . .

4. . . . then blend down to the base with the 2″ brush.

5. Highlight the mountain with the knife . . .

6. . . . then tap with the 2″ brush . . .

7. . . . and brush upward . . .

Pastel Winter

8. . . . to diffuse and mist.

9. Tap down evergreens with the fan brush . . .

10. . . . then use just the corner of the brush to add branches.

11. Tap the base of the evergreens with the 2" brush . . .

12. . . . to create the illusion of mist.

13. Tap down grassy areas with the 2" brush . . .

14. . . . then apply snowy highlights . . .

15. . . . paying close attention to the lay-of-the-land.

16. Use the 2" brush to extend the snow . . .

17. . . . to the bottom of the canvas.

18. Under-paint large leaf trees . . .

19. . . . and then highlight with the 2" brush.

20. Use the liner brush to add tree trunks . . .

21. . . . and limbs and branches.

22. Push in grassy areas with the fan brush . . .

23. . . . then use the 2" brush to pull in shadows . . .

24. . . . and your winter masterpiece is complete!

LONE MOUNTAIN

MATERIALS

2" Brush	Midnight Black
#6 Fan Brush	Dark Sienna
Large Knife	Van Dyke Brown
Small Knife	Alizarin Crimson
Liquid White	Cadmium Yellow
Titanium White	Yellow Ochre
Phthalo Green	Indian Yellow
Phthalo Blue	Bright Red
Prussian Blue	

Use the 2" brush to cover the entire canvas with a thin, even coat of Liquid White. With long horizontal and vertical strokes, work back and forth to ensure an even distribution of paint on the canvas. Do NOT allow the Liquid White to dry before you begin.

SKY

Load the 2" brush with a very small amount of Indian Yellow and begin painting the sky with criss-cross strokes, just above the horizon. Re-load the brush with a small amount of Phthalo Blue and make criss-cross strokes across the top of the sky. As you work down towards the horizon, notice how the color blends with the Liquid White already on the canvas. *(Photo 1.)*

Use a mixture of Phthalo Blue and Phthalo Green on the 2" brush to underpaint the water on the lower portion of the canvas. Starting at the bottom of the canvas and working upward, use horizontal strokes, pulling from the outside edges of the canvas in towards the center. *(Photo 2.)* You can create a sheen on the water by allowing the center of the canvas to remain light. With a clean, dry 2" brush, use criss-cross strokes to blend the sky and long horizontal strokes to blend the water. *(Photo 3.)*

MOUNTAIN

The mountain top is made with the knife and a mixture of Midnight Black, Van Dyke Brown and Phthalo Blue. Pull the mixture out very flat on your palette, hold the knife straight up and "cut" across the mixture to load the long edge of the blade with a small roll of paint. (Holding the knife *straight up* will force the small roll of paint to the very edge of the blade.) With firm pressure, shape just the top peak of the mountain. *(Photo 4.)*

Re-load the knife with a small roll of a mixture of Titanium White and Midnight Black and very lightly touch and bounce highlights to the right sides of the peaks. *(Photo 5.)* Use a darker mixture of Titanium White, Midnight Black and Prussian Blue on the small knife for the shadowed (left) sides of the peaks. Again, use so little pressure that the paint "breaks".

Use a small roll of Titanium White on the knife to shape the glacier under the top mountain peak. Pay close attention to angles and use so little pressure that the paint "breaks". Add shadowed areas to the glacier with a very small amount of Phthalo Blue. *(Photo 6.)* Lightly blend the base of the glacier with a clean, dry 2" brush. *(Photo 7.)*

Working in layers, continue adding mountain peaks with the dark mountain mixture, then add the highlights and shadows to the peaks. *(Photo 8.)*

Use a clean, dry 2" brush to tap the base of the mountain, paying close attention to angles *(Photo 9)* then upward strokes to create the illusion of mist *(Photo 10)*.

BACKGROUND

Load the fan brush with a mixture of Midnight Black, Prussian Blue, Phthalo Green, Van Dyke Brown, and Alizarin Crimson. Holding the brush vertically, just tap downward to indicate the small evergreen trees at the base of the mountain. *(Photo 11.)* Firmly tap the base of the evergreens with a clean, dry 2" brush *(Photo 12)* then lift upward to mist.

With the dark tree mixture on the 2" brush, pull straight down to reflect the evergreens into the water. *(Photo 13.)* Lightly brush across to give the reflections a "watery" appearance. With a very small amount of Titanium White on the fan brush, make short upward strokes to just indicate tiny tree trunks. *(Photo 14.)*

Re-load the 2″ brush with the dark tree mixture, hold the brush horizontally and tap in the soft grassy area at the base of the trees. Add the Yellows to the same brush to lightly tap highlights in the soft grass. *(Photo 15.)*

Use a mixture of Titanium White and Dark Sienna on the knife to firmly scrub in the banks along the water's edge *(Photo 16)* then use a small roll of Liquid White (tinted with a very small amount of Phthalo Blue) on the knife to cut in water lines and ripples *(Photo 17)*.

FOREGROUND

Working in layers, load the 2″ brush with the Midnight Black-Phthalo Blue-Phthalo Green-Van Dyke Brown-Alizarin Crimson mixture to tap in the grassy area on the right side of the foreground. *(Photo 18.)* Pull down to reflect the dark color into the water *(Photo 19)* then lightly brush across.

Use various mixtures of all of the Yellows and Bright Red on the 2″ brush to highlight the soft grassy areas. Load the 2″ brush by holding it at a 45-degree angle and tapping the bristles into the various paint mixtures. Allow the brush to "slide" slightly forward in the paint each time you tap (this assures that the very tips of the bristles are fully loaded with paint). Hold the brush horizontally and gently tap downward. Work in layers, carefully creating the lay-of-the-land. If you are also careful not to destroy all of the dark color already on the canvas, you can create grassy highlights that look almost like velvet.

Use the Titanium White-Dark Sienna mixture on the knife

to add the water's edge, then a small roll of Liquid White-Phthalo Blue mixture *(Photo 20)* to cut in water lines and ripples *(Photo 21)*.

LARGE EVERGREENS

For the larger evergreens, load the fan brush to a chiseled edge with the dark tree mixture. Holding the brush vertically, touch the canvas to create the center line of each tree. Use just the corner of the brush to begin adding the small top branches. Working from side to side, as you move down each tree, apply more pressure to the brush, forcing the bristles to bend downward *(Photo 22)* and automatically the branches will become larger as you near the base of each tree.

Use the dark mixture on the 2″ brush to tap in the entire foreground grassy area. *(Photo 23.)* Again, use all of the Yellows and Bright Red to tap in the soft grassy highlights, carefully creating the lay-of-the-land.

Add the evergreen trunks with a small roll of a mixture of Titanium White and Dark Sienna on the knife *(Photo 24)* then use the fan brush to very lightly touch highlights to the branches with a mixture of the dark tree color and the Yellows *(Photo 19)*.

FINISHING TOUCHES

Use the point of the knife to scratch in the indication of small sticks and twigs and your painting is ready for a signature.

Lone Mountain

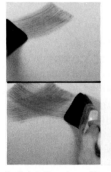      

1. Paint the sky with criss-cross strokes . . .

2. . . . then use horizontal strokes . . .

3. . . . to add the water.

4. Shape just the mountain top with the knife . . .

5. . . . then apply highlights and shadows.

6. Add the glacier with the knife . . .

7. . . . then use the 2″ brush . . .

Lone Mountain

8. . . .to blend and mist.

9. Tap with the 2" brush . . .

10. . . . to blend and mist the base of the mountain.

11. Tap down tiny evergreens . . .

12. . . . then firmly tap the base of the trees to mist.

13. Reflect trees into the water with the 2" brush . . .

14. . . . and add tiny trunks with the fan brush.

15. Use the 2" brush to tap in soft grassy areas.

16. Use Liquid White on the knife . . .

17. . . . to cut in water lines and ripples.

18. Tap in the foreground grass . . .

19. . . . and pull down to reflect it into the water.

20. Again, use the knife . . .

21. . . . to cut in foreground water lines.

22. Add large evergreens in the foreground with the fan brush . . .

23. . . . then tap in the soft grassy areas.

24. Add trunks to the evergreens . . .

25. . . . to complete the painting.

AUTUMN IMAGES

MATERIALS

2" Brush	Midnight Black
1" Brush	Dark Sienna
1" Round Brush	Van Dyke Brown
#6 Fan Brush	Alizarin Crimson
#2 Script Liner Brush	Sap Green
Large Knife	Cadmium Yellow
Liquid White	Yellow Ochre
Titanium White	Indian Yellow
Prussian Blue	Bright Red

Start by using the 2" brush to cover the entire canvas with a thin, even coat of Liquid White. With long horizontal and vertical strokes, work back and forth to ensure an even distribution of paint on the canvas. Do NOT allow the Liquid White to dry before you begin.

SKY AND WATER

Load the 2" brush with a very small amount of a mixture of Prussian Blue and Midnight Black, tapping the bristles firmly against the palette to ensure an even distribution of paint throughout the bristles.

Starting at the top of the canvas and working downward, use criss-cross strokes to paint the sky. *(Photo 1.)* Notice how the color blends with the Liquid White already on the canvas and automatically the sky becomes lighter as it nears the horizon. Vary the color, leaving some areas of the sky quite light, to indicate cloud placement.

This is a good time to underpaint the water on the lower portion of the canvas. Re-load the 2" brush with the Prussian Blue-Midnight Black mixture. Starting at the bottom of the canvas (and working up towards the horizon) use horizontal strokes, pulling from the outside edges of the canvas in towards the center. You can create the illusion of shimmering light on the water by allowing the center of the canvas to remain light. *(Photo 2.)*

Use a clean, dry 2" brush and criss-cross strokes to blend the sky, then blend the entire canvas (sky and water) with long, horizontal strokes.

CLOUDS

With a mixture of Titanium White and a very small amount of Bright Red on the 1" brush, use tiny, circular strokes to shape the clouds. *(Photo 3.)*

With the top corner of a clean, dry 2" brush, again make circular strokes to blend out just the base of the clouds *(Photo 4)* then lightly lift upward to "fluff". *(Photo 5.)*

MOUNTAIN

The mountain is painted with the knife and a mixture of Midnight Black, Prussian Blue, Van Dyke Brown and Alizarin Crimson. Pull the mixture out very flat on your palette, hold the knife straight up and "cut" across the mixture to load the long edge of the blade with a small roll of paint. (Holding the knife straight up will force the small roll of paint to the very edge of the blade.) With firm pressure, shape just the top edge of the mountain. *(Photo 6.)* When you are satisfied with the basic shape of the mountain top, use the knife to remove any excess paint. Then, with the 2" brush, blend the paint down to the base of the mountain, creating the illusion of mist. *(Photo 7.)*

Highlight the mountain with Titanium White. Again, load the long edge of the knife blade with a small roll of paint. Starting at the top (and paying close attention to angles) glide the knife down the right side of each peak, using so little pressure that the paint "breaks". *(Photo 8.)*

Use a mixture of Titanium White with a small amount of Prussian Blue on the short edge of the knife for the shadowed sides of the peaks. Apply the paint in the opposing direction, again using so little pressure that the paint "breaks". *(Photo 9.)*

With a clean, dry 2" brush, tap to diffuse the base of the mountain (carefully following the angles) *(Photo 10)* and then gently lift upward to create the illusion of mist.

BACKGROUND

Load the round brush by tapping the bristles into various

mixtures of Sap Green and the mountain color (Midnight Black, Prussian Blue, Van Dyke Brown, Alizarin Crimson and Sap Green). Tap downward with just the top edge of the bristles to block-in just the basic shape of the background trees. *(Photo 11.)*

Continue using the round brush to reflect the trees into the water and then with a clean, dry 2" brush, pull straight down and lightly brush across to give the reflections a "watery" appearance. *(Photo 12.)*

Highlight the trees with the round brush and various mixtures of all of the Yellows, Sap Green and Bright Red. Working in layers, tap downward with the brush to carefully create individual leaf clusters; try not to just hit at random. *(Photo 13.)* Do not completely cover all of the dark base-color already on the canvas; use it to separate the individual tree and bush shapes. *(Photo 14.)*

FOREGROUND

Add the tree trunks with a mixture of Van Dyke Brown and Dark Sienna on the liner brush. (To load the liner brush, thin the mixture to an ink-like consistency by first dipping the liner brush into paint thinner. Slowly turn the brush as you pull the bristles through the mixture, forcing them to a sharp point.) Apply very little pressure to the brush as you shape the trunks. By turning and wiggling the brush, you can give your trunks a gnarled appearance. *(Photo 15.)* Highlight the

trunks with a thinned mixture of Titanium White with a very small amount of Bright Red on the liner brush.

Tap downward to add foliage to the tree trunks *(Photo 16)* this time using a mixture of Yellow Ochre and Bright Red on the round brush *(Photo 17)*.

With a small roll of Van Dyke Brown on the knife, add the banks to the water's edge. *(Photo 18.)* Highlight the banks with a mixture of Titanium White and Dark Sienna, using so little pressure that the paint "breaks". *(Photo 19.)*

With various mixtures of the Yellows and Sap Green on the fan brush, use push-upward strokes to add grassy areas to the banks, carefully following the lay-of-the-land. Don't kill the dark areas at the base of the trees; these shadow areas are very important! *(Photo 20.)*

Cut in the water lines with a small roll of Liquid White on the edge of the knife. *(Photo 21.)*

LARGE TREE TRUNK

Pull down the large foreground trunk with Van Dyke Brown on the fan brush. *(Photo 22.)* Touch highlights to the right side of the trunk with a mixture of Van Dyke Brown and Titanium White on the knife. *(Photo 23.)*

FINISHING TOUCHES

Complete the painting by using thinned Van Dyke Brown on the liner brush to add small limbs and branches to the large tree trunk. *(Photo 24.)*

Autumn Images

1. Use criss-cross strokes to paint the sky . . .

2. . . . and horizontal strokes to paint the water.

3. Paint the clouds with circular strokes . . .

4. . . . then use the 2" brush to blend . . .

5. . . . and "fluff" the clouds.

6. Shape just the mountain top with the knife . . .

Autumn Images

7. . . . then blend the paint down with the 2" brush.

8. Use the knife to add highlights . . .

9. . . . and shadows to the mountain.

10. Tap the base of the mountain to mist.

11. Tap down small background trees with the round brush.

12. Reflect the trees into the water with the 2" brush.

13. Continue tapping downward with the round brush . . .

14. . . . to paint the large foreground trees.

15. Paint the tree trunks with the liner brush . . .

16. . . . then again tap downward with the round brush . . .

17. . . . to highlight the foliage.

18. Add banks to the water's edge with the knife . . .

19. . . . then lightly highlight.

20. Use the fan brush to add grassy patches . . .

21. . . . and the knife to cut in water lines.

22. Paint the large tree trunk with the fan brush . . .

23. . . . then apply highlights with the knife.

24. Use the liner brush to add limbs to the completed painting.

WINTERTIME BLUES

MATERIALS

2″ Brush	Phthalo Blue
1″ Brush	Prussian Blue
#6 Fan Brush	Midnight Black
#2 Script Liner Brush	Dark Sienna
Large Knife	Van Dyke Brown
Liquid White	Alizarin Crimson
Titanium White	

Use the 2″ brush to cover the entire canvas with a thin, even coat of Liquid White. With long horizontal and vertical strokes, work back and forth to ensure an even distribution of paint on the canvas. Do NOT allow the Liquid White to dry before you begin.

SKY

Load the 2″ brush with a very small amount of Phthalo Blue, tapping the bristles firmly against the palette to ensure an even distribution of paint throughout the bristles.

Starting at the top of the canvas and working downward, use criss-cross strokes to paint the sky. (Photo 1.) Notice how the color blends with the Liquid White already on the canvas and automatically the sky becomes lighter as it nears the horizon.

This is a good time to underpaint the water on the lower portion of the canvas. Re-load the brush with Phthalo Blue. Starting at the bottom of the canvas (and working up towards the horizon) use horizontal strokes, pulling from the outside edges of the canvas in towards the center. You can create the illusion of shimmering light on the water by allowing the center of the canvas to remain light. (Photo 2.)

Use a clean, dry 2″ brush and criss-cross strokes to blend the sky, then blend the entire canvas (sky and water) with long, horizontal strokes.

Use Titanium White on the fan brush to shape the clouds by making tiny, circular strokes with just the corner of the brush. (Photo 3.)

With the top corner of a clean, dry 2″ brush, again make circular strokes to blend out just the base of the clouds (Photo 4) then lightly lift upward to "fluff". Blend the entire sky. (Photo 5.)

MOUNTAINS

Use the knife to make a Lavender color on your palette by mixing a small amount of Phthalo Blue with some Alizarin Crimson. To a portion of this dark mixture, add a small amount of Titanium White to make a light Lavender color.

Load the long edge of the knife with a small roll of the lightest Lavender mixture and with firm pressure, shape just the top edge of the most distant mountain. (Photo 6.) Remove any excess paint with the knife, then firmly pull the paint down to the base of the mountain with a clean, dry 2″ brush. (Photo 7.) The color will blend and mix with the Liquid White already on the canvas to create a misty appearance at the base of the distant hill. Just with brush strokes you can create the illusion of highlights and shadows. (Photo 8.)

Add Prussian Blue and Alizarin Crimson to the darker Lavender color and again use the knife to shape the closer, darker mountain. (Photo 9.) After removing the excess paint, again use the 2″ brush to blend the paint down to the base of the mountain, creating the illusion of mist. (Photo 10.)

BACKGROUND

Load the fan brush with a mixture of Phthalo Blue, Titanium White and Midnight Black. Holding the brush vertically, just tap downward to indicate the small trees at the base of the mountains. You can "sparkle" a few of the trees with additional Titanium White on the brush. (Photo 11.)

Use the top corner of the 2″ brush to firmly tap the base of the trees to create the illusion of mist. (Photo 12.)

With Titanium White on the knife, paying close attention to the lay-of-the-land, add snow to the base of the tiny trees. (Photo 13.)

Load the 2″ brush with the tree color, pull straight down for reflections, then lightly brush across to give the reflections a "watery" appearance. *(Photo 14.)*

Use a small roll of Liquid White on the knife to add water lines and ripples *(Photo 15)* to complete the background *(Photo 16).*

EVERGREENS

The large evergreens are painted with the 2″ brush and a dark-tree mixture of Prussian Blue, Midnight Black, Alizarin Crimson and Van Dyke Brown. Load the brush to a chiseled edge by wiggling both sides of the bristles through the mixture.

Holding the brush horizontally, use just the corner of the brush to begin adding the small top branches. Working from side to side, as you move down each tree, apply more pressure to the brush, forcing the bristles to bend UPWARD and automatically the branches will become larger as you near the base of each tree. *(Photo 17.)*

Continue using the dark mixture on the 2″ brush to underpaint the small leaf trees and bushes in the foreground. *(Photo 18.)*

To add snow to the evergreens, load the 2″ brush to a chiseled edge with a mixture of Titanium White and Phthalo Blue, then pull just one corner of the bristles through Titanium White. (There should be Blue deep in the bristles and White on one corner.) Lightly apply snow to the large evergreens, again forcing the bristles to bend UPWARD. Be very careful not to overdo, these trees should remain quite dark. *(Photo 19.)*

To add snow to the small trees and bushes at the base of the evergreen, first dip the 1″ brush into Liquid White. Then, with the handle straight up, pull the brush (several times in one direction, to round one corner of the bristles) through Titanium White.

With the rounded corner of the brush up, force the bristles to bend upward to highlight the individual trees and bushes. Concentrate on shape and form—try not to just "hit" at random. If you are careful to not completely destroy all of the dark under-color, you can use it to separate the individual, lacy tree and bush shapes. *(Photo 20.)*

Complete the foreground by using Titanium White on the knife to add the snow to the base of the foreground trees. Pay close attention to the lay-of-the-land, using so little pressure that the paint "breaks". *(Photo 21.)*

FINISHING TOUCHES

Use a double-loaded liner brush to paint tiny tree trunks, sticks and twigs. (To double-load the liner brush, thin some Dark Sienna to an ink-like consistency by first dipping the liner brush into paint thinner. Slowly turn the brush as you pull the bristles through the paint, forcing them to a sharp point. Then, pull ONE side of the bristles through a very thin mixture of Liquid White and Dark Sienna.) With single strokes you can paint highlights and shadows. Applying very little pressure, turn and wiggle the brush to give your trunks a gnarled appearance. *(Photo 22.)* Your finished painting is ready for a signature. *(Photo 23.)*

Wintertime Blues

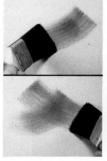

1. Use criss-cross strokes to paint the sky . . .

2. . . . and horizontal strokes to paint the water.

3. Paint clouds with the fan brush . . .

4. . . . then use the 2″ brush to blend . . .

5. . . . and "fluff" the clouds.

6. Shape the mountain top with the knife . . .

Wintertime Blues

7. . . . then blend the paint down with the 2" brush . . .

8. . . . to create the illusion of mist.

9. Use a darker color . . .

10. . . . to shape the closer range of mountains.

11. Tap down evergreens with the fan brush . . .

12. . . . then firmly tap to mist with the 2" brush.

13. Use the knife to add snow to the base of the trees.

14. Paint reflections in the water with the 2" brush . . .

15. . . . then use the knife . . .

16. . . . to add the water lines and ripples.

17. Underpaint foreground evergreens . . .

18. . . . and bushes with the 2" brush.

19. Add snow to the evergreens . . .

21. Use the knife to lay in the snow . . .

22. . . . the liner brush for small twigs . . .

23. . . . and the painting is complete.

LITTLE HOME IN THE MEADOW

MATERIALS

2″ Brush	Prussian Blue
#6 Fan Brush	Midnight Black
#2 Script Liner Brush	Alizarin Crimson
Large Knife	Sap Green
Adhesive-Backed Plastic	Cadmium Yellow
Black Gesso	Yellow Ochre
Liquid Clear	Indian Yellow
Titanium White	Bright Red
Phthalo Blue	

Start by covering the entire canvas with a piece of adhesive-backed plastic (such as Con-Tact Paper) from which you have removed a center oval shape. (A 16x20 oval for an 18x24 canvas.)

Use a foam applicator to cover the exposed area of the canvas with a thin, even coat of Black Gesso and allow to DRY COMPLETELY before you proceed. (Photo 1.)

When the Black Gesso is dry, use the 2″ brush to completely cover the exposed oval with a VERY SMALL AMOUNT of Liquid Clear. Use a paper towel to firmly rub the oval, removing as much of the Liquid Clear from the canvas as possible. The remaining Liquid Clear will be sufficient to proceed with the painting. Do NOT allow the canvas to dry before you begin.

SKY

Load a clean, dry 2″ brush by tapping the bristles into a small amount of a mixture of Titanium White and Phthalo Blue. Starting at the top of the oval, working down towards the horizon, paint the sky with small criss-cross strokes. (Photo 2.)

Load a clean, dry 2″ brush by holding the brush vertically and tapping the top corner of the bristles into a mixture of Titanium White and a very small amount of Bright Red. Working in layers, hold the brush horizontally and tap downward to shape the clouds (Photo 3) then blend the base of each cloud with a clean, dry 2″ brush using tiny criss-cross strokes (Photo 4).

BACKGROUND

Use the knife to make a Brown mixture with equal parts of Alizarin Crimson and Sap Green. To a portion of this Brown mixture add a small amount of Midnight Black, Phthalo Blue and Titanium White, to make a misty tree-color.

To paint the tall, background evergreens, load the 2″ brush to a chiseled edge by pulling both sides of the bristles through the misty tree-mixture. Starting at the base of each tree, simply hold the brush vertically and *press* the *side* of the brush against the canvas. As you work upward, apply less pressure on the brush, creating the tapered tree top. Complete first one side, and then the other, of each tree. (Photo 5.) With a very small amount of Titanium White on a clean, dry 2″ brush, mist the base of the trees by firmly tapping downward. (Photo 6.)

Working forward in layers, use a darker mixture of the misty tree color on the 2″ brush and tap downward with just the top corner of the brush to shape the small trees and bushes at the base of the tall evergreens. (Photo 7.) Again, diffuse the base of the trees by firmly tapping downward with a very small amount of Titanium White on the brush. (Photo 8.)

EVERGREENS

To paint the large evergreens, load the 2″ brush to a chiseled edge with a mixture of the Brown color, Midnight Black and Phthalo Blue. Holding the brush vertically, touch the canvas to create the center line of each tree. Use just the corner of the brush to begin adding the small top branches. Working from side to side, as you move down each tree, apply more pressure to the brush, forcing the bristles to bend downward and automatically the branches will become larger as you near the base of each tree. (Photo 9.)

Use the same dark mixture on the 2″ brush to tap in the small trees and bushes at the base of the evergreens.

Add trunks to the large evergreens with a small roll of a mixture of Titanium White and Brown on the knife (Photo 10) then reload the 2" brush with various mixtures of all of the Yellows and Midnight Black (to make a dark Green) and very lightly touch highlights to the evergreen branches.

To add the soft grassy area at the base of the trees, use the 2" brush and various mixtures of Midnight Black, all of the Yellows and Bright Red. Load the brush by holding it at a 45-degree angle and tapping the bristles into the various paint mixtures. Allow the brush to "slide" slightly forward in the paint each time you tap (this assures that the very tips of the bristles are fully loaded with paint). Hold the brush horizontally and gently tap downward to paint the soft grass. Working forward in layers, carefully creating the lay-of-the-land, use a very small amount of Titanium White to "sparkle" the lightest areas. If you are careful not to destroy all of the dark color already on the canvas, you can create grassy highlights that look almost like velvet. *(Photo 11.)*

Working forward in layers, add the darker evergreens with a mixture of Midnight Black, Prussian Blue and a small amount of Brown on the 2" brush. *(Photo 12.)*

CABIN

Use a clean knife to remove paint from the canvas in the basic shape of the cabin. With a small roll of Brown on the knife, paint the back edge of the roof, then pull down the front and the side of the cabin. Use a mixture of the Brown, Yellow Ochre and Titanium White to highlight the front of the cabin. With Brown on the knife, add logs to the front and

side of the cabin. Highlight the logs with Titanium White.

Use a mixture of Midnight Black and Titanium White on the short edge of the knife to paint the roof shingles. Start at the bottom of the roof and work up to the top. Finish the cabin with a Van Dyke Brown door and window. *(Photo 13.)*

FOREGROUND

Working forward in layers, use the 2" brush and the Yellow highlight mixtures to continue adding the soft grassy areas in the foreground, paying close attention to the contour of the land. *(Photo 14.)*

Use the fan brush and the Brown mixture to add the path with short, horizontal strokes. Highlight the path with Titanium White on the fan brush. *(Photo 15.)*

To paint the foreground tree, use the Brown mixture and the liner brush. (To load the liner brush, thin the Brown to an ink-like consistency by first dipping the liner brush into paint thinner. Slowly turn the brush as you pull the bristles through the mixture, forcing them to a sharp point.) Apply very little pressure to the brush, as you shape the tree. By turning and wiggling the brush, you can give your tree a gnarled appearance. *(Photo 16.)*

FINISHING TOUCHES

Carefully remove the Con-tact Paper from the canvas. *(Photo 17.)* With the thinned Brown mixture on the liner brush, you can extend the branches of the tree outside the oval and your painting is complete. *(Photo 18.)*

Little Home In The Meadow

1. Paint the exposed oval with Black Gesso.

2. Paint the sky with the 2" brush and criss-cross strokes . . .

3. . . . then use the 1" brush . . .

4. . . . to add the clouds.

5. Press with the side of the 2" brush to paint evergreens . . .

6. . . . then tap with the corner of the brush to mist.

Little Home In The Meadow

7. Tap down to paint small trees and bushes . . .

8. . . . then tap to mist the base of the trees.

9. Paint large evergreens with the 2" brush . . .

10. . . . then add the trunks with the knife.

11. Tap downward with the 2" brush . . .

12. . . . to paint the soft velvet grass.

13. Progressional steps used to paint the cabin.

14. Paint soft foreground grass with the 2" brush . . .

15. . . . then add the path with the fan brush.

16. Paint the tree trunk with the liner brush . . .

17. . . . then carefully remove the Con-Tact Paper . . .

18 . . . to expose your finished masterpiece.

SNOWBOUND CABIN

MATERIALS

2″ Brush	Titanium White
#6 Fan Brush	Phthalo Blue
#2 Script Liner Brush	Prussian Blue
Large Knife	Midnight Black
Small Knife	Alizarin Crimson
Liquid White	Sap Green
Liquid Clear	

Use a foam applicator to cover the entire canvas with a thin, even coat of Black Gesso and allow to DRY COMPLETELY before you begin.

When the Black Gesso is dry, use the 2″ brush to completely cover the canvas with a VERY SMALL AMOUNT of Liquid Clear. Use a paper towel* to firmly scrub the canvas, removing as much of the Liquid Clear as possible. The remaining Liquid Clear will be sufficient to proceed with the painting. Do NOT allow the canvas to dry before you begin. (Photo 1.)

(*I suggest that you use a very good quality, lint-free paper towel, such as Bounty brand.)

SKY

With a very small amount of Phthalo Blue on the 2″ brush, use criss-cross strokes to randomly place this color in the sky. (Photo 2.)

Load a clean, dry 2″ brush by holding it vertically and tapping the top corner into a small amount of Titanium White. Hold the brush vertically and tap in the cloud shapes with the top corner of the brush. (Photo 3.) Use a clean, dry 2″ brush and small criss-cross strokes to diffuse the base of the clouds. Continue layering and diffusing clouds, using a mixture of Midnight Black, Prussian Blue and Alizarin Crimson for the dark clouds. (Photo 4.) Use long, horizontal strokes to lightly blend the entire sky. (Photo 5.)

BACKGROUND

Use the knife to make a Brown mixture on your palette by mixing equal parts of Alizarin Crimson and Sap Green. Load the 2″ brush with this mixture, hold the brush vertically, and tap downward with the top corner of the brush to block in the basic shapes of the misty background trees. (Photo 6.)

Reload the 2″ brush with a mixture of Alizarin Crimson, Midnight Black, Prussian Blue and Phthalo Blue. Holding the brush horizontally, tap downward to shape the distant hills. You can create tiny tree tops on the hills with short, upward strokes. (Photo 7.)

Add trunks to the background trees with the Brown mixture and the liner brush. (To load the liner brush, thin the mixture to an ink-like consistency by first dipping the liner brush into paint thinner. Slowly turn the brush as you pull the bristles through the mixture, forcing them to a sharp point.) With very little pressure, shape the trunks with just the tips of the bristles. (Photo 8.) By turning and wiggling the brush, you can give your trunks a gnarled appearance. (Photo 9.)

EVERGREENS

To paint the evergreen trees, load the fan brush to a chiseled edge with a mixture of Midnight Black, Prussian Blue and Alizarin Crimson. Holding the brush vertically, touch the canvas to create the center line of each tree. Use just the corner of the brush to begin adding the small top branches. Working from side to side, as you move down each tree, apply more pressure to the brush, forcing the bristles to bend downward and automatically the branches will become larger as you near the base of each tree. (Photo 10.)

Dip a clean, dry fan brush into Liquid Clear, then load it to a chiseled edge with a mixture of Titanium White and Phthalo Blue to apply the snowy highlights to the evergreen branches. (Photo 11.)

With Titanium White on the 2″ brush, use long, horizontal strokes to add the snow to the base of the trees. (Photo 12.)

Double-load the liner brush to paint the background tree trunks. (To double-load the liner brush, fill the bristles with a very thin mixture of paint thinner, Titanium White and Van Dyke Brown, then pull one side of the bristles through very thinned Titanium White.) With single strokes you can paint the trunks with highlights and shadows *(Photo 13)* to complete the background *(Photo 14)*.

CABIN

Use the knife to remove paint from the canvas in the basic shape of the cabin. With a small roll of Van Dyke Brown on the knife, paint the front of the cabin. Highlight the front side with a mixture of Titanium White, Van Dyke Brown and Alizarin Crimson, using so little pressure that the paint "breaks". Add the door and the side of the cabin with Van Dyke Brown. "Bounce" pure Titanium White on the roof, then scrape out the windows on the side of the building with the small knife. Outline the windows with thinned light mixture on the liner brush. Add snow to the base of the cabin with various mixtures of Titanium White with a very small amount of Phthalo Blue. *(Photo 15.)*

Add the fence with thinned Van Dyke Brown on the liner brush; highlight with thinned Titanium White. Use Titanium White on the knife to add snow to the base of the fence; apply the snow with so little pressure that the paint "breaks" and the cabin is complete. *(Photo 16.)*

FOREGROUND

Load the fan brush to a chiseled edge with Van Dyke Brown. Holding the brush vertically, start at the top of the tree and just pull down the large tree trunk. *(Photo 17.)*

Use the Midnight Black-Prussian Blue-Alizarin Crimson mixture on the 2" brush to tap in the foliage at the base of the large tree.

Highlight the tree trunk with a small roll of a mixture of Van Dyke Brown and Titanium White on the knife. Hold the knife vertically and curve the strokes around the trunk. Be sure the paint "breaks". *(Photo 18.)* Use thinned Van Dyke Brown on the liner brush to add limbs and branches to the tree. *(Photo 19.)*

Continue adding foreground snow with Titanium White on the 2" brush, paying close attention to the lay of the land. *(Photo 20.)*

Paint the foreground fence with Van Dyke Brown on the knife *(Photo 21)* then highlight the fence with Titanium White.

FINISHING TOUCHES

Use thinned mixtures on the liner brush to add small sticks and twigs and your painting is complete. *(Photo 22.)*

Don't forget to sign your name with pride: Again, load the liner brush with thinned color of your choice. Sign just your initials, first name, last name or all of your names. Sign in the left corner, the right corner or one artist signs right in the middle of the canvas! The choice is yours. You might also consider including the date when you sign your painting. Whatever your choices, have fun, for hopefully with this painting you have truly experienced THE JOY OF PAINTING.

Snowbound Cabin

   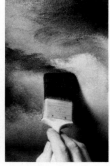   

1. Prepaint the canvas with Black Gesso . . .

2. . . . then use criss-cross strokes to paint the sky.

3. Tap down with the 2" brush to paint light . . .

4. . . . and dark clouds.

5. Blend the sky.

6. Block in background trees . . .

7. . . . and distant hills with the 2" brush.

Snowbound Cabin

8. Use the liner brush to add trunks . . .

9. . . . to the background trees.

10. Paint evergreen trees . . .

11. . . . and then highlight with the fan brush.

12. Use the 2" brush to lay in the snow . . .

13. . . . and the liner brush to paint the trunks . . .

14. . . . in the background.

15. Progressional steps used to paint the cabin.

16. Add a fence to complete the cabin.

17. Pull down tree trunks with the fan brush . . .

18. . . . then highlight with the knife.

19. Complete the tree with limbs and branches.

20. After painting the foreground snow . . .

21. . . . use the knife to add the foreground fence . . .

22. . . . and the painting is complete.

IN THE STILLNESS OF MORNING

MATERIALS

2" Brush
#2 Script Liner Brush
Large Knife
Liquid White
Titanium White
Prussian Blue
Midnight Black

Dark Sienna
Van Dyke Brown
Alizarin Crimson
Sap Green
Cadmium Yellow
Yellow Ochre
Indian Yellow

Begin by using the 2" brush to cover the entire canvas with a thin, even coat of Liquid White. With long horizontal and vertical strokes, work back and forth to ensure an even distribution of paint on the canvas. Do NOT allow the Liquid White to dry before you begin.

SKY AND WATER

Load the 2" brush with a small amount of Phthalo Blue. Starting at the top of the canvas and working downward, use criss-cross strokes to paint the sky. (Photo 1.) Allow some areas of the sky to remain quite light, for cloud placement. Reload the brush with a small amount of Prussian Blue and darken just the top corners of the sky, still using criss-cross strokes.

This is a good time to under-paint the water on the lower portion of the canvas. Reload the brush with Prussian Blue. Starting at the bottom of the canvas (and working up towards the horizon) use horizontal strokes, pulling from the outside edges of the canvas in towards the center. (Photo 2.) You can create the illusion of shimmering light on the water by allowing the center of the canvas to remain light.

Use a clean, dry 2" brush and criss-cross strokes to blend the sky, then blend the entire canvas (sky and water) with long, horizontal strokes.

Load the 2" brush with a small amount of Titanium White. Holding the brush vertically, use just the top corner of the brush to tap in the basic cloud shapes. (Photo 3.) Blend out the base of the clouds with a clean, dry 2" brush and circular strokes (Photo 4) then use sweeping upward strokes to "fluff" (Photo 5).

BACKGROUND

The misty background evergreens are painted with a Gray-Lavender mixture of Midnight Black, Prussian Blue, Alizarin Crimson and Titanium White. Load the 2" brush by wiggling the brush as you pull both sides of the bristles through the mixture, forcing the bristles to a sharp chiseled edge. Starting at the base of each tree, simply hold the brush vertically and press the side of the brush against the canvas. As you work upward, apply less pressure to the brush, creating the tapered tree top. Complete first one side and then the other of each tree. (Photo 6.)

Diffuse the base of the trees by firmly tapping downward with the top corner of the 2" brush, creating the illusion of mist. (Photo 7.)

Reload the 2" brush with the Lavender mixture to add the grassy area at the base of the background trees. (Photo 8.) Pull the color straight down into the water (Photo 9) then lightly brush across to create reflections.

Water lines and ripples can be added with the knife and a mixture of Titanium White and Liquid White. To load the knife, pull the mixture out very flat on your palette, then cut across to load the top of the blade with a small roll of paint. Push the blade straight into the canvas and use firm pressure to cut in the water lines and ripples. (Photo 10.) Be sure the lines are perfectly straight, parallel to the top and bottom of the canvas. (Photo 11.)

EVERGREENS

Start by painting the large evergreens on the right side of the painting. Load the 2" brush to a chiseled edge with a dark tree-mixture of Prussian Blue, Midnight Black, Alizarin Crimson, Sap Green and Van Dyke Brown. Holding the brush vertically, touch the canvas to create the center line of each tree. Use just the corner of the brush to begin adding the small top branches. Working from side to side, as you move down each tree, apply more pressure to the brush, forcing the bristles to bend downward and automatically the branches will become larger as you near the base of each tree. (Photo 12.)

Use the dark-tree color on the 2" brush to pull down reflections, then lightly brush across. *(Photo 13.)*

Add the tree trunks with a small roll of a mixture of Titanium White and Dark Sienna on the knife. *(Photo 14.)* Working in stages, paint the trees on the left side *(Photo 15)* before working forward with the evergreens on the right side of the painting *(Photo 16)*.

Without cleaning the brush, reload it to a chiseled edge with various mixtures of the Yellows and lightly touch highlights to the evergreen trees. *(Photo 17.)* Liquid White or paint thinner can be added to the mixtures to thin the consistency of the paint, if necessary. *(Photo 18.)*

SOFT GRASS

Use the 2" brush and various mixtures of all of the Yellows and Sap Green to highlight the soft grassy areas at the base of the evergreen trees. Load the 2" brush by holding it at a 45-degree angle and tapping the bristles into the various paint mixtures. Allow the brush to "slide" slightly forward in the paint each time you tap (this assures that the very tips of the bristles are fully loaded with paint). Hold the brush horizontally and gently tap downward. *(Photo 19.)* Work in layers, carefully creating the lay-of-the-land. If you are also careful not to destroy all of the dark color already on the canvas, you can create grassy highlights that look almost like velvet. *(Photo 20.)*

SMALL TREES AND BUSHES

To highlight the small trees and bushes at the base of the evergreens, first dip the 2" brush into Liquid White (or paint thinner). Then, with the handle straight up, pull the brush (several times in one direction, to round one corner of the bristles) through the various Yellow highlight mixtures. With the rounded corner of the brush up, force the bristles to bend upward to highlight the individual trees and bushes. Concentrate on shape and form—try not to just "hit" at random. *(Photo 21.)*

FINISHING TOUCHES

Cut in water lines and ripples with a small roll of Liquid White on the knife. *(Photo 22.)* Use the point of the knife to scratch in the indication of tiny trunks, sticks and twigs and your painting is complete. *(Photo 23.)*

Don't forget to sign your name with pride: load the liner brush with thinned color of your choice. Sign just your initials, first name, last name or all of your names. Sign in the left corner, the right corner or one artist we know signs right in the middle of the canvas! The choice is yours. Whatever your choices, have fun, for hopefully with this painting you have truly experienced THE JOY OF PAINTING!

In The Stillness Of Morning

1. Use criss-cross strokes to paint the sky . . .

2. . . . and horizontal strokes to paint the water.

3. Use the 2" brush to paint clouds . . .

4. . . . then blend with circular strokes . . .

5. . . . to complete the sky.

6. Press in evergreens with the 2" brush . . .

In The Stillness Of Morning

7. . . . then firmly tap the base to mist.

8. Use the 2" brush to tap in the grassy area . . .

9. . . . and to pull down reflections.

10. With Liquid White on the knife . . .

11. . . . cut in water lines and ripples.

12. Use the 2" brush to paint large evergreens . . .

13. . . . and to pull down reflections.

14. Add trunks with the knife . . .

15. . . . to the large evergreens.

16. Underpaint the foreground with the 2" brush . . .

17. . . . then use the 2" brush to highlight . . .

18. . . . the large evergreens.

19. Highlight the grassy area . . .

20. . . . paying close attention to the lay-of-the-land.

21. Highlight small trees and bushes with the 2" brush . . .

22. . . . then use the knife to cut in water lines . . .

23. . . . to complete the painting.

FIRST SNOW

MATERIALS

2" Brush	Dark Sienna
#6 Fan Brush	Van Dyke Brown
Large Knife	Alizarin Crimson
Liquid White	Sap Green
Titanium White	Cadmium Yellow
Phthalo Blue	Yellow Ochre
Prussian Blue	Indian Yellow
Midnight Black	Bright Red

Begin by using the 2" brush to cover the entire canvas with a thin, even coat of Liquid White. With long horizontal and vertical strokes, work back and forth to ensure an even distribution of paint on the canvas. Do NOT allow the Liquid White to dry before you begin.

SKY AND WATER

Load the 2" brush with a very small amount of Phthalo Blue, tapping the bristles firmly against the palette to ensure an even distribution of paint throughout the bristles. Use criss-cross strokes to paint the sky, starting at the top of the canvas and working downward. *(Photo 1.)* Allow some areas of the sky to remain quite light for cloud placement.

This is a good time to under-paint the water on the lower portion of the canvas. Reload the brush with Phthalo Blue. Starting at the bottom of the canvas (and working up towards the horizon) use horizontal strokes, pulling from the outside edges of the canvas in towards the center. You can create the illusion of shimmering light on the water by allowing the center of the canvas to remain light.

Load a clean, dry 2" brush with a very small amount of Alizarin Crimson and use criss-cross strokes just above the horizon to add the Pinkish glow to the sky. Blend with long, horizontal strokes.

With Titanium White on a clean, dry 2" brush, tap in the basic cloud shapes. *(Photo 2.)* Use the 2" brush and circular strokes to lightly blend the base of the clouds, then sweeping upward strokes to "fluff". Blend the entire canvas (sky and water) with long, horizontal strokes. *(Photo 3.)*

MOUNTAIN

Paint the mountain with the knife and a mixture of Prussian Blue, Midnight Black, and Alizarin Crimson. Pull the mixture out very flat on your palette, hold the knife straight up and "cut" across the mixture to load the long edge of the blade with a small roll of paint. (Holding the knife straight up will force the small roll of paint to the very edge of the blade.) With firm pressure, shape just the top edge of the mountain. *(Photo 4.)* When you are satisfied with the basic shape of the mountain top, use the knife to remove any excess paint. Then, with the 2" brush, pull the paint down to the base of the mountain to blend and complete the entire mountain shape. *(Photo 5.)*

Highlight the mountain with various mixtures of Titanium White, Midnight Black and a small amount of Bright Red. Again, load the long edge of the knife blade with a small roll of paint. Paying close attention to angles, apply highlights to the right side of each peak, using so little pressure that the paint "breaks". *(Photo 6.)* Use a mixture of Titanium White, Prussian Blue, Midnight Black and Van Dyke Brown, applied in the opposing direction, for the shadow sides of the peaks.

With a clean, dry 2" brush, tap to diffuse the base of the mountain (carefully following the angles) *(Photo 7)* then lightly brush upward to create the illusion of mist *(Photo 8)*.

FOOTHILLS

Load the 2" brush with the mountain shadow-mixture (Titanium White, Prussian Blue, Midnight Black and Van Dyke Brown). Shape the foothills at the base of the mountain by holding the brush horizontally and tapping downward. *(Photo 9.)* With very short upward strokes you can create the impression of tiny tree tops. *(Photo 10.)*

Working forward in layers, darken the mixture to add the closer range of foothills. Paying close attention to angles, allow these hills to "climb" right up the base of the mountain. Again, use short upward strokes to indicate the tiny tree tops.

Reload the 2" brush with the foothill mixture, hold the brush flat against the canvas and pull straight down to reflect the foothills into the water and then lightly brush across. *(Photo 11.)*

Add water lines and ripples with a small roll of Liquid White, blended with a very small amount of Bright Red, to cut in water lines and ripples. *(Photo 12.)* Be sure the lines are perfectly straight, parallel to the top and bottom of the canvas. *(Photo 13.)*

SOFT GRASS

Use a dark mixture of Prussian Blue, Van Dyke Brown, Midnight Black and Alizarin Crimson on the 2" brush *(Photo 14)* to underpaint the foreground land area *(Photo 15)*.

Without cleaning the 2" brush, reload it with various mixtures of the Yellows, Sap Green, Prussian Blue and a small amount of Bright Red. Hold the brush horizontally and gently tap downward to begin highlighting the soft grassy areas. Work in layers, creating the lay-of-the-land. If you are careful not to destroy all of the dark undercolor, you can create grassy highlights that look almost like velvet. *(Photo 16.)*

EVERGREENS

Load the fan brush to a chiseled edge with a mixture of Prussian Blue, Midnight Black, Van Dyke Brown, Alizarin Crimson and Sap Green. Hold the brush vertically and touch the canvas to create the center line of each tree. Use just the corner of the brush to begin adding the small top branches.

Working from side to side, as you move down each tree, apply more pressure to the brush, forcing the bristles to bend UPWARD and automatically the branches will become larger as you near the base of each tree. *(Photo 17.)*

To indicate the tiny evergreens, hold the brush vertically and just tap downward. *(Photo 18.)*

FOREGROUND

Reload the fan brush with various mixtures of all of the Yellows, Sap Green and a small amount of Bright Red. Hold the brush horizontally and force the bristles to bend upward *(Photo 19)* to paint the foreground grassy patches *(Photo 20)*.

Again, use the dark tree mixture on the fan brush to paint the large, foreground evergreens. *(Photo 21.)*

Use a small roll of the mountain highlight mixture (Titanium White-Midnight Black-Bright Red) on the knife to add patches of snow in the foreground. Again, pay close attention to the lay-of-the-land and use very little pressure on the knife, allowing the paint to "break". *(Photo 22.)*

Add the large evergreen trunks with a small roll of a mixture of Titanium White, Dark Sienna and Van Dyke Brown on the knife. *(Photo 23.)*

FINISHING TOUCHES

Use a mixture of the Yellows, Sap Green and a small amount of Midnight Black on the fan brush to lightly touch highlights to the evergreens and your painting is complete. *(Photo 24.)*

First Snow

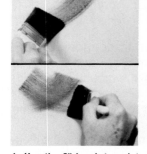   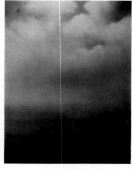  

1. Use the 2" brush to paint the sky . . .

2. . . . . to tap in clouds . . .

3. . . . . and to blend the entire sky.

4. Shape the mountain with the knife . . .

5. . . . . then blend with the 2" brush.

6. Add snow with the knife . . .

First Snow

7. . . . then firmly tap the base of the mountain . . .

8. . . . to create mist.

9. Continue using the 2" brush . . .

10. . . . to tap in the foothills.

11. Pull down reflections with the 2" brush . . .

12. . . . then use the knife . . .

13. . . . to cut in water lines and ripples.

14. Tap down with the 2" brush . . .

15. . . . to underpaint the foreground . . .

16. . . . and to add the soft grassy highlights.

17. Paint evergreens . . .

18. . . . and the indication of evergreens with the fan brush.

19. Continue using the fan brush . . .

20. . . . to add grassy patches in the foreground . . .

21. . . . before adding the large evergreens.

22. With the knife, add tree trunks . . .

23. . . .and patches of snow . . .

24. . . . to complete the painting.

ANGLER'S HAVEN

MATERIALS

2" Brush
2" Blender Brush
#6 Filbert Brush
#6 Fan Brush
#2 Script Liner Brush
Large Knife
Liquid White
Liquid Black
Titanium White
Phthalo Green
Phthalo Blue

Prussian Blue
Midnight Black
Dark Sienna
Van Dyke Brown
Alizarin Crimson
Sap Green
Cadmium Yellow
Yellow Ochre
Indian Yellow
Bright Red

Use the 2" brush to cover the top half of the canvas with a thin, even coat of Liquid White and the bottom half of the canvas with a thin, even coat of Liquid Black. With horizontal and vertical strokes, work back and forth to ensure an even distribution of paint on the canvas, while softly blending the two colors near the horizon. Do NOT allow the Liquids to dry before you begin. *(Photo 1.)*

SKY

Load a clean, dry 2" brush with a small amount of Phthalo Blue. Starting at the upper left corner of the canvas, working down towards the horizon, use criss-cross strokes to begin painting the sky. *(Photo 2.)*

Reload the 2" brush with Phthalo Blue. Using just the top corner of the brush, tap downward to add the basic cloud shapes to the sky, then use criss-cross strokes to blend and sweeping upward strokes to "fluff". *(Photo 3.)*

With a small amount of Titanium White on a clean, dry 2" brush, add the indication of light areas in the sky. *(Photo 4.)* Use the blender brush and criss-cross strokes to lightly blend these light areas. *(Photo 5.)* Use the blender brush and criss-cross strokes to blend the entire sky area. *(Photo 6.)*

MOUNTAIN

The mountain is made using the knife and a mixture of Midnight Black, Alizarin Crimson, Phthalo Blue and Van Dyke Brown. Pull the mixture out very flat on your palette, hold the knife straight up and "cut" across the mixture to load the long edge of the blade with a small roll of paint. (Holding the knife straight up will force the small roll of paint to the very edge of the blade.) With firm pressure, shape just the top edge of the mountain. *(Photo 7.)* When you are satisfied with the basic shape of the mountain top, use the knife to remove any excess paint. Then, with the 2" brush, pull the paint down to the base of the mountain, to blend and complete the entire mountain shape. *(Photo 8.)*

Highlight the mountain with a mixture of Titanium White and small amounts of Midnight Black and Bright Red. Again, load the long edge of the knife blade with a small roll of paint. Starting at the top (and paying close attention to angles) apply highlights to the left side of each peak, using so little pressure that the paint "breaks". *(Photo 9.)* Use a mixture of Titanium White, Phthalo Blue and a small amount of Midnight Black, applied in the opposing direction, for the shadow sides of the peaks. Again, use so little pressure that the paint "breaks".

Use a clean, dry blender brush to tap to diffuse the base of the mountain (carefully following the angles) *(Photo 10)* then gently lift upward to create the illusion of mist *(Photo 11)*.

TREES AND BUSHES

Tap the bristles of a clean, dry 2" brush into a mixture of the original dark mountain color and Sap Green. Moving forward in the painting, use just the corner of the brush to underpaint *(Photo 12)* the basic shapes of trees and bushes *(Photo 13)*.

Add branches and limbs to the trees with a mixture of Dark Sienna and a very small amount of Titanium White on the liner brush. *(Photo 14.)* (To load the liner brush, thin the mixture to an ink-like consistency by first dipping the liner brush into paint thinner. Slowly turn the brush as you pull the bristles through the mixture, forcing them to a sharp point.)

Load a clean, dry 2" brush with a small amount of Prussian Blue to color the water. Starting at the bottom of the canvas and working up towards the base of the trees, use long, horizontal strokes to apply this color to the dark underpaint (Liquid Black). *(Photo 15.)*

Reload the 2" brush, with various mixtures of Cadmium Yellow, Indian Yellow, Yellow Ochre and small amounts of Bright Red to highlight the trees and bushes. Concentrate on shape and form – try not to just "hit" at random. *(Photo 16.)*

EVERGREENS

For the evergreens, load the fan brush to a chiseled edge with a mixture of Midnight Black, Prussian Blue, Van Dyke Brown, Phthalo Green and Alizarin Crimson. Holding the brush vertically, touch the canvas to create the center line of each tree. Use just the corner of the brush to begin adding the small top branches. Working from side to side, as you move down each tree, apply more pressure to the brush, forcing the bristles to bend downward and automatically the branches will become larger as you near the base of each tree. *(Photo 17.)*

Add the trunks with a small roll of a mixture of Titanium White, Van Dyke Brown and Dark Sienna on the knife. *(Photo 18.)*

Use the fan brush to very lightly touch highlights to the branches with a mixture of the dark evergreen color and the Yellows.

LAND AND WATER

Add banks to the water's edge with the knife and a small roll of Van Dyke Brown. *(Photo 19.)* Highlight the banks with a mixture of Titanium White, Van Dyke Brown and Dark Sienna on

the knife, using so little pressure that the paint "breaks".

Add foliage to the banks with the Green highlight mixture on the fan brush. *(Photo 20.)*

Load the filbert brush with a thin mixture of Midnight Black and Van Dyke Brown, then pull ONE side of the bristles through a thin mixture of Titanium White, Van Dyke Brown and a very small amount of Midnight Black. With the light side of the brush UP, use a single, curved stroke to shape each of the rocks and stones in the water. *(Photo 21.)*

Load a clean, dry 2" brush with a small amount of Titanium White and, holding the brush horizontally, pull straight down from the banks at the water's edge. *(Photo 22.)* Brush lightly across to blend the water.

Use a small roll of a mixture of Titanium White and Phthalo Blue on the edge of the knife to add water lines and ripples. *(Photo 23.)* Be sure that the water lines are parallel to the bottom of the canvas. *(Photo 24.)*

Use the dark evergreen mixture on the 2" brush to underpaint another mass of land in the foreground of the painting. Add highlights to the land with mixtures of Yellow and Green on the 2" brush. Work in layers, concentrating on the lay-of-the-land. *(Photo 25.)*

FINISHING TOUCHES

Add rocks and stones to the water with the Browns on the filbert brush and the last water lines and ripples with Blue-White on the knife. *(Photo 26.)* Don't forget to sign your masterpiece! *(Photo 27.)*

Angler's Haven

   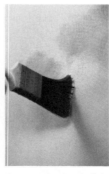 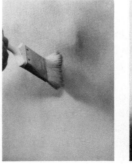  

1. Prepare the canvas with Liquid White and Black.

2. Use criss-cross strokes to paint the sky.

3. Then use the 2" brush to paint dark clouds . . .

4. . . . and to tap in light clouds.

5. Use the 2" soft blender . . .

6. . . . to blend the entire sky.

7. Shape the mountain top with the knife . . .

Angler's Haven

8. . . . then blend the paint down with the 2" brush.

9. Apply highlights with the knife . . .

10. . . . then tap the base of the mountain with the blender . . .

11. . . . to create the illusion of mist.

12. Use the 2" brush . . .

13. . . . to underpaint large trees and bushes.

14. Use the liner brush . . .

15. . . . to add trunks, limbs and branches.

16. Highlight the trees and bushes with the 2" brush.

17. Paint evergreens with the fan brush . . .

18. . . . then add trunks with the knife.

19. Add the land area with the knife . . .

20. . . . then add grassy areas with the fan brush.

21. Paint rocks with the filbert brush . . .

     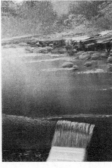 

22. . . . then pull down reflections with the 2" brush.

23. Use the knife . . .

24. . . . to cut in water lines and ripples.

25. Add the foreground with the 2" brush . . .

26. . . . then add water lines with the knife . . .

27. . . . to complete your painting.

WILDERNESS FALLS

MATERIALS

2" Brush	Prussian Blue
2" Blender Brush	Midnight Black
1" Oval Brush	Dark Sienna
#6 Fan Brush	Van Dyke Brown
Large Knife	Alizarin Crimson
Liquid White	Sap Green
Liquid Black	Cadmium Yellow
Titanium White	Yellow Ochre
Phthalo Green	Indian Yellow
Phthalo Blue	Bright Red

Use the 2" brush to cover the top half of the canvas with a thin, even coat of Liquid White and the bottom half of the canvas with a thin, even coat of Liquid Black. Softly blend the two colors near the horizon. *(Photo 1.)* Do NOT allow the Liquids to dry before you begin.

SKY

Load a clean, dry 2" brush with a small amount of Phthalo Blue and begin painting the large cloud shapes in the sky. Make circular strokes with the top corner of the brush to shape the fluffy clouds; stringy clouds are made by just tapping the brush. *(Photo 2.)*

Without cleaning the brush, reload it with a small amount of Alizarin Crimson and Titanium White to continue shaping the clouds.

Load the 2" brush with a small amount of Prussian Blue. Use long horizontal strokes to underpaint the water on the lower portion of the canvas. *(Photo 3.)*

MOUNTAIN

Paint the mountain with the knife and a mixture of Midnight Black, Prussian Blue, and Alizarin Crimson. Load the knife with a small roll of the mixture and use firm pressure to shape just the top edge of the mountain. *(Photo 4.)* When you are satisfied with the basic shape of the mountain top, use the knife to remove any excess paint. Then, with the 2" brush, pull the paint down to the base of the mountain, to blend and complete the entire mountain shape. *(Photo 5.)*

Highlight the mountain with a mixture of Titanium White and a small amount of Bright Red. Again, load the long edge of the knife blade with a small roll of paint. Starting at the top (and paying close attention to angles) glide the knife down the right side of each peak, using so little pressure that the paint "breaks". *(Photo 6.)* Use a mixture of Titanium White and Prussian Blue, applied in the opposing direction, for the shadow sides of the peaks.

Use the blender brush to tap to diffuse the base of the mountain *(Photo 7)* then gently lift upward to create the illusion of mist *(Photo 8)*.

Load a clean, dry 2" brush with a small amount of Indian Yellow and use criss-cross strokes to blend this color into the base of the mountain.

FOOTHILLS

Load a clean, dry 2" brush with the mountain-shadow mixture (Titanium White and Prussian Blue). Tap downward to shape the most distant foothills at the base of the mountain. *(Photo 9.)* (Notice how the Blue-White mixture blends with the underpainted Yellow to make Green.) With very short upward strokes you can create the impression of tiny tree tops. *(Photo 10.)* Working forward in layers, you can create darker tree lines by adding a small amount of Midnight Black to the mixture. *(Photo 11.)* Use a clean, dry 2" brush to tap the base of the foothills (Photo 12) creating the illusion of mist *(Photo 13)*.

The closer foothills are made with a mixture of Midnight Black, Alizarin Crimson, Prussian Blue, Sap Green and Titanium White on the 2" brush. *(Photo 14.)* To create the illusion of mist, firmly tap to diffuse the base of the foothills with the top corner of a clean, dry 2" brush, then gently lift upward.

Hold the 2" brush flat against the canvas and pull straight down to reflect the foothills into the water *(Photo 15)* then brush lightly across. (A small amount of Titanium White can be added to the 2" brush to "sparkle" the water.)

Without cleaning the brush, tap the bristles into various mixtures of Sap Green and the Yellows and lightly touch highlights to the closest range of foothills.

The grassy areas at the base of the foothills are made with the same highlight color (thinned with a small amount of Liquid White) and the fan brush. Hold the brush horizontally and push upward at the base of the foothills. *(Photo 16.)*

Cut in water lines and ripples with Titanium White and a very small amount of Bright Red on the knife *(Photo 17)* to complete the background *(Photo 18).*

WATERFALL

To paint the waterfall, load a clean fan brush with a thin mixture of Liquid White, Titanium White and a small amount of Phthalo Blue. Holding the brush horizontally, and starting at the top of the waterfall, make short horizontal strokes, each time pulling the brush straight down to the base of the falls. *(Photo 19.)*

Use Van Dyke Brown on the knife to block in the waterfall rock. *(Photo 20.)* Load the oval brush with a thin, dark mixture of paint thinner, Midnight Black, Prussian Blue, Van Dyke Brown, Dark Sienna and Alizarin Crimson. Then pull one side of the bristles through a thin Gray mixture of Titanium White, Midnight Black and a very small amount of Phthalo Blue, to double-load the brush. With the light side of the brush up, highlight and contour the waterfall rock. *(Photo 21.)*

TREES AND BUSHES

Use a mixture of Prussian Blue, Sap Green and Phthalo

Green on the fan brush to paint the large evergreen. Holding the brush vertically, touch the canvas to create the center line of each tree. Use just the corner of the brush to begin adding the small top branches. Working from side to side, as you move down each tree, apply more pressure to the brush, forcing the bristles to bend upward and automatically the branches will become larger as you near the base of the tree. *(Photo 22.)* Touch highlights to the evergreen with mixtures of the Yellows on the fan brush. *(Photo 23.)*

The leaf trees and bushes are underpainted with the same dark tree color on the 2" brush. *(Photo 24.)* Apply the highlights to the bushes with mixtures of Sap Green, the Yellows and small amounts of Bright Red. Concentrate on shape and form. *(Photo 25.)*

FOREGROUND

Working forward in layers, continue highlighting the foliage with the 2" brush *(Photo 26)* and shaping rocks and stones with the oval brush *(Photo 27).* When you are satisfied with the foliage *(Photo 28)* add spray, foam and water lines to the water at the base of the falls with Titanium White and a small amount of Phthalo Blue on the fan brush *(Photo 29).*

FINISHING TOUCHES

Use thinned Van Dyke Brown on the liner brush to add a tiny leafless tree to the foreground *(Photo 30)* and your painting is complete *(Photo 31).*

Wilderness Falls

 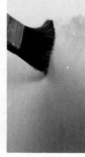      

1. Begin by painting the canvas with Liquid Black and White.

2. Use the 2" brush . . .

3. . . . to paint the sky.

4. Shape the mountain top with the knife . . .

5. . . . then blend the paint down with the 2" brush.

6. Apply snow with the knife . . .

7. . . . then tap with the 2" brush . . .

8. . . . to create the illusion of mist.

Wilderness Falls

9. Tap down with the 2" brush . . .

10. . . . to begin shaping the foothills.

11. Add the closer hills . . .

12. . . . then firmly tap the base . . .

13. . . . to create the illusion of mist.

14. Tap in background trees . . .

15. . . . and pull down reflections.

16. Add grassy areas with the fan brush . . .

17. . . . then use the knife . . .

18. . . . to cut in water lines and ripples.

19. Use the fan brush to paint the waterfall.

20. Underpaint the rocks with the knife . . .

21. . . . then highlight with the oval brush.

22. Use the fan brush . . .

23. . . . to paint the large evergreen.

24. Use the 2" brush to underpaint . . .

25. . . . and highlight leaf trees and bushes.

26. Layer foliage . . .

27. . . . and rocks . . .

28. . . . near the waterfall.

29. Add foreground water with the fan brush . . .

30. . . . and a tree trunk with the liner brush . . .

31. . . . to complete your painting.

FISHERMAN'S TRAIL

MATERIALS

2" Brush	Midnight Black
1" Brush	Dark Sienna
#6 Fan Brush	Van Dyke Brown
#2 Script Liner Brush	Alizarin Crimson
Large Knife	Sap Green
Liquid White	Cadmium Yellow
Liquid Clear	Yellow Ochre
Titanium White	Indian Yellow
Phthalo Blue	Bright Red
Prussian Blue	

Use the 2" brush to completely cover the canvas with a VERY THIN coat of Liquid Clear. (It is important to stress that the Liquid Clear should be applied VERY, VERY sparingly and really scrubbed into the canvas! You can use a paper towel to remove excess Liquid Clear from the canvas, if necessary.) Do not allow the Liquid Clear to dry before you proceed with your painting.

WOOD BACKGROUND

Use the knife to make a Brown mixture using equal parts of Alizarin Crimson and Sap Green.

Load a clean, very dry 2" brush with a mixture of the Brown color and Titanium White and, holding the brush horizontally and starting from the right side of the canvas and working across, use long, vertical strokes to apply this "wood" color to the canvas. (Photo 1.)

Vary the amounts of Titanium White, Alizarin Crimson and Sap Green used for the mixture. A small amount of Midnight Black may also be added to the mixture. Notice that by changing the value of the color a "boarded" or "paneled" wood effect is created. (Photo 2.)

Dip a fan brush into paint thinner and shake off the excess. Hold the brush horizontally and, starting at the top of each board and walking downward, lightly brush the bristles against the canvas. Vary the direction of the brush strokes to create the effect of wood grain. (Photo 3.) (Notice that the reaction between the paint thinner and the Liquid Clear causes the paint to "break up", producing a wood grain effect.) (Photo 4.)

MOUNTAIN

The mountain is made using the knife and a mixture of Van Dyke Brown, Midnight Black, Prussian Blue and Alizarin Crimson. Pull the mixture out very flat on your palette, hold the knife straight up and "cut" across the mixture to load the long edge of the blade with a small roll of paint. (Holding the knife straight up will force the small roll of paint to the very edge of the blade.) With firm pressure, shape just the top edge of the mountain. (Photo 5.) When you are satisfied with the basic shape of the mountain top, use the knife to remove any excess paint. Then, with the 2" brush, pull the paint down to the base of the mountain, to blend and complete the entire mountain shape. (Photo 6.)

Highlight the mountain with a mixture of Titanium White and a small amount of Bright Red. Again, load the long edge of the knife blade with a small roll of paint. Starting at the top (and paying close attention to angles) glide the knife down the right side of each peak, using so little pressure that the paint "breaks". (Photo 7.) Use a mixture of Titanium White and Phthalo Blue applied in the opposing direction, for the shadow sides of the peaks. Again, use so little pressure that the paint "breaks".

Use a clean, dry 2" brush to tap to diffuse the base of the mountain, carefully following the angle of each peak (Photo 8) then gently lift upward with the brush to create the illusion of mist (Photo 9).

BACKGROUND EVERGREENS

Load the fan brush with a mixture of the original dark mountain color and Sap Green. Holding the brush vertically, touch the canvas to create the center line of each tree. Use just the corner of the brush to begin adding the small top branches. Working from side to side, as you move down each tree, apply more pressure to the brush, forcing the bristles to bend downward and automatically the branches will become larger as you near the base of each tree. *(Photo 10.)*

Add the trunks with a small roll of a mixture of Titanium White and Dark Sienna on the knife. *(Photo 11.)* Use the fan brush to very lightly touch highlights to the branches with a mixture of the dark tree color and the Yellows. *(Photo 12.)*

Use a clean, dry 2" brush and holding the brush horizontally, pull straight down from the base of the trees to create reflections in the water. Brush lightly across. *(Photo 13.)*

Reload the fan brush with various mixtures of the Yellow-Green highlight colors and small amounts of Bright Red and tap in the small bushes at the base of the background evergreen trees. *(Photo 14.)*

Use a small roll of Liquid White on the knife to cut in water lines and ripples *(Photo 15)* to complete the background *(Photo 16)*.

FOREGROUND

The bushes in the foreground of the painting are underpainted with the original dark mountain-mixture on the 1" brush. *(Photo 17.)*

Use various mixtures of Sap Green and all of the Yellows to highlight the trees and bushes. Begin by dipping the 1" brush into Liquid White (or paint thinner) to thin the mixture. Then, with the handle of the brush straight up, pull the brush (several times in one direction, to round one corner of the bristles) through the various highlight mixtures. With the rounded corner of the bristles "up", very lightly touch the canvas, forcing the bristles to bend upward the apply highlights to each individual small tree and bush. Try not to just "hit" at random; carefully shape individual trees and bushes. Be very careful not to completely cover all of the dark undercolor, these are the shadow areas which will help to separate the individual shapes.

Use a small roll of Van Dyke Brown on the knife and horizontal strokes to add the path. Pay close attention to perspective; the path is wider as it comes forward. Highlight the path with a small roll of a mixture of Van Dyke Brown and Titanium White on the knife. Again, use horizontal strokes, but this time with so little pressure that the paint "breaks". *(Photo 18.)*

FINISHING TOUCHES

Use the point of the knife to scratch in the indication of sticks and twigs or add tiny details with the liner brush. (To load the liner brush, thin the Brown mixture to an ink-like consistency by first dipping the liner brush into paint thinner. Slowly turn the brush as you pull the bristles through the mixture, forcing them to a sharp point.) Use just the point of the brush and very little pressure to add tiny limbs and branches or small sticks and twigs.

Use thinned paint on the liner brush to sign the painting and your masterpiece is complete. *(Photo 19.)*

Fisherman's Trail

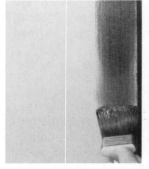     

1. Use the 2" brush to apply . . .

2. . . . . long vertical strokes of color.

3. With paint thinner on the fan brush . . .

4. . . . . create the wood grain.

5. Use the knife to paint the mountain top . . .

6. . . . . then blend the paint down with the 2" brush.

Fisherman's Trail

7. Apply highlights with the knife . . .

8. . . . then tap the base of the mountain . . .

9. . . . to create the illusion of mist.

10. Paint large evergreens with the fan brush . . .

11. . . . then use the knife to add trunks . . .

12. . . . to the background evergreens.

13. Pull down reflections with the 2" brush.

14. Add grassy areas with the fan brush . . .

15. . . . then use a small roll of Liquid White on the knife . . .

16. . . . to cut in water lines and ripples.

17. Paint foreground bushes with the 1" brush.

18. Use the knife and horizontal strokes . . .

19. . . . to add a path to the finished painting.

A WARM WINTER

MATERIALS

2" Brush	Titanium White
2" Blender Brush	Phthalo Blue
1" Brush	Prussian Blue
#6 Fan Brush	Midnight Black
#2 Script Liner Brush	Alizarin Crimson
Large Knife	Sap Green
Small Knife	Cadmium Yellow
Adhesive-Backed Plastic	Yellow Ochre
Liquid White	Bright Red

Start by covering the entire canvas with a piece of adhesive-backed plastic (such as Con-Tact Paper) from which you have removed a center oval shape. (A 16x20 oval for an 18x24 canvas.) *(Photo 1.)*

Use the 2" brush to cover the exposed area of the canvas with a thin, even coat of Liquid White. Do NOT allow the Liquid White to dry before you begin.

SKY

Load a clean, dry 2" brush with Cadmium Yellow and working outward from the center of the horizon, use criss-cross strokes to begin painting the brilliant glow in the sky. Without cleaning the brush, reload it with Yellow Ochre and working upward blend this color into the sky area. Still without cleaning the brush, reload it with Bright Red and add this color to the sky, above the Yellow Ochre. Softly blend with horizontal strokes.

Load a clean, dry 2" brush with a small amount of Phthalo Blue and Midnight Black. Working at the upper-most portion of the exposed canvas, use criss-cross strokes to complete the band of colors in the sky.

With Titanium White, use one corner of the fan brush and circular strokes to add clouds to the sky. *(Photo 2.)* Gently blend the base of the clouds with the top corner of the blender brush. *(Photo 3.)* Use a clean fan brush to paint the darker clouds with a mixture of Alizarin Crimson and Sap Green. *(Photo 4.)* Again blend the base of the clouds with the blender brush. *(Photo 5.)* Highlight these darker clouds with a mixture of Titanium White and a very small amount of Bright Red on the fan brush, at the same time tapping in the indication of "stringy" clouds. *(Photo 6.)* Use circular strokes and the blender brush to soften the highlights and then blend the entire sky with long, horizontal strokes. *(Photo 7.)*

BACKGROUND

Load a clean, dry 2" brush with a light mixture of Titanium White, Alizarin Crimson and Sap Green and, holding the brush horizontally, tap downward to shape the distant hills. *(Photo 8.)* With very short upward strokes you can create the impression of tiny tree tops along the top edges of the hills. To blend, hold the blender brush vertically and tap the base of the hills, then brush lightly across. Continue adding layers of hills, using slightly darker mixtures (less Titanium White) of the same color each time, as you move forward in the painting. *(Photo 9.)*

Use Titanium White on the fan brush to add snow to the base of the background hills. *(Photo 10.)* A small amount of Bright Red may also be used to create the illusion of the sky's reflection in the snow. *(Photo 11.)*

EVERGREENS

Load the fan brush with a mixture of Prussian Blue, Midnight Black and Alizarin Crimson. Holding the brush vertically, touch the canvas to create the center line of each tree. Use just the corner of the brush to begin adding the small top branches. Working from side to side, as you move down each tree, apply more pressure to the brush, forcing the bristles to bend downward and automatically the branches will become larger as you near the base of each tree. *(Photo 12.)* Load a clean fan brush with Titanium White and, touching the canvas at the base of the trees, pull shadows out into the surrounding snow. *(Photo 13.)*

Use the fan brush to very lightly touch highlights to the branches with a mixture of Liquid White, Titanium White and a small amount of Phthalo Blue. *(Photo 14.)*

CABIN

Use the knife to remove paint from the canvas in the basic shape of the cabin. Load the long edge of the knife with a small roll of a Brown mixture using Sap Green and Alizarin Crimson. To load the knife pull the paint out very flat on your palette and just cut across. Paint the back edge of the roof, then pull down the front and side of the cabin. Use the same Brown mixture and Titanium White to highlight the front and side of the cabin, using so little pressure that the paint "breaks".

Add the snow-covered roof with Titanium White. Don't forget to add a bit of snow to the back edges of the roof. (A small amount of Phthalo Blue may be used with the Titanium White to "deepen" the snow at the edges of the roof.) Shape the bottom edge of the cabin by removing the excess paint with a clean knife. Use the small knife and dark Brown to add the door to the cabin.

Add snow to the base of the cabin with Titanium White on the fan brush. (Again, a small amount of Bright Red can be used to indicate the reflection of the sky.) Use long, horizontal strokes to extend the snow to the bottom of the exposed oval. *(Photo 15.)*

FOREGROUND

Underpaint the small trees and bushes in the foreground with dark Brown on the 1" brush. *(Photo 16.)* Dip the 1" brush into Liquid White then load it with a mixture of Yellow Ochre and a very small amount of Bright Red. Concentrating on shape and form, touch highlights to the trees and bushes. (If you are careful not to destroy all of the dark undercolor, you can use it to separate the individual tree and bush shapes.) *(Photo 17.)*

Use the liner brush and thinned Brown to add the small barren tree in the foreground. *(Photo 18.)*

Load the fan brush with Titanium White and again pull out the shadows at the base of the foreground trees and bushes. *(Photo 19.)*

FINISHING TOUCHES

Carefully remove the Con-Tact Paper from your painted oval. *(Photo 20.)* Use the original dark tree-mixture on the fan brush to extend top branches of the largest evergreen outside the oval. Highlight the trees with a mixture of Liquid White, Titanium White and Phthalo Blue on the fan brush and your painting is ready for a signature! *(Photo 21.)*

A Warm Winter

1. Cover the canvas with Con-Tact Paper.

2. Add light clouds with the fan brush . . .

3. . . . then blend with the blender brush.

4. Add dark clouds . . .

5. . . . and again blend . . .

6. . . . then use the fan brush . . .

7. . . . to add "stringy" clouds.

A Warm Winter

8. Use the 2" brush . . .

9. . . . to tap in layers in hills.

10. Add snow . . .

11. . . . to the base of the hills.

12. Paint evergreens with the fan brush . . .

13. . . . then add snow to the base of the trees . . .

14. . . . and highlights to the branches.

15. Progressional steps used to paint the cabin.

16. Add foreground bushes . . .

17. . . . and highlights with the 1" brush.

18. Use the liner brush . . .

19. . . . to add the small foreground tree.

20. Remove the Con-Tact Paper from your canvas . . .

21. . . . then extend an evergreen tree outside the oval.

UNDER PASTEL SKIES

MATERIALS

2" Brush	Dark Sienna
#6 Fan Brush	Van Dyke Brown
#2 Script Liner Brush	Alizarin Crimson
Large Knife	Sap Green
Liquid White	Cadmium Yellow
Titanium White	Yellow Ochre
Phthalo Blue	Indian Yellow
Prussian Blue	Bright Red
Midnight Black	

Use the 2" brush to cover the entire canvas with a thin, even coat of Liquid White. Do NOT allow the Liquid White to dry before proceeding.

SKY

Load a clean, dry 2" brush with Indian Yellow and working outward from the center of the horizon, use criss-cross strokes to begin painting the Golden glow in the sky. *(Photo 1.)* Without cleaning the brush, reload it with Yellow Ochre and working upward blend this color into the sky area. Still without cleaning the brush, reload it with Alizarin Crimson and add this color to the sky, above the Yellow Ochre. Softly blend with horizontal strokes.

Load a clean, dry 2" brush with a small amount of Phthalo Blue and use criss-cross strokes to add this color to the upper most portion of the sky. With Phthalo Blue still on the brush, tap in the basic shapes of clouds in the sky. *(Photo 2.)*

Use a clean, dry 2" brush to blend the entire sky area with long, horizontal strokes. *(Photo 3.)*

Now is a good time to underpaint the water on the lower portion of the canvas. Reload the 2" brush with Phthalo Blue. Starting at the bottom of the canvas (and working up towards the horizon) use horizontal strokes, pulling from the outside edges of the canvas in towards the center.

MOUNTAIN

The small mountain in the background is made using the knife and a mixture of Phthalo Blue, Midnight Black and Titanium White. Pull the mixture out very flat on your palette, hold the knife straight up and "cut" across the mixture to load the long edge of the blade with a small roll of paint. (Holding the knife straight up will force the small roll of paint to the very edge of the blade.) With firm pressure, shape just the top edge of the mountain. *(Photo 4.)*

When you are satisfied with the basic shape of the mountain top, use the knife to remove any excess paint. Then, with the 2" brush, blend the paint down to the base of the mountain. *(Photo 5.)* Load a clean, dry 2" brush with a very small amount of Titanium White and tap to diffuse the base of the mountain (carefully following the angles) *(Photo 6)* then gently lift upward to create the illusion of mist *(Photo 7)*.

Moving forward in the painting, add a second mountain range with a mixture of Prussian Blue, Midnight Black, Alizarin Crimson and Van Dyke Brown on the knife. *(Photo 8.)* Use the 2" brush to blend the paint down to the base of the mountain. *(Photo 9.)*

Highlight the mountain with Titanium White. Again, load the long edge of the knife blade with a small roll of paint. Starting at the top (and paying close attention to angles) glide the knife down the right side of each peak, using so little pressure that the paint "breaks". *(Photo 10.)* Use a mixture of Phthalo Blue, Titanium White and a small amount of Midnight Black, applied in the opposing direction, for the shadow sides of the peaks. Again, use so little pressure that the paint "breaks".

Tap downward with a clean, dry 2" brush to diffuse the base of the mountain (carefully following the angles) and then gently lift upward to create the illusion of mist. *(Photo 11.)*

Use the mountain shadow-mixture (Phthalo Blue, Titanium White, Midnight Black) on the fan brush to indicate the foothills at the base of the second mountain range. Hold the brush horizontally and just tap downward. *(Photo 12.)* With the same color, hold the brush flat against the canvas and pull straight down to reflect the foothills into the water and then lightly brush across. With very short upward strokes you can create the impression of tiny tree tops along the top edges of the hills. *(Photo 13.)* Add water lines to the base of the foothills with a small roll of Liquid White on the edge of the knife. *(Photo 14.)*

Add the large mountain with a mixture of Prussian Blue, Midnight Black, Alizarin Crimson, Van Dyke Brown on the knife. *(Photo 15.)*

Use the dark mountain-mixture (Blue-Black-Crimson-Brown) on the 2" brush to extend the foothills out from the base of the large mountain. Pull the color straight down into the water for reflections. *(Photo 16.)* Brush lightly across.

Use Liquid White and a very small amount of Bright Red on the knife to cut in water lines and ripples. *(Photo 17.)*

Highlight the large mountain with a small roll of Titanium White on the knife. *(Photo 18.)* Use a mixture of Titanium White and Phthalo Blue for the highlights on the shadowed sides of the peaks. Tap to diffuse the base of the mountain *(Photo 19)* then lightly brush upward to create the illusion of mist *(Photo 20)*.

EVERGREENS

To paint the evergreens, load the fan brush with the dark mountain-mixture and Sap Green. Holding the brush vertically, touch the canvas to create the center line of each tree. Use just the corner of the brush to begin adding the small top branches. Working from side to side, as you move down each tree, apply more pressure to the brush, forcing the bristles to bend down-

ward and automatically the branches will become larger as you near the base of each tree. *(Photo 21.)*

Use the 2" brush to pick up some of the paint at the base of the trees and tap downward to underpaint the foreground land areas. *(Photo 22.)*

Very lightly touch highlights to the evergreen branches with a mixture of the dark tree color and the Yellows (to make Green).

FOREGROUND

The rocks and stones at the base of the evergreens are underpainted with a mixture of Dark Sienna and Van Dyke Brown on the knife. Use a mixture of the same Brown color and Titanium White on the knife and very little pressure to highlight the rocks. *(Photo 23.)*

Load a clean, dry 2" brush with the various mixtures of the evergreen color, all of the Yellows and a small amount of Titanium White and Bright Red to add the soft grassy highlights to the foreground. Hold the brush horizontally and gently tap downward. Work in layers, carefully creating the lay-of-the-land. If you are also careful not to destroy all of the dark color already on the canvas, you can create grassy highlights that look almost like velvet. *(Photo 24.)*

FINISHING TOUCHES

Use the point of the knife to scratch in just the indication of small sticks and twigs. Don't forget to sign your painting! *(Photo 25.)*

Under Pastel Skies

1. Paint the sky with criss-cross strokes . . .

2. . . . then tap downward with the 2" brush . . .

3. . . . to add cloud shapes to the sky.

4. Add the distant mountain top with the knife . . .

5. . . . then blend the paint down with the 2" brush.

6. Tap the base of the mountain with the 2" brush . . .

Under Pastel Skies

7. . . . to create the illusion of mist.

8. Shape the closer mountain top . . .

9. . . . and again blend with the 2" brush.

10. Highlight the closer mountain . . .

11. . . . then tap to mist the base.

12. Add the tree line with the fan brush . . .

13. . . . then pull up tiny tree tops.

14. Cut in water lines with the knife.

15. Shape the larger, closer mountain.

16. Pull down reflections with the 2" brush . . .

17. . . . then cut in water lines with the knife.

18. Highlight the large mountain . . .

19. . . . then use the 2" brush to diffuse . . .

20. . . . the base of the large mountain.

21. Paint large evergreens with the fan brush . . .

22. . . . then tap in grassy areas with the 2" brush.

23. Add the land areas with the knife . . .

24. . . . then use the 2" brush . . .

25. . . . to add soft grass to the finished painting.

GOLDEN RAYS OF SUNLIGHT

MATERIALS

2" Brush
#2 Script Liner Brush
Large Knife
White Gesso
Black Gesso
Gray Gesso
Liquid Clear

Titanium White
Phthalo Blue
Prussian Blue
Alizarin Crimson
Sap Green
Indian Yellow

Start by using a foam applicator to apply a thin, even coat of Black Gesso to your entire canvas and allow to DRY COMPLETELY.

Dip a crumpled paper towel into White Gesso and, starting in the middle of the canvas (just above the horizon) and working outward, "tap in" the light source in the sky. *(Photo 1.)* Working away from the center of the light source, gradually add Gray Gesso to the outer portions of the canvas. Allow the Gessos to DRY COMPLETELY before proceeding. *(Photo 2.)*

In this painting, it is important to understand the use of the three Gesso colors. These underpainted colors are used to define the value of light in the painting, in much the same way that a black and white photograph consists of black, white and shades of gray. The trees nearest the light source are painted with Black Gesso. Load both sides of the foam applicator with Black Gesso. Holding the applicator vertically and starting at the top of the canvas, just pull straight down, to begin painting the tree trunks, applying more pressure against the canvas as you near the base of each tree. *(Photo 3.)*

Working away from the light source, use Gray Gesso to paint the tree trunks. *(Photo 4.)* For the trees furthest away from the light source, use White Gesso.

Thin the Gessos with water and use the liner brush to add smaller trees *(Photo 5)* limbs *(Photo 6)* and branches *(Photo 7)*. (To load the liner brush, dip the brush into water. Slowly turn the brush as you pull the bristles through the thinned Gesso, forcing the bristles to a sharp point.) Use just the tip of the bristles and very little pressure to paint the trunks, limbs and branches.

By turning and wiggling the brush, you can give the trees a gnarled appearance. *(Photo 8.)*

Working forward in layers, continue using the foam applicator and Black Gesso to add the largest tree trunk. *(Photo 9.)* Again, use Black Gesso, thinned with water, and the liner brush to add limbs and branches *(Photo 10)* to the large tree *(Photo 11)*.

Use the White and Gray Gessos on the foam applicator *(Photo 12)* to block in the foliage at the base of the trees *(Photo 13)*. With Black Gesso on the foam applicator, use horizontal strokes to add the indication of a path in the foreground. *(Photo 14.)* When you are satisfied with your underpainting, allow the Gessos to DRY COMPLETELY before you continue. *(Photo 15.)*

When the Black Gesso is dry, use the 2" brush to completely cover the canvas with a VERY THIN coat of Liquid Clear. (It is important to stress that the Liquid Clear should be applied VERY, VERY sparingly and really scrubbed into the canvas! If necessary, you can remove excess Liquid Clear from the canvas with a paper towel. The remaining Liquid Clear will not only ease the application of the firmer paint, but will allow you to apply very little color, creating a glazed effect.)

SKY

Load a clean, dry 2" brush with a very small amount of Phthalo Blue and begin coloring the sky, using criss-cross strokes at the upper portion of the canvas and working downward. *(Photo 16.)* Reload the 2" brush with a small amount of Prussian Blue and darken the upper corners of the canvas.

FOREGROUND

Load a clean, dry 2" brush with a small amount of Indian Yellow and use criss-cross strokes below the horizon to begin coloring (or glazing) the bushes, grass and foliage. (Notice the Green highlight color that is produced when the Yellow blends with the Blue already on the canvas.)

Use the knife to make a Brown mixture on your palette with

equal parts of Alizarin Crimson and Sap Green. Load a clean, dry 2" brush with this color and again use criss-cross strokes to glaze the foreground land area, working from the very bottom of the canvas up to the base of the trees. (Notice the "shadowy" effect that is created by glazing the Gessos with this Brown color.) *(Photo 17.)*

SKY

Load just the corner of a clean, dry 2" brush with Titanium White. Starting in the lightest area of the sky and working outward, use small criss-cross strokes to add the indication of light coming through the trees. *(Photo 18.)* Continue using the 2" brush to pull out the rays of light. *(Photo 19.)*

FINISHING TOUCHES

Use the 2" brush and various mixtures of Phthalo Blue and Indian Yellow to lightly touch final highlights to the bushes, grass and foliage at the base of the trees. *(Photo 20.)*

Sign your painting with pride; load the liner brush with thinned oil color of your choice. Sign just your initials, first name, last name or all of your names. Sign in the left corner, the right corner or one artist signs right in the middle of the canvas! The choice is yours. You might also consider including the date when you sign your painting. Whatever your choices, have fun, for hopefully with this painting you have truly experienced THE JOY OF PAINTING!

Golden Rays of Sunlight

1. Use a crumpled paper towel and White Gesso . . .

2. . . . to underpaint the light in the sky.

3. Use Black Gesso . . .

4. . . . and White Gesso to underpaint tree trunks.

5. Use thinned Gesso on the liner brush to add small trunks . . .

Golden Rays of Sunlight

6. . . . and limbs . . .

7. . . . and branches . . .

8. . . . to the underpainted background.

9. Underpaint the large trunk with the applicator . . .

10. . . . then use the liner brush . . .

11. . . . to add small limbs and branches.

12. Use the foam applicator . . .

13. . . . to add foliage to the base of the trees.

14. With horizontal strokes . . .

15. . . . add the foreground path.

16. Use criss-cross strokes . . .

17. . . . to paint the sky.

18. Add the light glow . . .

19. . . . then blend outward . . .

20. . . . to complete the painting.

GLACIER LAKE

MATERIALS

2" Brush	Prussian Blue
2" Blender Brush	Midnight Black
#6 Filbert Brush	Dark Sienna
#6 Fan Brush	Van Dyke Brown
#3 Fan Brush	Alizarin Crimson
#2 Script Liner Brush	Sap Green
Large Knife	Cadmium Yellow
Small Knife	Yellow Ochre
Liquid White	Indian Yellow
Titanium White	Bright Red
Phthalo Blue	

Use the 2" brush to cover the canvas with a thin, even coat of Liquid White. Do NOT allow the Liquid White to dry before you proceed.

SKY

Load a clean, dry 2" brush with a small amount of Phthalo Blue. Starting at the very top of the canvas, working down towards the horizon, paint the sky with criss-cross strokes. *(Photo 1.)* Reload the brush with Phthalo Blue and underpaint the water on the lower portion of the canvas with long, horizontal strokes. *(Photo 2.)* Clean and dry the 2" brush and blend the entire canvas with long, horizontal strokes.

To paint the clouds, load the 2" brush by holding it vertically and firmly tapping the bristles into Titanium White. Still holding the brush vertically, tap in the basic cloud shapes. *(Photo 3.)* Use criss-cross strokes to lightly blend the clouds, then lift upward to "fluff". *(Photo 4.)*

MOUNTAIN

To begin painting the mountain, load the knife with a small roll of a mixture of Midnight Black with a small amount of Prussian Blue. Use firm pressure to shape the most distant peaks. *(Photo 5.)* Use a mixture of Prussian Blue and Titanium White on the knife to add the shadowed (left) sides of the peaks.

(Photo 6.) Load a clean, dry 2" brush to a chiseled edge with Titanium White. (By "wiggling" and "pulling" both sides of the brush through the paint, the bristles are forced to a sharp edge.) Holding the brush horizontally and paying close attention to angles, use sweeping horizontal strokes to lay in the snow in and around the protruding peaks. *(Photo 7.)*

Use a mixture of Titanium White and Midnight Black (to make Gray) on the 2" brush to paint the "shaded" sides of the snow banks. *(Photo 8.)* Again, carefully follow the slopes and angles of the mountain. *(Photo 9.)*

Working in layers, continue adding the protruding peaks with Midnight Black on the knife – then add White (for the highlights) and Blue-White (for the shadows). *(Photo 10.)*

Use the small knife to blend the base of the peaks into the snow. *(Photo 11.)* Use the blender brush to softly blend these areas. *(Photo 12.)*

Working in layers, continue adding the dark peaks with the knife, the snowy areas with Titanium White on the 2" brush *(Photo 13)* and then softly blending with the blender brush *(Photo 14)* always paying close attention to angles.

To complete the mountain, tap downward with a clean, dry 2" brush to diffuse the base of the mountain, then make sweeping upward strokes to blend. *(Photo 15.)*

FOOTHILLS

Use the knife to make a Blue-Gray mixture on your palette with Prussian Blue, Midnight Black, Alizarin Crimson, Van Dyke Brown and Titanium White. To a portion of the mixture, add more Titanium White to make a light Blue-Gray mixture. Load the fan brush with the light Blue-Gray color, hold the brush vertically, just tap downward to paint the indication of tiny evergreens at the base of the mountain. *(Photo 16.)* Use a clean, dry 2" brush to tap to diffuse the base of the foothill trees then gently lift upward to create the illusion of mist. *(Photo 17.)* Use the darker Blue-Gray mixture on the fan brush to add another, closer range of foothill trees at the base of the mountain. Again, tap to diffuse the base of the trees and lift upward to mist.

Continue layering the foothills, making each range of trees progressively darker in value as you move forward in the painting. *(Photo 18.)* With a clean, dry 2" brush (held horizontally) touch the base of the closest range of trees and pull the color straight down into the water. Brush lightly across for a watery appearance. *(Photo 19.)*

WATERFALL

Use a thin mixture of Liquid White and Titanium White on the small fan brush to paint the waterfall. Hold the brush horizontally, start with a short horizontal stroke at the top of the falls, then pull the brush straight down, ending the stroke at the base of the falls. *(Photo 20.)* Use a small amount of the same White mixture on the blender brush and tap to mist the base of the falls. *(Photo 21.)* Use a small roll of Liquid White on the knife to cut in the indication of water lines and ripples *(Photo 22)* at the base of the background trees *(Photo 23)*.

LARGE EVERGREENS

To paint the evergreens, load the fan brush with a dark mixture of Midnight Black, Prussian Blue, Sap Green, Alizarin Crimson, Van Dyke Brown and Dark Sienna. Holding the brush vertically, touch the canvas to create the center line of each tree. Use just the corner of the brush to begin adding the small top branches. Working from side to side, as you move down each tree, apply more pressure to the brush, forcing the bristles to bend downward and automatically the branches will become larger as you near the base of each tree. *(Photo 24.)*

Without cleaning the fan brush, reload it with a mixture of Cadmium Yellow and Yellow Ochre (to make Green) and lightly touch highlights to the large evergreens. *(Photo 25.)*

FOREGROUND

With a clean, dry 2" brush, tap to diffuse the base of the larger evergreens, extending the dark tree color out into the land area at the base of the trees. *(Photo 26.)* Pull the dark color straight down into the water for reflections *(Photo 27)* then brush lightly across. Without cleaning the 2" brush, tap the bristles into various mixtures of the Yellows and very small amounts of Bright Red and, carefully creating the lay-of-the-land, add the grassy highlights to the land areas. *(Photo 28.)*

To paint the rocks and stones in the water, load the filbert brush with a dark Brown mixture of Midnight Black and Van Dyke Brown (thinned with paint thinner), then pull one side of the bristles through a mixture of Titanium White and Dark Sienna, to double-load the brush. With the light side of the brush up, use a single curved stroke to paint each rock and stone. *(Photo 29.)* Use a small roll of Liquid White on the knife to cut in the foreground water lines. *(Photo 30.)*

FINISHING TOUCHES

Use Yellow-Green on the 1" brush to tap in the small bush at the base of the large evergreens *(Photo 31)* and your painting is complete *(Photo 32)*.

Glacier Lake

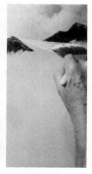

1. Use crisscross strokes to paint sky . . .

2. . . . and horizontal strokes to add the water.

3. Use the 2" brush and circular strokes . . .

4. . . . to add the clouds.

5. Use the knife to paint . . .

6. . . . the protruding mountain peaks.

7. Add highlights . . .

8. . . . and shadows to mountain snow . . .

Glacier Lake

9. . . . paying close attention to angles.

10. Continue adding peaks . . .

11. . . . then use the small knife to blend . . .

12. . . . the base of the peaks into the snow.

13. Continue adding snow with the 2" brush . . .

14. . . . then use the blender brush . . .

15. . . . to soften the snow.

16. Add small evergreens with the fan brush . . .

17. . . . then tap down with the 2" brush . . .

18. . . . to mist the base of the trees.

19. Reflect the small trees into the water.

20. Use the fan brush to paint the waterfall . . .

21. . . . then mist the base of the falls with the blender.

22. Use Liquid White on the knife . . .

23. . . . to cut in water lines.

24. Paint large evergreens . . .

25. . . . as you work forward.

26. Use the 2" brush to add grass . . .

27. . . . and reflections to the base of the trees.

28. Highlight the grassy areas with the 2" brush.

29. Add rocks to the water's edge with the filbert brush.

30. Cut in water lines with the knife . . .

31. . . . and highlight small bushes . . .

32. . . . to complete your painting.

DEEP FOREST FALLS

MATERIALS

2" Brush	Titanium White
2" Blender Brush	Phthalo Blue
1" Brush	Prussian Blue
#6 Filbert Brush	Midnight Black
#6 Fan Brush	Dark Sienna
#2 Script Liner Brush	Van Dyke Brown
Large Knife	Alizarin Crimson
Small Knife	Sap Green
White Gesso	Cadmium Yellow
Black Gesso	Yellow Ochre
Gray Gesso	Indian Yellow
Liquid Clear	Bright Red

I used a 16 x 20 oval canvas for this painting, but if you prefer, you could also use a rectangular-shaped canvas, 16 x 20, 18 x 24, etc.

Start by using a foam applicator to apply a thin, even coat of Black Gesso to your entire canvas and allow to DRY COMPLETELY.

Use a liner brush (preferably an old one) and the three Gessos (White, Black and Gray) to paint the background tree trunks, branches and limbs, then tap in the foliage shapes with a crumpled paper towel. Use Black Gesso and Gray Gesso on the filbert brush to underpaint the indication of rocks and stones on the riverbed. Allow the canvas to DRY COMPLETELY. *(Photo 1.)*

When the Gessos are dry, use a 2" brush to cover the entire canvas with a VERY THIN coat of Liquid Clear. The Liquid Clear should be applied VERY, VERY sparingly and really scrubbed into the canvas! The Liquid Clear will not only ease with the application of the firmer paint, but will allow you to apply very little color, creating a glazed effect. Use a paper towel to remove excess Liquid Clear from the canvas, if necessary. Do NOT allow the canvas to dry before proceeding.

SKY

Load a clean, dry 2" brush with a small amount of Phthalo Blue and use criss-cross strokes to apply this color to the entire canvas (sky and water). *(Photo 2.)*

WATERFALL

Use a mixture of Van Dyke Brown and Dark Sienna on the knife to shape the distant waterfall rock. Pull the mixture out very flat on your palette, hold the knife straight up and "cut" across the mixture to load the long edge of the knife with a small roll of paint. Highlight the rock with a marbled mixture of Titanium White, Midnight Black, Prussian Blue and Dark Sienna, on the knife, using so little pressure that the paint just "breaks". *(Photo 3.)*

To add the waterfall, first dip the fan brush into Liquid Clear (to thin the mixture) and then load it with Titanium White and a small amount of Phthalo Blue. Hold the brush horizontally, start with a short horizontal stroke at the top of the falls *(Photo 4)*, then pull the brush straight down *(Photo 5)* ending the stroke at the base of the falls *(Photo 6)*.

Load just one corner of the blender brush with the same Blue-White mixture and tap in the mist and bubbling action at the base of the falls *(Photo 7)* then use the other corner of the bristles to blend *(Photo 8)*.

Working forward, continue by adding the larger, closer waterfall rocks with a mixture of Dark Sienna and Van Dyke Brown on the knife. Allow the base of the rocks to disappear in the misty area at the base of the falls. Highlight the closer rocks with the White-Black-Blue-Sienna mixture on the knife, again using so little pressure that the paint "breaks". *(Photo 9.)* You can extend the misty area forward to the base of the rocks. *(Photo 10.)*

LARGE TREES, BUSHES AND FOLIAGE

Load a clean, dry 2" brush with a dark mixture of Midnight Black, Prussian Blue, Alizarin Crimson and Sap Green. With just the corner of the brush, tap in the basic shapes of the large trees, bushes and foliage. *(Photo 11.)*

Add highlights to the large trees and bushes with the 1" brush and various mixtures of the dark tree undercolor, the Yellows and small amounts of Bright Red. (Paint thinner may be used to thin the mixtures.) Load the brush by holding it at a 45-degree angle and tapping the bristles into the various paint mixtures. Allow the brush to "slide" slightly forward in the paint each time you tap (this assures that the very tips of the bristles are fully loaded with paint). Use just the corner of the brush to apply the highlights, concentrating on individual shapes and form. *(Photo 12.)* Be very careful not to completely destroy all of the dark underpaint. *(Photo 13.)*

LAND AND WATER

The land areas at the base of the trees and bushes are under-painted with a mixture of Van Dyke Brown and Dark Sienna on the knife. Add the grassy highlights to the land areas with Green-Yellow and very small amounts of Bright Red on the 1" brush. Work in layers, carefully creating the lay-of-the-land. *(Photo 14.)*

Use a thin Brown-White mixture on the liner brush to add small trunks, limbs, branches, sticks and twigs. (To load the liner brush, thin the paint mixture to an ink-like consistency by first dipping the liner brush into paint thinner. Slowly turn the brush as you pull the bristles through the mixture, forcing them to a sharp point.) *(Photo 15.)*

Use the knife to make a dark Brown mixture consisting of Midnight Black and Van Dyke Brown and a Gray mixture consisting of Titanium White, Midnight Black, Van Dyke Brown and a small amount of Phthalo Blue. Thin both mixtures with paint

thinner. To paint the rocks and stones at the edge of the water, load the filbert brush with the dark Brown-mixture, then pull one side of the bristles through the Gray mixture, to double-load the brush. With the light side of the brush on the up, use a curved stroke to paint each rock and stone. By double-loading the brush, you can highlight and shadow each rock and stone with just a single stroke. *(Photo 16.)*

Load both sides of a clean fan brush with a mixture of Titanium White and a small amount of Phthalo Blue (thinned with Liquid Clear). Hold the brush horizontally and "pull" the water over the rocks. *(Photo 17.)* Use short horizontal strokes to add water lines, ripples and "splashes" to the water. *(Photo 18.)*

FINISHING TOUCHES

Use a marbled mixture of Titanium White, Van Dyke Brown and Midnight Black on the small knife to add final highlights to the land areas and you have a finished painting, ready for your signature. *(Photo 19.)*

To sign your painting, load the liner brush with thinned color of your choice. Sign just your initials, first name, last name or all of your names. Sign in the left corner, the right corner or one artist signs right in the middle of the canvas! The choice is yours. You might also consider including the date when you sign your painting. Whatever your choices, have fun, for hopefully with this painting you have truly experienced THE JOY OF PAINTING!

Deep Forest Falls

1. Use the three Gessos for the underpainting.

2. Paint the sky with the 2" brush and criss-cross strokes.

3. Paint the distant rock . . .

4. . . . . before starting the waterfall.

Deep Forest Falls

5. Use one long continuous stroke . . .

6. . . . . to paint the waterfall with the fan brush.

7. Use one corner of the blender brush . . .

8. . . . . to add mist to the base of the falls.

9. Use the knife to paint . . .

10. . . . . and highlight the closer waterfall rock.

11. Underpaint foliage with the 2" brush . . .

12. . . . . then use the 1" brush . . .

13. . . . . to apply highlights to the foliage.

14. Add water with the 1" brush . . .

15. . . . . and twigs with the liner brush . . .

16. . . . . and rocks with the filbert brush.

17. Use the fan brush . . .

18. . . . . to paint the foreground water . . .

19. . . . . to complete the painting.

WINTER'S GRACE

MATERIALS

2" Brush	Titanium White
#6 Fan Brush	Phthalo Blue
Large Knife	Prussian Blue
Small Knife	Midnight Black
Liquid White	

Use the 2" brush to cover the entire canvas with a thin, even coat of Liquid White. With long horizontal and vertical strokes, work back and forth to ensure an even distribution of paint on the canvas. Do NOT allow the Liquid White to dry before you begin.

SKY

Load a clean, dry 2" brush by tapping the bristles into a small amount of Phthalo Blue. Using criss-cross strokes, create a large Blue circle in the sky, just above the horizon. *(Photo 1.)*

Reload the 2" brush with Prussian Blue and continue working outward (in all directions) with criss-cross strokes.

Reload the 2" brush with a mixture of Prussian Blue and Midnight Black and, still working outward, add this color to the sky (and the land area, below the horizon) with criss-cross strokes.

Reload the 2" brush with Midnight Black and paint the outer most edges of the canvas with criss-cross strokes.

Load a clean, dry 2" brush by tapping just one corner of the bristles into Titanium White. Hold the brush vertically (with the loaded corner of the bristles on top) and, working in a circle, use small criss-cross strokes to paint the center of the light source in the sky. *(Photo 2.)* Use sweeping semi-circular strokes and then long, horizontal strokes to blend the sky area. These same steps may be repeated to further "brighten" the source of light in the sky. *(Photo 3.)*

BACKGROUND

Use the knife to make a light Blue mixture on your palette with Phthalo Blue, Prussian Blue and Titanium White. Load both sides of a fan brush with this mixture and, holding the brush horizontally, use horizontal strokes to trace the top edges of the background hills. *(Photo 4.)* Then, paying close attention to angles, use the 2" brush to pull the paint down to the base of the hills. *(Photo 5.)* Brush lightly across to blend. *(Photo 6.)*

Load the 2" brush with a slightly darker Blue-White mixture and, moving forward, continue layering the background hills. *(Photo 7.)* With very short upward strokes you can create the impression of tiny tree tops *(Photo 8)* along the top edges of the hills *(Photo 9)*.

Load the fan brush with Titanium White. Holding the brush horizontally, use short horizontal strokes to lay in the snow in and around the base of the distant hills. *(Photo 10.)*

Load a clean fan brush with a mixture of the Blues, Midnight Black and Titanium White. Holding the brush vertically, just tap downward to paint the indication of the small background evergreen trees. *(Photo 11.)* Use the 2" brush to tap to diffuse the base of the trees and then gently lift upward to create the illusion of mist. *(Photo 12.)*

Working forward in layers, continue adding the snowy land areas *(Photo 13)* to the base of the background evergreens *(Photo 14)*.

Use a mixture of the tree color and Titanium White on the small knife to add the indication of the "icy" river with short horizontal strokes. *(Photo 15.)* Blend with a clean, dry 2" brush and horizontal strokes *(Photo 16)* to complete the background *(Photo 17)*.

EVERGREENS

Use the knife to make a dark mixture using the Blues, Midnight Black and a small amount of Titanium White. For the larger evergreens, load the fan brush to a chiseled edge with this mixture. Holding the brush vertically, touch the canvas to create the center line of each tree. Use just the corner of the brush to begin adding the small top branches. Working from side to side, as you move down each tree, apply more pressure to the brush, forcing the bristles to bend downward and automatically the branches will become larger as you near the base of each tree. *(Photo 18.)*

Use a mixture of Liquid White, Titanium White and Phthalo Blue on the fan to lightly touch highlights to the branches of the large evergreens. *(Photo 19.)*

Add snow to the base of the large evergreens with Titanium White on the fan brush. *(Photo 20.)* The impressions of shadows and rock in the snow can also be created with Blue-White on the fan brush. *(Photo 21.)*

FOREGROUND

Working forward, use the fan brush and the dark-tree mixture to add the large evergreens *(Photo 22)* and the grassy areas in the foreground *(Photo 23)*.

FINISHING TOUCHES

Use the point of the knife to scratch in tiny sticks and twigs and your masterpiece is complete. *(Photo 24.)* Don't forget to sign your finished work!

Winter's Grace

1. Use criss-cross strokes to paint the sky . . .

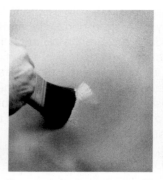

2. . . . and circular strokes to add the light source . . .

3. . . . to complete the sky.

4. Use the fan brush to shape the distant hills . . .

5. . . . then blend down with the 2" brush . . .

6. . . . to complete the first range of hills.

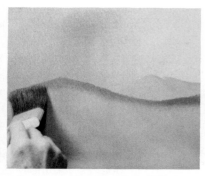

7. Continue shaping hills with the 2" brush . . .

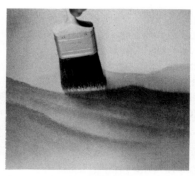

8. . . . then make short upward strokes . . .

9. . . . to create tiny tree tops.

Winter's Grace

10. Lay in snow around the base of the hills.

11. Create the impression of tiny evergreens . . .

12. . . . then firmly tap the base of the trees to mist.

13. Use the fan brush to continue adding snow . . .

14. . . . to the base of the background trees.

15. Add the "icy" river with the small knife . . .

16. . . . then use horizontal strokes with the 2" brush . . .

17. . . . to blend and complete the background.

18. Paint large evergreens with the fan brush . . .

19. . . . then very lightly highlight the branches.

20. Use the fan brush . . .

21. . . . to continue adding foreground snow.

22. Add large foreground evergreens . . .

23. . . . and grassy areas with the fan brush . . .

24. . . . to complete the painting.

TRANQUIL SEAS

MATERIALS

2" Brush	Liquid Clear
2" Blender Brush	Titanium White
#6 Filbert Brush	Phthalo Green
#6 Fan Brush	Phthalo Blue
#3 Fan Brush	Midnight Black
#2 Script Liner Brush	Alizarin Crimson
Small Knife	Sap Green
Adhesive-Backed Plastic	Cadmium Yellow
Black Gesso	Yellow Ochre
Gray Gesso	Indian Yellow
Liquid White	Bright Red

Start by covering the entire canvas with a piece of adhesive-backed plastic (such as Con-Tact Paper) from which you have removed a center oval shape. (A 16 x 20 oval for an 18 x 24 canvas.) Use a foam applicator to cover the area of exposed canvas above the horizon with Gray Gesso and the area below the horizon with Black Gesso. Allow the Gessos to DRY COMPLETELY. (Photo 1.)

When the Gessos are dry, use the 2" brush to cover the entire oval with a VERY THIN coat of Liquid Clear. Do NOT allow the canvas to dry before proceeding.

SKY

Load the 2" brush with a small amount of Indian Yellow and use horizontal strokes to begin painting the sunset, just above the horizon. Reload the brush with Yellow Ochre and continue working upward in the sky with criss-cross strokes. Reload the 2" brush with a small amount of Bright Red and continue using criss-cross strokes to complete the uppermost portion of the sky.

Load a clean, dry 2" brush with Titanium White and use small criss-cross strokes to add the brightest area of the light source, just above the horizon line. (Photo 2.) Blend upward. Use long, horizontal strokes to blend the entire sky.

Use the knife to make a dark Lavender mixture on your palette with Alizarin Crimson and a small amount of Phthalo Blue, then load both sides of a fan brush with this mixture. Use just the corner of the brush and tiny circular strokes to shape the cloud masses in the sky. (Photo 3.) Blend out the base of the cloud shapes with the 2" brush and circular strokes, then use the corner of the soft blender brush to continue blending the clouds. (Photo 4.) Lightly blend the entire sky with long, horizontal strokes. (Photo 5.)

BACKGROUND

Load the 2" brush with a mixture of Phthalo Blue and Phthalo Green and, with horizontal strokes, add this color just below the horizon.

Use the knife to make a Brown mixture on your palette with equal parts of Alizarin Crimson and Sap Green. With the 2" brush, apply this color to the very bottom of the oval with horizontal strokes.

Use Titanium White on the fan brush to sketch just the basic shape of the large wave and background swells. (Photo 6.)

With a mixture of the Lavender, Titanium White and Midnight Black on the fan brush, shape the distant headlands just above the horizon. (Photo 7.)

Re-enforce the top edges of the background swells and large wave with Titanium White on the fan brush. With a clean, dry small fan brush, use short, rocking strokes, pull just the top edges of the wave and swells back, to blend. Be very careful not to destroy the dark undercolor that separates the individual waves. (Photo 8.)

LARGE WAVE

Use the small fan brush and a mixture of Titanium White with a very small amount of Cadmium Yellow to scrub in the "eye" of the large wave. (Photo 9.) Blend the "eye" with circular strokes using the top corner of the blender brush. (Photo 10.)

With Titanium White on the small fan brush, pull the water over the top of the crashing wave. Be very careful of the angle here. (Photo 11.)

Load the small fan brush with Lavender and make small circular strokes with one corner of the brush to scrub in the foam shadows at the base of the large wave.

Highlight the foam edges with Titanium White on the small fan brush, using just the corner of the brush and small circular strokes. *(Photo 12.)* Lightly blend the base of the highlights with the top corner of the blender brush and small circular strokes. *(Photo 13.)*

Use thinned Titanium White on the liner brush to highlight the top edges of the background swells *(Photo 14)* and to add foam patterns *(Photo 15)* to the background water and the large wave *(Photo 16).*

LARGE ROCK

Shape the large foreground rock with the Brown mixture (Alizarin Crimson-Sap Green) on the filbert brush. *(Photo 17.)* Reload the filbert brush with a mixture of Lavender and Bright Red to highlight and contour the large rock. Use Titanium White on the fan brush to add the "splashes" and foaming action at the base of the large rock. *(Photo 18.)*

FOREGROUND

In the lightest area of the foreground beach, pull down long, vertical strokes with a mixture of Titanium White and a small amount of Cadmium Yellow on the 2" brush. *(Photo 19.)* Lightly brush across to create the reflected light on the beach.

Load the "bottom" of the long edge of the small knife with a very small roll of Titanium White (thinned with Liquid White). Hold the knife flat against the canvas and use firm pressure and long horizontal strokes to add the foamy water action on the beach. *(Photo 20.)* Use a clean fan brush to pull the top edge of this line of paint back towards the large wave *(Photo 21)* creating swirling foam patterns *(Photo 22).*

Use Titanium White on the filbert brush to add more details of foam patterns, splashes and ripples to the foreground water. The finer details can be indicated with thinned Titanium White (and Phthalo Blue) on the liner brush.

Shape the small rocks and stones on the beach with Brown on the filbert brush, then add the highlights with Bright Red. *(Photo 23.)* Use Liquid White on the knife to add the water lines at the base of the small rocks and stones. *(Photo 24.)*

SMALL TREE

Use the liner brush and thinned Brown to paint the small tree in the foreground. By turning and wiggling the brush, you can give your tree a gnarled appearance. *(Photo 25.)*

FINISHING TOUCHES

Use the liner brush and thinned Lavender to add the line of shadow at the base of the foam of the large wave *(Photo 26)* then use a thin mixture of Titanium White and Cadmium Yellow on the liner brush to add the final highlights to the background water. Carefully remove the Con-Tact Paper from the canvas to expose your beautiful oval seascape. *(Photo 27.)*

Tranquil Seas

1. Paint the canvas with Black and Gray Gesso.

2. Add light area to the sky with 2" brush.

3. Use the fan brush to shape clouds.

4. Blend clouds with blender brush . . .

5. . . . to complete the sky.

6. Sketch the large wave.

7. Use the fan brush to paint the headlands.

Tranquil Seas

8. Blend back the tops of the waves . . .

9. . . . before painting the "eye" of the wave.

10. Blend the "eye" with the soft blender.

11. Pull water over the wave with the fan brush.

12. Add foam with the fan brush . . .

13. . . . then blend with the blender brush.

14. Use the liner brush to highlight waves . . .

15. . . . and to add foam patterns . . .

16. . . . to the water.

17. Use the filbert brush . . .

18. . . . to shape the foreground rock.

19. Add reflections to the beach with the 2" brush . . .

20. . . . then add the water line with the knife.

21. Use the fan brush . . .

22. . . . to blend back the water line.

23. Paint rocks on the beach with the filbert brush . . .

24. . . . then use the knife to add water lines.

25. Use the liner brush to paint the small tree . . .

26. . . . and the large wave foam shadow . . .

27. . . . to complete the painting.

MOUNTAIN SERENITY

MATERIALS

2" Brush	Midnight Black
1" Brush	Dark Sienna
#6 Fan Brush	Van Dyke Brown
Large Knife	Alizarin Crimson
Liquid White	Sap Green
Titanium White	Cadmium Yellow
Phthalo Green	Yellow Ochre
Phthalo Blue	Indian Yellow
Prussian Blue	Bright Red

Use the 2" brush to cover the entire canvas with a thin, even coat of Liquid White. With long horizontal and vertical strokes, work back and forth to ensure an even distribution of paint on the canvas. Do NOT allow the Liquid White to dry before you begin.

SKY AND WATER

Load the 2" brush with a small amount of Alizarin Crimson and, using criss-cross strokes, begin painting the Pink glow in the sky above the horizon. *(Photo 1.)*

Reflect the color into the water with horizontal strokes on the lower portion of the canvas, pulling from the outside edges in towards the center.

Without cleaning the brush, reload it with Phthalo Blue and continue with criss-cross strokes in the upper portion of the sky. Still without cleaning the brush, reload it with Prussian Blue and darken just the corners of the sky.

With Blue still on the 2" brush, use horizontal strokes at the bottom of the canvas, again pulling from the outside edges of the canvas in towards the center. You can create a Pink shimmer of light in the water by allowing the center of the canvas to remain light.

Use a clean, dry 2" brush and criss-cross strokes to blend the colors in the sky and then blend the entire canvas with long, horizontal strokes.

With Titanium White on the 2" brush, tap in the basic cloud shapes. *(Photo 2.)* Use a clean, dry 2" brush to gently blend the clouds, then sweeping upward strokes to "fluff". Blend the entire sky area with long, horizontal strokes.

MOUNTAIN

The large mountain is painted with the knife and a mixture of Prussian Blue, Van Dyke Brown, Midnight Black and Alizarin Crimson. Pull the mixture out very flat on your palette, hold the knife straight up and "cut" across the mixture to load the long edge of the blade with a small roll of paint. (Holding the knife straight up will force the small roll of paint to the very edge of the blade.) With firm pressure, shape just the top edge of the mountain. *(Photo 3.)* When you are satisfied with the basic shape of the mountain top, use the knife to remove any excess paint. Then, with the 2" brush, pull the paint down to the base of the mountain, to blend and complete the entire mountain shape. *(Photo 4.)*

Highlight the mountain with a marbled mixture of Titanium White and small amounts of Midnight Black and Bright Red. Again, load the long edge of the knife blade with a small roll of paint. Starting at the top (and paying close attention to angles) glide the knife down the right side of each peak, using so little pressure that the paint "breaks". *(Photo 5.)* Use a mixture of Titanium White and Prussian Blue, applied in the opposing direction, for the shadow sides of the peaks. Again, use so little pressure that the paint "breaks".

Use a clean, dry 2" brush to tap to diffuse the base of the mountain (carefully following the angles) *(Photo 6)* and then gently lift upward to create the illusion of mist.

Working forward, add the small ridge of mountains with the knife and the same dark mountain mixture. *(Photo 7.)* Again, blend the paint down to the base of the ridge with the 2" brush. *(Photo 8.)* Highlight the ridge of mountains with a mixture of Titanium White and a small amount of Midnight Black. *(Photo 9.)* Use the 2" brush to tap and diffuse the base of the ridge of mountains *(Photo 10)* creating the illusion of mist *(Photo 11)*.

BACKGROUND

Load the fan brush with a mixture of Titanium White, Prussian

Blue and a small amount of Midnight Black. Holding the brush vertically, just tap downward to indicate the small trees at the base of the mountain. *(Photo 12.)*

Firmly tap the base of the trees with a clean, dry 2" brush creating the illusion of mist. *(Photo 13.)* Lift upward to blend. *(Photo 14.)*

EVERGREENS

For the larger evergreens, load the fan brush to a chiseled edge with a mixture of Prussian Blue, Phthalo Green, Van Dyke Brown, and Alizarin Crimson. Holding the brush vertically, touch the canvas to create the center line of each tree. Use just the corner of the brush to begin adding the small top branches. Working from side to side, as you move down each tree, apply more pressure to the brush, forcing the bristles to bend downward and automatically the branches will become larger as you near the base of each tree. *(Photo 15.)*

Use the same dark tree-mixture on the 2" brush to underpaint the land areas at the base of the evergreens. *(Photo 16.)* Holding the brush horizontally, pull the color straight down into the water. *(Photo 17.)* Brush lightly across for reflections.

Use the fan brush to very lightly touch highlights to the branches of the evergreens with mixtures of the dark tree color and the Yellows.

Use the same mixtures (and small amounts of Bright Red) to highlight the soft grassy area at the base of the trees. *(Photo 18.)*

FOREGROUND

Use Van Dyke Brown and Dark Sienna on the knife to add the land areas at the water's edge. *(Photo 19.)* Highlight these areas with a Brown-White mixture on the knife. *(Photo 20.)*

To add the small trees and bushes at the base of the evergreens, first dip the 1" brush into Liquid White. Then, with the handle straight up, pull the brush (several times in one direction, to round one corner of the bristles) through various mixtures of Sap Green, the Yellows and small amounts of Bright Red. With the rounded corner of the brush up, force the bristles to bend upward to highlight the individual trees and bushes. *(Photo 21.)* Concentrate on shape and form – try not to just "hit" at random.

Use a small roll of Liquid White on the knife to add water lines and ripples *(Photo 22)* to the foreground *(Photo 23)*.

Use the dark tree color on the 1" brush to underpaint the last bushes in the foreground *(Photo 24)* then highlight with Yellow-Green *(Photo 25)*.

FINISHING TOUCHES

Use thinned mixtures on the liner brush to add small sticks and twigs *(Photo 26)* to complete your painting *(Photo 27)*.

Mountain Serenity

1. Paint the sky with criss-cross strokes . . .

2. . . . and the clouds with circular strokes.

3. Shape the mountain with the knife . . .

4. . . . then blend with the 2" brush.

5. Highlight the mountain . . .

6. . . . then firmly tap with the 2" brush to mist.

7. Add the closer range of mountains . . .

Mountain Serenity

8. . . . and blend with the 2" brush.

9. Highlight the mountain . . .

10. . . . and again tap the base . . .

11. . . . to create the illusion of mist.

12. Tap in small evergreens with the fan brush . . .

13. . . . then firmly tap the base of the trees . . .

14. . . . to create the misty area.

15. Paint large evergreens with the fan brush.

16. Use the 2" brush to underpaint grassy areas . . .

17. . . . and to pull down reflections . . .

18. . . . and to highlight the grassy areas.

19. Add banks to the water's edge . . .

20. . . . then apply highlights with the knife.

21. Highlight small bushes with the 1" brush . . .

22. . . . then use the knife . . .

23. . . . to cut in water lines and ripples.

24. Add foreground bushes . . .

25. . . . and highlights with the 1" brush.

26. Use thinned paint on the liner brush . . .

27. . . . to complete the painting with small sticks and twigs.

HOME BEFORE NIGHTFALL

MATERIALS

2" Brush	Phthalo Blue
2" Blender Brush	Midnight Black
1" Round Brush	Alizarin Crimson
#6 Filbert Brush	Sap Green
#2 Script Liner Brush	Cadmium Yellow
Large Knife	Yellow Ochre
Liquid White	Bright Red
Titanium White	

Use the 2" brush and criss-cross strokes to cover the entire canvas with a thin, even coat of Phthalo Blue. *(Photo 1.)* With long horizontal and vertical strokes, work back and forth to ensure an even distribution of paint on the canvas. Do NOT allow the paint to dry before you begin.

SKY

Load the 2" brush by tapping just one corner into Midnight Black. With the same corner of the brush, use small, circular strokes to paint the cloud shapes in the evening sky. *(Photo 2.)*

Load one corner of the blender brush with a very small amount of Titanium White. Again, use just the corner of the brush and small, circular strokes to indicate the subtle source of light in the sky. *(Photo 3.)* Gently blend the entire sky with long, horizontal strokes. *(Photo 4.)*

BACKGROUND

Use the knife to make a Brown mixture on your palette with equal parts of Alizarin Crimson and Sap Green. Tap the bristles of the round brush into this Brown mixture and begin tapping in the basic shapes of the background trees. *(Photo 5.)*

Clean and dry the round brush then tap the bristles into mixtures of the Yellows and Bright Red (to make Orange). Concentrating on individual tree shapes and forms, apply the highlights to the background trees. *(Photo 6.)* Less of the highlight color should be applied to the bases of the trees, for a "shadowy" appearance. *(Photo 7.)*

Load a clean, dry 2" brush with the Brown mixture. Holding the brush horizontally, tap downward to underpaint the land areas that extend from the base of the background trees to the bottom of the canvas. *(Photo 8.)* Be very careful not to completely cover the Blue already on the canvas. *(Photo 9.)*

Load the 2" brush by tapping the bristles into various mixtures of the Yellow-Red, Gray (made with Liquid White, Titanium White and Midnight Black), and small amounts of Phthalo Blue. Highlight the soft grassy area at the base of the trees by holding the brush horizontally and tapping downward *(Photo 10)* carefully creating the lay-of-the-land *(Photo 11)*.

MIDDLEGROUND

To make the larger trees in the middleground of the painting, first load the filbert brush with the Brown mixture (Alizarin Crimson-Sap Green). Touch the top of each tree trunk and pull straight down to the base of the tree. *(Photo 12.)* The smaller limbs and branches are added with thinned Brown mixture to an ink-like consistency by first dipping the liner brush into paint thinner.) Slowly turn the brush as you pull the bristles through the mixture, forcing them to a sharp point.) Apply very little pressure to the brush, as you shape the limbs and branches. By turning and wiggling the brush, you can give your branches a gnarled appearance. *(Photo 13.)*

Reload the liner brush with a thin Gray mixture (Titanium White and Midnight Black) and add the small fence at the base of the middleground trees. *(Photo 14.)*

Underpaint the leaf clusters on the middleground trees with Brown on the round brush *(Photo 15)* then apply the highlights with mixtures of the Yellows, Bright Red and Liquid White *(Photo 16)*.

CABIN

Use a clean knife to remove paint from the canvas in the basic shape of the cabin. Load the long edge of the knife with a small roll of the Brown mixture by pulling the paint out very flat on your palette and just cutting across. Shape the left side of the roof, the back under-roof (and the back under-roof of the porch), then pull down to add the side and then the front of the cabin.

With a marbled mixture of Titanium White, Brown and a small amount of Midnight Black on the short edge of the knife, add the shingles to the roof. Use the same mixture to highlight the front and side of the cabin, holding the knife vertically and using so little pressure that the paint "breaks". Use Titanium White on the knife to highlight just the edges of the roof's frame.

Use dark Brown to add boards to the front of the cabin. Just scrape off paint to add the window then add the light source from within the cabin with Cadmium Yellow and a small amount of Yellow Ochre on the knife. Add the window frame with Brown on the knife to complete the cabin. *(Photo 17.)*

Use the 2" brush to continue adding the grassy highlights (Yellow-Red-Gray-Blue) to the land areas that extend from the base of the cabin into the foreground of the painting.

FINISHING TOUCHES

Use thin mixtures of Yellow and Red on the liner brush to add the weeds, grass and bushes in the foreground *(Photo 18)* and your painting is complete *(Photo 19).*

Home Before Nightfall

1. Start painting the sky with criss-cross strokes . . .

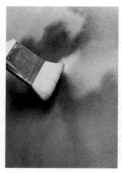

2. . . . then tap in dark cloud shapes.

3. Use the blender brush . . .

4. . . . to add light areas to the sky.

5. Underpaint background trees with the round brush . . .

6. . . . then tap on highlights . . .

7. . . . to create individual bush and tree shapes.

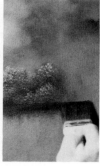

8. Tap down with the 2" brush . . .

9. . . . to underpaint the grassy areas.

10. Highlight grassy areas . . .

11. . . . paying close attention to the lay-of-the-land.

Home Before Nightfall

12. Add trunks with the filbert brush . . .

13. . . . and branches with the liner brush.

14. Paint the small fence.

15. Use the round brush . . .

16. . . . to add foliage to the trees.

17. Progressional steps used to paint the cabin.

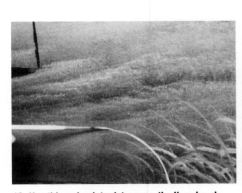

18. Use thinned paint mixtures on the liner brush . . .

19. . . . to pull up long grasses to complete your painting.

LIGHT AT THE SUMMIT

MATERIALS

2" Brush	Prussian Blue
#6 Filbert Brush	Midnight Black
#6 Fan Brush	Dark Sienna
#2 Script Liner Brush	Van Dyke Brown
Large Knife	Alizarin Crimson
Black Gesso	Sap Green
Gray Gesso	Cadmium Yellow
Liquid Clear	Yellow Ochre
Titanium White	Indian Yellow
Phthalo Blue	Bright Red

Start by using a foam applicator to block in the basic shapes of the mountains with Black and Gray Gessos. (The Gray Gesso is used to indicate highlight and distance.) Allow the Gessos to DRY COMPLETELY before proceeding. (Photo 1.)

When the Gessos are dry, use the 2" brush to completely cover the canvas with a VERY THIN coat of Liquid Clear. (It is important to stress that the Liquid Clear should be applied VERY, VERY sparingly and really scrubbed into the canvas! If necessary, you can use a paper towel to remove any excess Liquid Clear from the canvas.) Liquid Clear will not only ease with the application of the firmer paint, but will allow you to apply very little color, creating a glazed effect.

Still using the 2" brush, cover the Liquid Clear with a very thin, even coat of a Lavender mixture made with Alizarin Crimson and Phthalo Blue. (The mixture should contain proportionately much more Crimson than Blue.)

SKY

Load the 2" brush with a small amount of Phthalo Blue and begin painting the sky, using criss-cross strokes on the upper portion of the canvas. (Photo 2.)

Without cleaning the brush, reload it with a small amount of Prussian Blue and darken just the edges of the sky.

Still without cleaning the brush, reload it with a mixture of the Blues and apply a thin coat of this mixture to the lower portion of the canvas.

Load a clean, dry 2" brush with Titanium White. Using just the corner of the brush and working outward from the center of the canvas, add the source of light just above the horizon (Photo 3) to complete the sky (Photo 4).

SOFT GRASS

Use mixtures of Sap Green and all of the Yellows to highlight the soft grassy area at the base of the mountains. Load the 2" brush by holding it at a 45-degree angle and tapping the bristles into the various paint mixtures. Allow the brush to "slide" slightly forward in the paint each time you tap (this assures that the very tips of the bristles are fully loaded with paint). Hold the brush horizontally and gently tap downward. Work in layers, carefully creating the lay-of-the-land. If you are also careful not to destroy all of the dark color already on the canvas, you can create grassy highlights that look almost like velvet. (Photo 5.)

Load the fan brush with a mixture of Van Dyke Brown and Dark Sienna and, holding the brush horizontally, use short, horizontal strokes to add the path. (Photo 6.) Lightly touch highlights to the path with a mixture of the Browns and a small amount of Titanium White on the fan brush. (Photo 7.) Pay close attention to perspective here, the path should get progressively wider as you work forward. (Photo 8.)

FOREGROUND

Use the knife to make a dark mixture using Midnight Black, Prussian Blue, Alizarin Crimson and Sap Green. Load a clean, dry 2" brush with this mixture and again, tap downward to underpaint the foreground grassy areas. (Photo 9.)

Use various mixtures of Sap Green, the Yellows and small amounts of Midnight Black on the 2" brush to highlight the foreground grass. Working forward in layers, pay close attention to the lay-of-the-land. (Photo 10.)

Extend the path into the foreground with the Browns on the fan brush and again, highlight with a Brown-White mixture. (Photo 11.)

FOREGROUND TREES

To paint the small foreground tree trunks, first load the fan brush with a mixture of Van Dyke Brown and Dark Sienna. (Be sure that both sides of the bristles are fully loaded with paint.)

Holding the brush vertically, start at the top of each tree and just pull down to the base of the trunk. *(Photo 12.)*

Continue using the Brown mixture on the fan brush to shape the large foreground trunks.

Highlight the trunks with a mixture of Titanium White and Van Dyke Brown on the knife. (To load the knife, pull the mixture out very flat on your palette, hold the knife straight up and "cut" across the mixture to load the long edge of the blade with a small roll of paint.) Hold the knife vertically and curve the strokes around the trunk. Be sure the paint "breaks" and that the highlights are facing the light source. (Highlight the left sides of the trunks on the right side of the canvas, and the right sides of the trunks on the left side of the canvas.) *(Photo 13.)*

Use thinned Brown on the liner brush to add limbs and branches to the foreground trees. (To load the liner brush, thin the Brown mixture to an ink-like consistency by first dipping the liner brush into paint thinner. Slowly turn the brush as you pull the bristles through the mixture, forcing them to a sharp point.) Apply very little pressure to the brush when you paint the branches. By turning and wiggling the brush, you can give your limbs and branches a gnarled appearance. *(Photo 14.)*

Use dark Brown on the corner of the 2" brush to underpaint the foliage on the large trees. *(Photo 15.)* Apply the highlights with various mixtures of Sap Green, all of the Yellows and small amounts of Bright Red on the 2" brush. Concentrate on individual shapes and form, carefully creating individual leaf clusters. *(Photo 16.)*

FINISHING TOUCHES

Use dark Brown on the filbert brush to add the fence posts *(Photo 17)* then highlight the light side of each post with a Brown and White mixture on the filbert brush. Add tiny sticks and twigs and other final details with thinned Brown on the liner brush *(Photo 18)* to complete your painting *(Photo 19)*.

Don't forget to sign your masterpiece with pride: Load the liner brush with thinned color of your choice. Sign just your initials, first name, last name or all of your names. Sign in the left corner, the right corner or one artist signs right in the middle of the canvas! The choice is yours. You might also consider including the date when you sign your painting. Whatever your choices, have fun, for hopefully with this painting you have truly experienced THE JOY OF PAINTING!

Light at the Summit

1. Underpaint the mountain and foreground with Black and Gray Gesso.

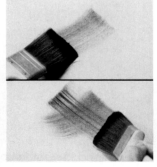

2. Use the 2" brush and criss-cross strokes to paint the sky.

3. Continue using the 2" brush to add the light source . . .

4. . . . just above the horizon.

Light at the Summit

5. Begin tapping in the grassy areas with the 2" brush.

6. Underpaint the path with the fan brush . . .

7. . . . then use short horizontal strokes to apply highlight . . .

8. . . . paying close attention to perspective.

9. Working forward in layers, tap in the foreground grass . . .

10. . . . apply highlights with the 2" brush . . .

11. . . . and continue painting the path with the fan brush.

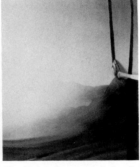

12. Paint foreground trunks with the fan brush.

13. Apply highlights with the knife . . .

14. . . . and limbs and branches with the liner brush.

15. Underpaint tree foliage with the 2" brush . . .

16. . . . and highlight carefully shaping branches.

17. Add fence posts with the filbert brush . . .

18. . . . small sticks and twigs with the liner brush . . .

19. . . . and your masterpiece is ready for a signature.

CYPRESS CREEK

MATERIALS

2" Brush	Midnight Black
#6 Filbert Brush	Dark Sienna
#3 Fan Brush	Van Dyke Brown
#2 Script Liner Brush	Alizarin Crimson
Large Knife	Sap Green
Black Gesso	Cadmium Yellow
Gray Gesso	Yellow Ochre
Liquid Clear	Indian Yellow
Titanium White	Bright Red

Use Gray Gesso on the fan brush and the liner brush (it is preferable to use old brushes) to paint the indication of the palm trees in the background. Use Black Gesso on the same brushes for the foreground palm trees, then use a natural sponge to block in the basic shapes of the foliage in the foreground with Black Gesso. Allow the Gessos to DRY COMPLETELY before proceeding. *(Photo 1.)*

When the Gessos are dry, use the 2" brush to completely cover the canvas with a VERY THIN coat of Liquid Clear. (It is important to stress that the Liquid Clear should be applied VERY, VERY sparingly and really scrubbed into the canvas! Just to be safe, you could use a paper towel to remove any excess Liquid Clear. The remaining Liquid Clear will not only ease with the application of the firmer paint, but will allow you to apply very little color, creating a glazed effect.)

SKY

Load a clean, dry 2" brush with a very small amount of Yellow Ochre. Starting at the top of the canvas and working downward to the horizon, use criss-cross strokes *(Photo 2)* to paint the sky *(Photo 3)*.

FOREGROUND

Use the knife to make a Brown mixture on your palette with equal parts of Alizarin Crimson and Sap Green. Load the 2" brush with a small amount of this Brown color and, working upward from the bottom of the canvas, use criss-cross strokes to begin coloring (or glazing) the foreground trees, bushes and foliage.

Load the 2" brush by tapping the bristles into various mixtures of Sap Green, all of the Yellows and small amounts of Midnight Black and Bright Red. Using just the corner of the brush, begin adding the highlights to the trees *(Photo 4)* carefully forming individual branches *(Photo 5)*. Highlight the small bushes at the base of the trees. *(Photo 6.)* Be very careful not to completely cover all of the dark undercolor, allow it to separate the individual bushes. *(Photo 7.)*

CYPRESS TREES

To add the large foreground cypress trees, load the filbert brush with a mixture of Van Dyke Brown and Dark Sienna. (Make sure that both sides of the bristles are fully loaded with paint.) Touch the canvas at the top of each tree trunk and pull straight down. By applying more pressure to the brush the trunk will automatically become wider as you near the base of each tree. *(Photo 8.)* You can also shape some small cypress trunks, or "knees" at the base of the large trunks.

Load a clean, dry 2" brush with a very small amount of Titanium White. Holding the brush horizontally, touch the canvas at the base of the trees and bushes in the foreground and pull straight down into the water for reflections. *(Photo 9.)* Brush lightly across. *(Photo 10.)*

Use a Brown-White mixture on the filbert brush to add highlights to the right, light sides of the large cypress tree trunks. *(Photo 11.)*

The limbs and branches of the cypress trees are painted with a Brown mixture on the liner brush. (To load the liner brush, thin the Brown mixture to an ink-like consistency by first dipping the liner brush into paint thinner. Slowly turn the brush as you pull the bristles through the mixture, forcing them to a sharp point.) Apply very little pressure to the brush as you shape the branches. By turning and wiggling the brush you can give your branches a gnarled appearance. *(Photo 12.)* You can also use thinned color on the liner brush *(Photo 13)* to add tiny sticks and twigs *(Photo 14)*.

Use a mixture of Midnight Black and Sap Green on the 2" brush to underpaint the foliage on the cypress trees. *(Photo 15.)* For the highlights, use various mixtures of the dark tree under-color and all of the Yellows on the 2" brush. *(Photo 16.)*

Load the fan brush with a thin Gray mixture of paint thinner, Titanium White and Midnight Black. Holding the brush horizontally *(Photo 17)* pull down the Spanish moss hanging from the trees and bushes in the foreground *(Photo 18)*.

FOREGROUND

Push in patches of grass at the base of the cypress "knees" on the right side of the painting with a Yellow-Green mixture on the fan brush. *(Photo 19.)*

Working forward, use a mixture of Midnight Black and Sap Green on the fan brush to underpaint the grasses at the base of the closer cypress trunks. Highlight the grassy area with Yellow-Green mixtures. *(Photo 20.)* Scrub in the water's edge with a Brown-White mixture on the knife. *(Photo 21.)*

FINISHING TOUCHES

To complete your "swampy" masterpiece, don't forget to add your signature. Again, load the liner brush with thinned color of your choice. Sign just your initials, first name, last name or all of your names. Sign in the left corner, the right corner or one artist we know signs right in the middle of the canvas! The choice is yours. You might also consider including the date when you sign your painting. Whatever your choices, have fun, for hopefully with this painting you have truly experienced THE JOY OF PAINTING! *(Photo 22.)*

Cypress Creek

1. Underpaint palm trees and foliage with Black and Gray Gessos.

2. Starting in the sky area and working downward, use the 2" brush and criss-cross strokes . . .

3. . . . to "glaze" the canvas with color.

4. Tap down with the 2" brush to highlight the background trees . . .

5. . . . carefully forming leaf clusters.

6. Also use the 2" brush . . .

Cypress Creek

7. . . . to highlight small bushes and ground foliage.

8. Add cypress trunks and "knees" with the filbert brush.

9. Pull down with Titanium White on the 2" brush . . .

10. . . . to add foreground water.

11. Highlight cypress trunks with the filbert brush . . .

12. . . . then use thinned color on the liner brush to add limbs and branches. . .

13. . . . small sticks and twigs . . .

14. . . . and other small details to the painting.

15. Underpaint foliage on the cypress trees . . .

16. . . . then carefully add highlights with the 2" brush.

17. Use thinned Gray color on the fan brush . . .

18. . . . to hang the Spanish moss from the trees.

19. Use fan brush to add grass to the base of the "knees" . . .

20. . . . and large cypress tree trunks.

21. Scrub in the water's edge . . .

22. . . . to complete your "swampy" creation!

A PERFECT WINTER DAY

MATERIALS

2" Brush	Phthalo Blue
1" Brush	Prussian Blue
#6 Fan Brush	Midnight Black
#2 Script Liner Brush	Dark Sienna
Large Knife	Van Dyke Brown
Liquid White	Alizarin Crimson
Titanium White	

Use the 2" brush to cover the entire canvas with a thin, even coat of Liquid White. With long horizontal and vertical strokes, work back and forth to ensure an even distribution of paint on the canvas. Do NOT allow the Liquid White to dry before you begin.

SKY

Load the 2" brush with a small amount of Prussian Blue, tapping the bristles firmly against the palette to ensure an even distribution of paint throughout the bristles. Starting at the top of the canvas and working downward, use criss-cross strokes to paint the sky. *(Photo 1.)* Notice how the color blends with the Liquid White already on the canvas and automatically the sky becomes lighter as it nears the horizon. Blend the entire sky with long, horizontal strokes.

Reload the brush with Prussian Blue. Starting at the bottom of the canvas (and working up towards the horizon) use long, horizontal strokes to underpaint the snow to the lower portion.

Load a clean, dry 2" brush by holding it vertically and tapping the top corner into a small amount of Titanium White. Use just the top corner of the brush to tap in the cloud shapes. *(Photo 2.)* With a clean, dry 2" brush, use circular strokes to blend the base of the clouds *(Photo 3)* then use sweeping upward strokes to "fluff" the clouds *(Photo 4).* With long, horizontal strokes, blend the entire sky area.

MOUNTAIN

The mountain is made using the knife and a mixture of Midnight Black, Prussian Blue, Van Dyke Brown and Alizarin Crimson. Pull the mixture out flat on your palette, hold the knife straight up and "cut" across the mixture to load the long edge of the blade with a small roll of paint. (Holding the knife straight up will force the small roll of paint to the very edge of the blade.) With firm pressure, shape just the top edge of the mountain. *(Photo 5.)* When you are satisfied with the shape of the mountain top, use the knife to remove excess paint. With the 2" brush, pull the paint down to the base of the mountain, to blend and complete the entire mountain shape. *(Photo 6.)*

Highlight the mountain with Titanium White. Again, load the long edge of the knife blade with a small roll of paint. Starting at the top (and paying close attention to angles) glide the knife down the right side of each peak, using so little pressure that the paint "breaks". *(Photo 7.)* Use a mixture of Titanium White and Prussian Blue, applied in the opposing direction, for the shadow sides of the peaks. Again, use so little pressure that the paint "breaks".

Use a clean, dry 2" brush to tap to diffuse the base of the mountain, carefully following the angles *(Photo 8)* and then gently lift upward to create the illusion of mist *(Photo 9).*

FOOTHILLS

Load the 2" brush by tapping the bristles into Titanium White, Prussian Blue and the original mountain mixture. Use just the corner of the brush to shape the foothills at the base of the mountain. *(Photo 10.)* With very short upward strokes you can create the impression of tiny tree tops along the top edges of the hills. Use downward strokes to reflect the color in the snow.

Load the 2" brush liberally with Titanium White and, holding the brush horizontally, make long horizontal strokes *(Photo 11)* to lay in the snow at the base of the foothills *(Photo 12).*

EVERGREENS

For the evergreens, load the 2" brush to a chiseled edge with a mixture of Midnight Black, Prussian Blue and Alizarin Crimson. Holding the brush vertically, touch the canvas to create the center line of each tree. Use just the corner of the brush to begin adding the small top branches. Working from side to side, as you move down each tree, apply more pressure to the brush, forcing the bristles to bend downward and automatically the branches will become larger as you near the base of each tree. *(Photo 13.)* Use the fan brush to very lightly touch highlights to the branches with a mixture of Liquid White and Phthalo Blue. *(Photo 14.)*

Use the dark tree mixture (Midnight Black, Prussian Blue and Alizarin Crimson) on the 1" brush to underpaint the small trees and bushes at the base of the evergreen trees.

To highlight the small trees and bushes, first dip the 1" brush into Liquid White (or paint thinner). Then, with the handle straight up, pull the brush (several times in one direction, to round one corner of the bristles) through a mixture of Titanium White and Phthalo Blue. With the rounded corner of the brush up, force the bristles to bend upward to highlight the individual trees and bushes. Concentrate on shape and form–try not to just "hit" at random. *(Photo 15.)*

Extend the snow into the foreground with Titanium White on the 2" brush, intentionally pulling out some of the dark color from the base of the small trees and bushes to create a cool, "shadowy" effect. *(Photo 16.)*

CABIN

Use a clean knife to remove paint from the canvas in the basic shape of the cabin. Load the long edge of the knife with a small roll of a mixture of Midnight Black and Van Dyke Brown. Block in the back edge of the roof, the front and then the side of the cabin. Use a marbled mixture of Titanium White, Van Dyke Brown and Dark Sienna to highlight the front; hold the knife vertically and just touch the canvas to indicate boards. (Boards may also be touched holding the knife horizontally.) Apply so little pressure that the paint "breaks". Use less Titanium White in the mixture to highlight the darker side of the cabin.

"Bounce" snow on the roof with thick Titanium White. Don't forget to highlight the back edge of the roof. Finish the cabin with Van Dyke Brown for the door and then remove any excess paint from the base of the cabin with a clean knife. *(Photo 17.)*

Use Titanium White on the 2" brush and long horizontal strokes to add the snow to the base of the cabin, then use the dark tree mixture (Black-Blue-Crimson) on the 1" brush to underpaint bushes at the base of the cabin; highlight with a thin Blue-White mixture. *(Photo 18.)*

FOREGROUND

Load the 2" brush to a chiseled edge with the dark tree mixture and add the large foreground evergreen tree, then tap in the basic shapes of the smaller trees and bushes in the foreground. *(Photo 19.)* Apply highlights to the large evergreen with Blue-White on the fan brush; use Blue-White on the 1" brush for the smaller trees and bushes.

FINISHING TOUCHES

Use Titanium White on the 2" brush to extend snow into the foreground and use the knife to scratch in sticks and twigs. Use a thin Blue mixture on the liner brush to add the tiny barren tree *(Photo 20)* and your painting is complete *(Photo 21)*.

A Perfect Winter Day

1. Paint the sky with criss-cross strokes . . .

2. . . . then tap in cloud shapes.

3. Blend out the base of the clouds . . .

4. . . . then use sweeping upward strokes to "fluff".

5. Shape just the mountain top with the knife . . .

6. . . . then blend the paint down with the 2" brush.

7. Apply snowy highlights with the knife . . .

8. . . . then firmly tap the base of the mountain . . .

A Perfect Winter Day

9. . . . to create the illusion of mist.

10. With the 2" brush, tap in foothills . . .

11. . . . then make long horizontal strokes . . .

12. . . . to lay in the snow.

13. Paint large evergreens with the 2" brush . . .

14. . . . then highlight with the fan brush.

15. Highlight small trees and bushes with the 1" brush.

16. Continue adding snow with the 2" brush.

17. Progressional steps used to paint the cabin.

18. Add snow and small bushes to the base of the cabin.

19. Add foreground trees and bushes . . .

20. . . . tiny sticks and twigs . . .

21. . . . and your painting is ready for a signature.

BABBLING BROOK

MATERIALS

2" Brush	Titanium White
#6 Filbert Brush	Phthalo Blue
#6 Fan Brush	Midnight Black
#3 Fan Brush	Dark Sienna
#2 Script Liner Brush	Van Dyke Brown
Large Knife	Alizarin Crimson
Adhesive-Backed Plastic	Sap Green
Black Gesso	Cadmium Yellow
Gray Gesso	Yellow Ochre
Liquid White	Indian Yellow
Liquid Clear	Bright Red

Start by covering the entire canvas with a piece of adhesive-backed plastic (such as Con-Tact Paper) from which you have removed a center oval shape. (A 14 x 20 oval for an 18 x 24 canvas.)

Use Black and Gray Gesso on the liner brush to create the shapes of the distant tree trunks, limbs and branches; underpaint the foliage areas with a natural sponge. Allow the gessos to DRY COMPLETELY before proceeding. *(Photo 1.)*

When the canvas is dry, use the 2" brush to completely cover the exposed oval with a VERY THIN coat of Liquid Clear. (It is important to stress that the Liquid Clear should be applied VERY, VERY sparingly and really scrubbed into the canvas! The Liquid Clear will not only ease with the application of the firmer paint, but will allow you to apply very little color, creating a glazed effect.) Do NOT allow the Liquid Clear to dry before you proceed.

SKY

Load the 2" brush with a small amount of Yellow Ochre and use criss-cross strokes to apply a thin coat of this color to the entire exposed oval. (Allow the area at the center of the horizon to remain somewhat light, for placement of the light source.)

Without cleaning the 2" brush, reload it with a mixture using equal parts of Alizarin Crimson and Sap Green (to make Brown). Use criss-cross strokes to add this Brown color to the canvas,

blending inward from the outside edges of the oval. *(Photo 2.)*

Clean and dry the bristles of the 2" brush and load it by firmly tapping the bristles into a small amount of Titanium White. Using just the corner of the brush and working outward from the center of the light source, use tiny criss-cross strokes to brighten the sky. *(Photo 3.)* Blend the entire canvas with long, horizontal strokes. *(Photo 4.)*

BACKGROUND TREES AND FOLIAGE

Load a clean, dry 2" brush with a mixture of Midnight Black, Alizarin Crimson, Van Dyke Brown and Sap Green and tap in the basic tree and foliage shapes in the background. *(Photo 5.)*

Paint the indication of the background tree trunks and branches with a mixture of Van Dyke Brown, Dark Sienna and Titanium White on the liner brush. (To load the liner brush, thin the light Brown mixture to an ink-like consistency by first dipping the liner brush into paint thinner. Slowly turn the brush as you pull the bristles through the mixture, forcing them to a sharp point.) Apply very little pressure to the brush, as you shape the trunks and branches. *(Photo 6.)*

Tap the bristles of a clean, dry 2" brush into various mixtures of Midnight Black, Sap Green, all of the Yellows and small amounts of Bright Red. Using just the corner of the brush, touch highlights to the background trees and foliage. *(Photo 7.)* Concentrate on shape and form—try not to just "hit" at random. If you are careful to not completely destroy all of the dark undercolor, you can use it to separate the individual tree and foliage shapes. *(Photo 8.)*

WATERFALL

Load both sides of the fan brush with a mixture of Liquid White, Titanium White and a very small amount of Phthalo Blue. To paint the waterfall, start with a horizontal stroke, then pull straight down *(Photo 9)* to create the falling water *(Photo 10)*.

Add the foaming water action at the base of the falls by pressing the brush into the canvas and forcing the bristles to bend upward. *(Photo 11.)* Continue using horizontal strokes on the fan brush to extend the water into the foreground of the painting. *(Photo 12.)*

Load the filbert brush with a mixture of Midnight Black and the Browns (thinned with paint thinner), then pull one side of the bristles through a thin mixture of Liquid White, Titanium White and Black-Brown, to double-load the brush. With the light side of the brush up *(Photo 13)* use short curved strokes to add the waterfall rocks *(Photo 14)*. By double-loading the brush, you can highlight and shadow each rock in a single stroke. *(Photo 15.)*

FOREGROUND

To paint the large tree in the foreground, first load the small fan brush with a dark Black-Brown mixture. Holding the brush vertically, touch the canvas at the top of the tree and pull downward, applying more pressure to the brush as you near the base of the trunk. *(Photo 16.)* Add the larger branches to the tree in the same manner.

Use a thin mixture of the same color on the liner brush to add the smaller branches to the tree. *(Photo 17.)* By turning and wiggling the brush, you can give your branches a gnarled appearance. *(Photo 18.)*

Use the knife and a mixture of Titanium White and Midnight Black to highlight the trunks and branches. Pull the mixture out very flat on your palette, hold the knife straight up and "cut" across the mixture to load the long edge of the blade with a small roll of paint. Just graze the canvas as you apply the highlights using so little pressure that the paint just "breaks". *(Photo 19.)*

Underpaint the large tree foliage with a mixture of Midnight Black and Sap Green *(Photo 20)* then add subtle highlights with mixtures of Sap Green and the Yellows.

FINISHING TOUCHES

Use Yellow-Green on the corner of the 2" brush to add the grassy highlights in the foreground. With a thin Gray mixture on the liner brush *(Photo 21)* add final sticks and twigs *(Photo 22)*. Carefully remove the Con-Tact Paper *(Photo 23)* to reveal your finished masterpiece *(Photo 24)*. Don't forget to sign your name with pride: Again, load the liner brush with thinned color of your choice. Sign just your initials, first name, last name or all of your names. Sign in the left corner, the right corner or one artist signs right in the middle of the canvas! The choice is yours. You might also consider including the date when you sign your painting. Whatever your choices, have fun, for hopefully with this painting you have truly experienced THE JOY OF PAINTING!

Babbling Brook

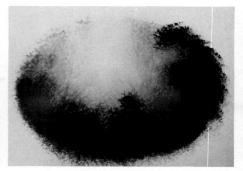

1. Underpaint the foliage with all of the Gessos . . .

2. . . . then use the 2" brush to glaze the canvas.

3. Add light filtering through the trees . . .

4. . . . to complete the sky.

5. Underpaint the foliage with the 2" brush . . .

6. . . . and add trunks with the liner brush.

Babbling Brook

  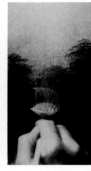   

7. Use the corner of the 2" brush . . .

8. . . . to highlight the foliage.

9. Start the waterfall with a short horizontal stroke . . .

10. . . . then pull straight down to the base of the falls.

11. Add the foaming action at the base of the falls . . .

12. . . . then swirl the water forward.

   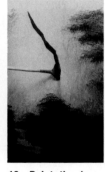   

13. Use single curved strokes . . .

14. . . . with the double-loaded filbert brush . . .

15. . . . to add rocks to the water's edge.

16. Paint the large foreground trunks with the fan brush . . .

17. . . . then use thinned color on the liner brush . . .

18. . . . to add limbs and branches.

19. Highlight the trunk with the knife . . .

20. . . . then use the 2" brush to add foliage to complete the tree.

21. Use thinned paint on the liner brush . . .

22. . . . to add final details.

23. Carefully remove the Con-Tact Paper . . .

24. . . . to expose your finished painting.

A COPPER WINTER

MATERIALS

2" Brush	Midnight Black
#6 Fan Brush	Dark Sienna
#2 Script Liner Brush	Van Dyke Brown
Large Knife	Alizarin Crimson
Liquid White	Sap Green
Liquid Clear	Cadmium Yellow
Titanium White	Yellow Ochre
Phthalo Blue	Indian Yellow
Prussian Blue	Bright Red

Use the 2" brush to cover the entire canvas with a thin, even coat of a mixture of Liquid Clear and Liquid White. With long horizontal and vertical strokes, work back and forth to ensure an even distribution of paint on the canvas. Do NOT allow the canvas to dry before you begin.

BACKGROUND

Use the knife to make a Brown mixture on your palette with equal parts of Alizarin Crimson and Sap Green. Load the 2" brush with this Brown mixture and, starting near the center of the canvas, use long, vertical strokes to paint the wide "streaks" of background color to the upper portion of the canvas. Without cleaning the brush, reload it with mixtures of Dark Sienna and Van Dyke Brown and, working outward, add several more streaks of background color.

Clean and dry the bristles of the 2" brush and reload it with Titanium White. Still using long, vertical strokes, blend this color between each of the Brown streaks. *(Photo 1.)*

With Brown-White still on the brush, use long, horizontal strokes to underpaint the lower portion of the canvas. *(Photo 2.)*

Add the background tree trunks with the liner brush and a mixture of Titanium White and the Alizarin Crimson-Sap Green mixture. (To load the liner brush, thin the paint mixture to an ink-like consistency by first dipping the liner brush into paint thinner. Slowly turn the brush as you pull the bristles through the mixture, forcing them to a sharp point.) Apply very little pressure to the brush, as you shape the trunks and branches. *(Photo 3.)*

To create a misty, mottled effect in the background, dip the fan brush into paint thinner (shake the brush to remove the excess thinner) then pull the bristles across the edge of the knife, allowing a spray of tiny droplets to interact with the Liquid Clear already on the canvas. *(Photo 4.)* Notice that the reaction between the paint thinner and the Liquid Clear creates the illusion of tiny leaves on the background trees. *(Photo 5.)*

Load the 2" brush with a mixture of the Brown color and Titanium White. Hold the brush vertically and tap in the basic shapes of the background trees and bushes. *(Photo 6.)*

Without cleaning the 2" brush, reload it with various mixtures of the Yellows and small amounts of Bright Red. Use just the top corner of the brush to highlight the individual bushes. Concentrate on shape and form–try not to just "hit" at random. *(Photo 7.)*

SNOW AND WATER

Load a clean, dry 2" brush with Titanium White and, holding the brush horizontally, use sweeping horizontal strokes to add snow to the base of the background trees and bushes. Pay close attention to the lay-of-the-land. *(Photo 8.)*

Reload the 2" brush with a mixture of Midnight Black, Van Dyke Brown and a small amount of Prussian Blue. Holding the brush horizontally, pull straight down to add the water *(Photo 9)* then brush lightly across to create reflections *(Photo 10)*.

MIDDLEGROUND

Working forward in the painting, use a mixture of Van Dyke Brown and Dark Sienna on the 2" brush to underpaint the small trees and bushes in the middleground. *(Photo 11.)* Add the highlights with mixtures of Liquid White (to thin the paint), all of the Yellows and small amounts of Bright Red. Again, concentrate on shapes and form. If you are careful not to destroy all of the dark undercolor, you can use it to separate the individual tree and bush shapes. *(Photo 12.)*

Load a clean, dry 2" brush with Titanium White to add the

snow to the base of the middleground trees and bushes. *(Photo 13.)* Allow the brush to pick up some of the dark undercolor to create the shadowed areas in the snow. You can also extend the snow out into the water to create a small peninsula in your painting. *(Photo 14.)*

FOREGROUND

To paint the large birch trees in the foreground, use a mixture of Midnight Black and Van Dyke Brown on the fan brush. Holding the brush vertically, just touch the canvas at the top of each trunk and pull straight down. By applying more pressure to the brush, the trunks automatically become wider as you near the base of the tree. *(Photo 15.)*

Load the knife with a small roll of Titanium White and, holding the knife vertically, use short curved strokes to highlight each trunk. *(Photo 16.)*

Use a thin Black-Brown mixture on the liner brush to add the smaller limbs *(Photo 17)* and branches to the birch trees *(Photo 18)*.

Load the fan brush to a chiseled edge with a dark mixture of Midnight Black, Van Dyke Brown, Prussian Blue and Alizarin Crimson. To paint the evergreen tree in the foreground, hold the brush vertically and touch the canvas to create the center line of each tree. Use just the corner of the brush to begin adding the small top branches. Working from side to side, as you move down each tree, apply more pressure to the brush, forcing the bristles to bend downward and automatically the branches will become larger as you near the base of each tree. *(Photo 19.)*

Add snow to the base of the evergreen tree *(Photo 20)* then use the knife to cut in the evergreen trunk *(Photo 21)*. Lightly touch snowy highlights to the evergreen tree with a mixture of Titanium White and Phthalo Blue on the fan brush. *(Photo 22.)*

FINISHING TOUCHES

Use Van Dyke Brown on the 2" brush to add the foreground bushes, then highlight with the Yellow-Green highlight colors.

Lay in the last of the foreground snow with Titanium White on the fan brush and your painting is complete. *(Photo 23.)*

A Copper Winter

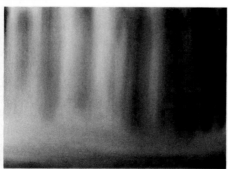

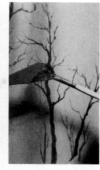

1. Use the 2" brush and long vertical strokes . . .

2. . . . . and horizontal strokes to prepaint the canvas.

3. Add tree trunks with the liner brush . . .

4. . . . . then spray the canvas with paint thinner . . .

5. . . . . to create the illusion of subtle foliage.

6. Tap downward with the 2" brush . . .

A Copper Winter

7. . . . to add small background trees and bushes.

8. Use the 2" brush to lay in the snow . . .

9. . . . and to pull down the water.

10. Brush lightly across to create reflections.

11. Tap down with the 2" brush . . .

12. . . . to add bushes along the water's edge.

13. Continue using the 2" brush to add snow . . .

14. . . . paying close attention to the lay-of-the-land.

15. Add large trunks with the fan brush . . .

16. . . . then highlight with the knife.

17. Use thinned paint on the liner brush . . .

18. . . . to add limbs and branches.

19. Add the evergreen tree with the fan brush . . .

20. . . . then add snow to base of the tree with 2" brush.

21. Paint the evergreen trunk with the knife . . .

22. . . . then use the fan brush to highlight the evergreen.

23. Add snow and final bushes to complete your painting.

MISTY FOOTHILLS

MATERIALS

2" Brush
#6 Fan Brush
#3 Fan Brush
#2 Script Liner Brush
Large Knife
Liquid White
Titanium White
Prussian Blue

Midnight Black
Dark Sienna
Van Dyke Brown
Alizarin Crimson
Sap Green
Cadmium Yellow
Yellow Ochre
Indian Yellow

Use the 2" brush and long horizontal and vertical strokes to cover the entire canvas with a thin, even coat of Liquid White. Do NOT allow the Liquid White to dry before you begin.

SKY

Load the 2" brush with a small amount of Prussian Blue. Starting at the top of the canvas and working downward, use criss-cross strokes to paint the sky. *(Photo 1.)* Allow some areas of the sky to remain quite light, for cloud placement.

This is a good time to underpaint the water on the lower portion of the canvas. Reload the brush with Prussian Blue. Starting at the bottom of the canvas (and working up towards the horizon) use horizontal strokes, pulling from the outside edges of the canvas in towards the center. You can create the illusion of shimmering light on the water by allowing the center of the canvas to remain light.

Without cleaning the 2" brush, reload it with Midnight Black and darken just the corners of the water, then add the darker patches to the sky area. Use a clean, dry 2" brush and long horizontal strokes to blend the entire canvas (sky and water).

Load the 2" brush by holding it vertically and tapping the top corner into a small amount of Titanium White. Hold the brush vertically and just tap in the basic cloud shapes with the top corner of the brush. *(Photo 2.)* Tap to diffuse the base of the clouds with a clean, dry 2" brush *(Photo 3)* then use sweeping upward strokes to "fluff" *(Photo 4)*.

MOUNTAIN

The mountain is made using the knife and a mixture of Midnight Black, Van Dyke Brown, Prussian Blue and Alizarin Crimson. Pull the mixture out very flat on your palette, hold the knife straight up and "cut" across the mixture to load the long edge of the blade with a small roll of paint. With firm pressure, shape just the top edge of the mountain. *(Photo 5.)* When you are satisfied with the basic shape of the mountain top, use the knife to remove any excess paint. Then, with the 2" brush, pull the paint down to the base of the mountain, to blend and complete the entire mountain shape. *(Photo 6.)*

Highlight the mountain with a Gray mixture of Titanium White and Midnight Black. Again, load the long edge of the knife blade with a small roll of paint. Starting at the top (and paying close attention to angles) glide the knife down the right side of each peak, using so little pressure that the paint "breaks". *(Photo 7.)* Use the original, dark mountain mixture, applied in the opposing direction, for the shadow sides of the peaks. Again, use so little pressure that the paint "breaks". *(Photo 8.)*

Load the 2" brush with Titanium White and, holding the brush vertically, tap in the mist at the base of the mountain. *(Photo 9.)* Use a clean, dry 2" brush to tap to diffuse the base of the mountain and then gently lift upward to blend out the mist. *(Photo 10.)*

Use a mixture of Titanium White, Sap Green and the original, dark mountain color on the knife *(Photo 11)* to add the smaller, closer mountain *(Photo 12)*.

GRASS AND WATER

Load the 2" brush with the dark mountain color and, holding the brush horizontally, tap downward to underpaint the grassy land area at the base of the smaller mountain. *(Photo 13.)* Without cleaning the brush, reload it with a mixture of Sap Green and the Yellows. To add the grassy highlights, hold the brush horizontally and gently tap downward. Concentrate on the lay-of-the-land. *(Photo 14.)*

Load the small fan brush with a mixture of Van Dyke Brown and Dark Sienna. Holding the brush horizontally, use short horizontal strokes to add the path that extends from the base of the smaller mountain to the water's edge. *(Photo 15.)* Without cleaning the brush, reload it with a small amount of Titanium White and just "graze" the canvas as you highlight the path. *(Photo 16.)*

Load the 2" brush with a mixture of Prussian Blue, Sap Green and the original mountain color. Holding the brush horizontally, pull reflections straight down from the base of the grassy area. *(Photo 17.)* Brush lightly across.

EVERGREENS

Load the large fan brush with a dark mixture of Midnight Black, Van Dyke Brown, Prussian Blue, Alizarin Crimson and Sap Green. Hold the brush vertically and just tap downward to indicate the small evergreens. *(Photo 18.)*

The large evergreen on the right side of the canvas is made with the same dark tree mixture and the knife. Hold the knife vertically and just touch the canvas to indicate the center line of the tree. Turn the knife horizontally and work from side to side as you shape the smaller top branches of the tree. Gradually work outward and use more of the blade's width to make the larger branches as you near the base of the tree. *(Photo 19.)* Continue by adding the land area *(Photo 20)* at the base of the tree *(Photo 21)*.

The cluster of evergreens on the left side of the canvas are made with the dark tree color and the fan brush. Holding the brush vertically, touch the canvas to create the center line of each tree. Use just the corner of the brush to begin adding the small top branches. Working from side to side, as you move down each tree, apply more pressure to the brush, forcing the bristles to bend downward and automatically the branches will become larger as you near the base of each tree. *(Photo 22.)*

Use either the knife or the fan brush to add highlights to the large evergreens with a mixture of Sap Green and the Yellows. *(Photo 23.)*

Highlight the land area at the base of the trees with Yellow-Green mixtures on the knife. Use so little pressure that the paint "breaks". *(Photo 24.)*

Reload the knife with a mixture of Liquid White and Dark Sienna to add the water's edge *(Photo 25)* then use Liquid White on the knife to cut in the water lines and ripples.

FINISHING TOUCHES

Load the knife with dark Brown and add the indication of the rock at the water's edge; highlight with Brown-White. Don't forget to sign your finished painting with pride! *(Photo 26.)*

Misty Foothills

1. Paint the sky with criss-cross strokes . . .

2. . . . then use the 2" brush to add clouds.

3. Blend the clouds with the 2" brush . . .

4. . . . then lift upward to "fluff".

5. Shape the mountain top with the knife . . .

6. . . . then blend the paint down with the 2" brush.

7. Use the knife to apply highlights . . .

Misty Foothills

8. . . . and shadows to the mountains.

9. Tap the base of the mountain with White . . .

10. . . . to create the illusion of mist.

11. Use a small roll of paint on the knife . . .

12. . . . to add the smaller, closer mountain.

13. Underpaint the grassy area at base of mountain . . .

14. . . . and apply highlights with the 2" brush.

15. Make short horizontal strokes with the fan brush . . .

16. . . . to paint the path.

17. Pull down reflections with the 2" brush.

18. Tap in small evergreen trees with the fan brush.

19. Use the knife to paint the large evergreen . . .

20. . . . and the land area . . .

21. . . . at the base of the tree.

22. Also paint evergreens with the fan brush.

23. Highlight the evergreen . . .

24. . . . and the land area with the knife.

25. Add the water's edge . . .

26. . . . then cut in water lines and ripples to complete the painting.

SEASIDE HARMONY

MATERIALS

2" Brush
2" Blender Brush
#3 Fan Brush
#2 Script Liner Brush
Large Knife
Small Knife
Black Gesso
Alizarin Crimson Acrylic Paint
Liquid Clear
Titanium White

Phthalo Blue
Prussian Blue
Midnight Black
Dark Sienna
Van Dyke Brown
Alizarin Crimson
Sap Green
Cadmium Yellow
Indian Yellow

Use a foam applicator to underpaint the area below the horizon with a thin, even coat of Black Gesso. When the Black Gesso is dry, mark the horizon, just below the center, with a strip of masking tape. The Alizarin Crimson Acrylic Paint is also applied with a foam applicator to the area above the horizon. Allow the canvas to dry completely.

When the canvas is dry, use the 2" brush to cover the area above and below the horizon with a VERY THIN coat of Liquid Clear. (It is important to stress that the Liquid Clear should be applied VERY, VERY sparingly and really scrubbed into the canvas! The Liquid Clear will not only ease with the application of the firmer paint, but will allow you to apply very little color, creating a glazed effect.)

Still using the 2" brush, apply a very small amount of a mixture of Prussian Blue and Sap Green just below the horizon. Apply a Brown mixture made from equal parts of Alizarin Crimson and Sap Green to the lower portion of the canvas. Do NOT allow the canvas to dry before proceeding. *(Photo 1.)*

SKY

Use a small amount of Titanium White and Midnight Black on the 2" brush and criss-cross strokes to sparingly add color to the sky, being very careful not to completely cover the Alizarin Crimson underpainting. Also add a very small amount of Phthalo Blue to the sky, again with criss-cross strokes. *(Photo 2.)*

Continue painting the sky with a small amount of Titanium White on the 2" brush to tap in the cloud shapes. *(Photo 3.)* Lightly blend the clouds with the soft blender brush. *(Photo 4.)* Working in layers, continue tapping in clouds with Titanium White on the 2" brush, then blending with the blender brush. When you are satisfied with your clouds, lightly blend the entire sky with the blender brush. *(Photo 5.)*

BACKGROUND WATER

Carefully remove the masking tape to expose your horizon line. *(Photo 6.)* With the 2" brush, use a mixture of Prussian Blue and Sap Green to cover the area left dry by the tape, before proceeding.

With a small amount of Titanium White on the small knife, roughly sketch the basic shape of the large wave. *(Photo 7.)* Continue using Titanium White on the small knife to add the top edges of the background swells, below the horizon. Then use the fan brush and short, rocking strokes to pull the top edges of the swells back to blend. *(Photo 8.)* Be very careful not to destroy the dark color that separates the individual swells (or background waves).

LARGE WAVE

Use a small roll of Titanium White on the knife to add water to the top of the crashing wave *(Photo 9)* then "pull" the water down towards the base of the breaker with the fan brush, paying close attention to the angle of the water *(Photo 10)*.

The "eye" of the wave is scrubbed in with a small amount of Titanium White on the knife. *(Photo 11.)* Blend a very small amount of Cadmium Yellow near the top of the "eye", still using the knife.

Use a mixture of Alizarin Crimson and Phthalo Blue on the knife to scrub in the foam shadows at the base of the breaker. *(Photo 12.)* Allow the foam to "break" the horizon. *(Photo 13.)*

Working forward, use a mixture of Titanium White and Phthalo Blue on the knife to add the foamy water line at the base of the large wave. *(Photo 14.)* Blend the top edge of the water line back towards the wave using a rubbing motion with the knife. Be very careful not to completely cover the dark at the base of the wave.

Highlight the top edge of the large wave with a small amount of Titanium White on the knife. Continue using Titanium White on the knife and circular strokes to add highlights to the foam at the base of the crashing wave. *(Photo 15.)*

ROCK

Shape the large rock with a mixture of Van Dyke Brown, Dark Sienna and Midnight Black on the knife. *(Photo 16.)* Add Titanium White to the mixture to highlight, shape and contour the rock. *(Photo 17.)*

With Titanium White on the knife, scrub in the foam at the base of the large rock. *(Photo 18.)*

Use a small amount of a mixture of Titanium White and Indian Yellow on the 2" brush to pull down the reflections on the beach. *(Photo 19.)*

Again, use Titanium White and Phthalo Blue on the knife to scrub in the water lines on the beach. *(Photo 20.)* Work forward with the water lines *(Photo 21)* then use horizontal strokes with the fan brush to blend the top edges of the water lines back towards the base of the large wave *(Photo 22)*.

FINISHING TOUCHES

Use various thinned mixtures of Titanium White and Phthalo Blue on the liner brush to add small sparkling details to the water. Add foam shadows with a thinned mixture of Alizarin Crimson and Phthalo Blue on the liner brush *(Photo 23)* and your painting is ready for a signature *(Photo 24)*.

Seaside Harmony

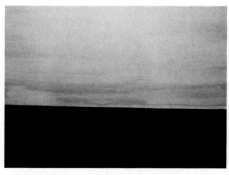

1. Prepaint the canvas with Gesso and Acrylic paint.

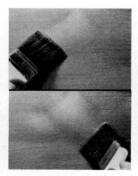

2. Paint the sky with criss-cross strokes . . .

3. . . . then tap in cloud shapes.

4. Blend clouds with the soft blender brush . . .

5. . . . then lightly blend the entire sky.

Seaside Harmony

6. Carefully remove the masking tape from the horizon.

7. Use the knife to sketch the large wave and swells.

8. Blend the top edges of the waves back with the fan brush.

9. Pull the water over the large wave with the knife . . .

10. . . . then blend downward with the fan brush.

11. Scrub in the "eye" of the wave with the knife.

12. Use the knife to scrub in the foam . . .

13. . . . allowing it to "break" the horizon.

14. Add water lines . . .

15. . . . and foam highlights with the knife.

16. Continue using the knife to shape the large rock . . .

17. . . . then use the highlights . . .

18. . . . to shape and contour the rock.

19. Add reflections to the beach . . .

20. . . . before adding the water lines.

21. Continue working forward with water lines . . .

22. . . . then blend the water back with the fan brush.

23. Add final details with the liner brush . . .

24. . . . to complete your painting.

A COLD SPRING DAY

MATERIALS

2" Brush	Midnight Black
1" Brush	Dark Sienna
#6 Fan Brush	Van Dyke Brown
#2 Script Liner Brush	Alizarin Crimson
Large Knife	Sap Green
Liquid White	Cadmium Yellow
Titanium White	Yellow Ochre
Phthalo Green	Indian Yellow
Phthalo Blue	Bright Red
Prussian Blue	

Use the 2" brush to cover the entire canvas with a thin, even coat of Liquid White. With long horizontal and vertical strokes, work back and forth to ensure an even distribution of paint on the canvas. Do NOT allow the Liquid White to dry before you begin.

SKY

Load the 2" brush with a very small amount of Prussian Blue, tapping the bristles firmly against the palette to ensure an even distribution of paint throughout the bristles. Starting at the top of the canvas and working downward, use criss-cross strokes to paint the sky. (Photo 1.) Notice how the color blends with the Liquid White already on the canvas and automatically the sky becomes lighter as it nears the horizon. Blend the entire sky with long, horizontal strokes.

This is a good time to under-paint the water on the lower portion of the canvas. Reload the brush with Prussian Blue. Starting at the bottom of the canvas (and working up towards the horizon) use horizontal strokes, pulling from the outside edges of the canvas in towards the center. You can create the illusion of shimmering light on the water by allowing the center of the canvas to remain light. Use a clean, dry 2" brush and criss-cross strokes to blend the sky, then blend the entire canvas (sky and water) with long, horizontal strokes.

MOUNTAIN

The mountain is made using the knife and a mixture of Prussian Blue and Midnight Black. Pull the mixture out very flat on your palette. Holding the knife handle straight up, "cut" across the mixture to load the long edge of the blade with a small roll of paint. (Holding the knife straight up will force the small roll of paint to the very edge of the blade.) With firm pressure, begin shaping the tops of the mountain peaks. (Photo 2.) Working in layers, use various mixtures of Titanium White and Midnight Black on the knife to add the snow (or glacier) using so little pressure that the paint "breaks". (Photo 3.) Continue adding peaks, then adding the snow. (Photo 4.) When you are satisfied with your peaks, use a small amount of Titanium White on the 2" brush to firmly tap the base of the mountain (Photo 5) creating the illusion of mist (Photo 6).

BACKGROUND TREES

Load a clean, dry 2" brush by tapping the bristles into Midnight Black, Prussian Blue, Sap Green and Alizarin Crimson. Holding the brush vertically, tap downward (Photo 7) to underpaint the leaf trees at the base of the mountain (Photo 8).

To paint the evergreen trees, load the fan brush to a chiseled edge with a dark-tree mixture of Prussian Blue, Midnight Black, Phthalo Green and Van Dyke Brown. Hold the brush vertically and touch the canvas to create the center line of each evergreen tree. Use just the corner of the brush to begin adding the small top branches. Working from side to side, as you move down each tree, apply more pressure to the brush, forcing the bristles to bend downward and automatically the branches will become larger as you near the base of each tree. (Photo 9.)

To highlight the background leaf trees, load the 2" brush by tapping the bristles into various mixtures of the dark-tree color and all of the Yellows. Holding the brush vertically, tap downward with one corner of the brush to add subtle highlights to individual background trees. (Photo 10.)

Firmly tap the base of the trees with a small amount of Titanium White on a clean, dry 2" brush to create the illusion of mist. (Photo 11.)

With the dark tree mixture on a clean 2" brush, hold the brush horizontally and tap downward to underpaint the grassy area at the base of the background trees. *(Photo 12.)* Pull this color straight down, into the water, for reflections. *(Photo 13.)*

Working forward in layers, use the corner of the brush to also underpaint small trees and bushes along the water's edge. Again, highlight the small trees and bushes by adding mixtures of all of the Yellows to the corner of the brush.

Continue using the Yellow mixtures on the 2" brush to highlight the soft grass at the base of the trees. *(Photo 14.)*

With a small roll of Liquid White on the knife, cut in the water lines and ripples *(Photo 15)* at the base of the soft grassy area *(Photo 16)*.

FOREGROUND

Use a mixture of Prussian Blue, Midnight Black, Phthalo Green and Alizarin Crimson on the fan brush to add the large foreground evergreens. *(Photo 17.)* Underpaint the foreground leaf trees *(Photo 18)* and bushes with the same dark mixture on the 2" brush *(Photo 19)*.

Load the knife with a small roll of a mixture of Titanium White, Dark Sienna and Van Dyke Brown to suggest the evergreen tree trunks. *(Photo 20.)*

Lightly touch highlights to the large evergreen branches with a mixture of Liquid White, Titanium White and Phthalo Blue on the fan brush.

To highlight the foreground leaf trees and bushes, first dip the 1" brush into Liquid White. Then, with the handle straight up, pull the brush (several times in one direction, to round one corner of the bristles) through various mixtures of Sap Green, the Yellows and Bright Red. With the rounded corner of the brush up, touch the canvas, forcing the bristles to bend upward to apply highlights to the individual trees and bushes. Concentrate on shape and form–try not to just "hit" at random. If you are careful to not completely destroy all of the dark undercolor, you can use it to separate the individual tree and bush shapes. *(Photo 21.)*

PATH

Use a mixture of Van Dyke Brown and Dark Sienna on the knife and short horizontal strokes to add the foreground path. *(Photo 22.)* Highlight the path with a mixture of the path color and Titanium White on the knife, using so little pressure that the paint "breaks". *(Photo 23.)* With the Yellow highlight mixtures on the 1" brush, add grassy areas and bushes along the edges of the path.

FINISHING TOUCHES

Use thinned Brown mixtures on the liner brush to add small sticks and twigs and your painting is complete. *(Photo 24.)*

A Cold Spring Day

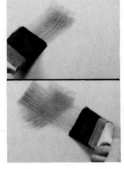

1. Paint the sky with criss-cross strokes.

2. Add the mountain top with the knife . . .

3. . . . then begin adding snow.

4. Continue shaping mountain peaks.

5. Tap downward with the 2" brush . . .

6. . . . to mist the base of the mountain.

A Cold Spring Day

7. Also tap downward with the 2" brush . . .

8. . . . to add leaf trees to the base of the mountain.

9. Paint evergreens with the fan brush . . .

10. . . . then highlight leaf trees with the 2" brush.

11. Tap the base of the background trees to mist.

12. Underpaint grassy area at the base of the trees . . .

13. . . . then pull down reflections with 2" brush.

14. Highlight grass with the 2" brush . . .

15. . . . then use Liquid White on the knife . . .

16. . . . to cut in water lines and ripples.

17. Paint large evergreens with the fan brush . . .

18. . . . and large leaf trees . . .

19. . . . and bushes with the 2" brush.

20. Add evergreen trunks with the knife . . .

21. . . . then highlight leaf trees and bushes with the 1" brush.

22. Use the knife and horizontal strokes . . .

23. . . . to add the path . . .

24. . . . and your painting is complete.

BLUE RIDGE FALLS

MATERIALS

2" Brush	Phthalo Blue
2" Blender Brush	Prussian Blue
#6 Filbert Brush	Midnight Black
#6 Fan Brush	Dark Sienna
#3 Fan Brush	Van Dyke Brown
#2 Script Liner Brush	Alizarin Crimson
Large Knife	Sap Green
Black Gesso	Cadmium Yellow
Liquid Clear	Yellow Ochre
Titanium White	Indian Yellow

Begin by underpainting the dark shapes on the lower portion of the canvas with a natural sponge and Black Gesso. When the Black Gesso is dry, use the 2" brush to completely cover the canvas with a VERY THIN coat of Liquid Clear. (It is important to stress that the Liquid Clear should be applied VERY, VERY sparingly and really scrubbed into the canvas! The Liquid Clear will not only ease with the application of firmer paint, but will allow you to apply very little color, creating a glazed effect.)

Still using the 2" brush, apply a very small amount of a mixture of Sap Green, Prussian Blue and Van Dyke Brown just to the dark lower portion of the canvas. Do NOT allow the canvas to dry before you proceed. *(Photo 1.)*

SKY

Load the 2" brush with a very small amount of Phthalo Blue, tapping the brush against the palette to ensure an even distribution of paint throughout the bristles. Starting at the top of the canvas and working downward, use criss-cross strokes to paint the sky. *(Photo 2.)* You can add small amounts of Titanium White to the brush to create light cloudy areas. *(Photo 3.)*

MOUNTAINS

With a mixture of Prussian Blue, Sap Green, Midnight Black and a small amount of Van Dyke Brown and Dark Sienna on the 2" brush, tap in the basic shape of the mountain. *(Photo 4.)* Use a clean, dry 2" brush to firmly tap the base of the mountain to create the illusion of mist. *(Photo 5.)*

Working forward in layers, continue using the mountain mixture on the 2" brush to tap in a small mountain or hill at the base of the large mountain. Firmly tap the base of the hill, adding small amounts of Titanium White to the 2" brush, to again create the illusion of mist. *(Photo 6.)*

BACKGROUND

To paint the evergreens at the base of the mountains, load the small fan brush to a chiseled edge with a mixture of Prussian Blue, Midnight Black, Alizarin Crimson and Sap Green. Holding the brush vertically, touch the canvas to create the center line of each tree. Use just the corner of the brush to begin adding the small top branches. Working from side to side, as you move down each tree, apply more pressure to the brush, forcing the bristles to bend downward and automatically the branches will become larger as you near the base of each tree. *(Photo 7.)*

Use the point of the knife to scratch in the indication of small tree trunks. With the same dark-tree mixture on the fan brush, punch in the land area at the base of the trees and brush upward to create just a suggestion of tiny distant trees. *(Photo 8.)*

Continue using the fan brush to very lightly touch highlights to the evergreens and the grassy area at the base of the trees with a mixture of the dark-tree color and Cadmium Yellow. *(Photo 9.)*

Use the knife to make two thin mixtures on your palette. One mixture is Midnight Black, Van Dyke Brown and paint thinner; the other mixture is Midnight Black, Van Dyke Brown, Titanium White and paint thinner. Load both sides of the filbert brush with the dark-Brown mixture, then pull one side of the bristles through the lighter mixture, to double-load the brush. With the light side of the brush up, use curved strokes to paint the background rocks along the water's edge. By double-loading the brush, you can shape and highlight each rock with just a single stroke. *(Photo 10.)*

WATERFALL

Use a mixture of Liquid Clear, Titanium White and a small

amount of Phthalo Blue on the fan brush and short horizontal strokes to begin painting the background water. *(Photo 11.)* As you work forward, make a series of long vertical strokes *(Photo 12)* to paint the waterfall *(Photo 13)*. Tap the base of the waterfall with a small amount of Titanium White on the corner of the soft blender brush *(Photo 14)* to create the illusion of mist *(Photo 15)*. Again, use the two thin Brown mixtures on the filbert brush to shape the large rocks containing the waterfall. *(Photo 16.)*

Working forward, use the dark-tree mixture on the large fan brush to add the large evergreen trees *(Photo 17)* in the foreground *(Photo 18)*. Add various mixtures of the Yellows to the dark-tree mixture on the fan brush and very lightly touch highlights to the branches.

With Titanium White on the corner of the blender brush, tap in the misty areas at the base of the foreground evergreens. *(Photo 19.)*

Continue swirling the water forward with the Titanium White-Liquid Clear-Phthalo Blue mixture on the fan brush. *(Photo 20.)*

Use Van Dyke Brown, Midnight Black and Dark Sienna on the knife to shape the foreground rocks, then highlight with a mixture of Van Dyke Brown and Titanium White on the knife. *(Photo 21.)*

Working forward in layers, continue by adding the tiny waterfalls *(Photo 22)* and large rocks *(Photo 23)* in the foreground *(Photo 24)*.

Underpaint the foreground leaf trees and bushes with the dark-tree mixture on the 2" brush. Use the 2" brush to highlight the trees and bushes using various mixtures of the dark-tree color and all of the Yellows. Load the 2" brush by holding it at a 45-degree angle and tapping the bristles into the various paint mixtures. Allow the brush to "slide" slightly forward in the paint each time you tap (this assures that the very tips of the bristles are fully loaded with paint). Hold the brush horizontally and gently tap downward with one corner of the brush to shape the individual leaf trees *(Photo 25)* and bushes *(Photo 26)*. Work in layers, carefully preserving the dark undercolor to distinguish individual leaf clusters. If you are very careful not to completely cover all of the dark under-color, you can create delicate, lacy highlights.

Add the small rocks and stones in the foreground with the double-loaded filbert brush, then use the fan brush with the White-water mixture to swirl water around the base of the stones.

FINISHING TOUCHES
Use thinned paint on the liner brush to add final details, not the least of which is your signature! *(Photo 27.)*

Blue Ridge Falls

1. Underpaint the canvas with Black Gesso . . .

2. . . . then use the 2" brush and criss-cross strokes . . .

3. . . . to paint the sky.

4. Shape background hills with the 2" brush . . .

5. . . . then use the soft blender brush . . .

6. . . . to mist the base of the hills.

Blue Ridge Falls

7. Add tiny ever-greens . . .

8. . . . and pull up the grassy area with the fan brush.

9. Highlight the grassy area . . .

10. . . . before adding rocks and stones with the filbert brush.

11. Use fan brush and horizontal strokes to paint the water . . .

12. . . . and a series of downward strokes . . .

13. . . . to add the waterfall.

14. With the soft blender brush . . .

15. . . . add mist to the base of the falls.

16. Shape large rocks with the filbert brush . . .

17. . . . then use the fan brush . . .

18. . . . to add large evergreen trees.

19. Continue adding mist with the blender brush . . .

20. . . . and swirling water forward with the fan brush.

21. Shape water rocks with the knife . . .

22. . . . then pull down with fan brush . . .

23. . . . to shape the small water falls.

24. Add foreground cliffs with knife . . .

25. . . . and foreground trees . . .

26. . . . and bushes with 2" brush . . .

27. . . . to complete the painting.

BEFORE THE SNOWFALL

MATERIALS

2" Brush	Titanium White
1" Brush	Phthalo Blue
#6 Fan Brush	Prussian Blue
#2 Script Liner Brush	Midnight Black
2" Blender Brush	Dark Sienna
Large Knife	Van Dyke Brown
Liquid White	Alizarin Crimson

Use the 2" brush to cover the entire canvas with a thin, even coat of Liquid White. With long horizontal and vertical strokes, work back and forth to ensure an even distribution of paint on the canvas. Do NOT allow the Liquid White to dry before you begin.

SKY

Load the 2" brush with a very small amount of a mixture of Midnight Black and Prussian Blue. Starting at the top of the canvas and working downward, use criss-cross strokes to paint the sky. *(Photo 1.)*

Reload the 2" brush with the same Midnight Black-Prussian Blue mixture and use long, horizontal strokes to underpaint the lower portion of the canvas.

Load a clean, dry 2" brush by holding it vertically and tapping the top corner of the bristles into a small amount of Titanium White. With the top corner of the brush, tap in the basic cloud shapes. *(Photo 2.)* Blend out the base of the clouds with criss-cross strokes and the blender brush. *(Photo 3.)*

Reload the 2" brush with the Midnight Black-Prussian Blue mixture. Holding the brush vertically, tap in the shapes of the darker clouds in the sky. Blend the entire sky area with long, horizontal strokes. *(Photo 4.)*

BACKGROUND

Load a clean, dry 2" brush with the dark sky color and again use the top corner of the brush to tap in small background trees and bushes. *(Photo 5.)*

The indication of tall, misty, background evergreens is made still using the sky mixture and the 2" brush. To load the brush, pull both sides of the bristles through the Blue-Black mixture, forcing them to a chiseled edge. Starting at the base of each tree, simply hold the brush vertically and press the side of the bristles against the canvas. As you work upward, apply less pressure on the brush, creating the tapered tree top. Complete first one side and then the other of each tree. *(Photo 6.)*

Use a clean, dry 2" brush to tap to diffuse the base of the background trees and bushes, then use long, horizontal strokes to blend out the lower portion of the canvas. *(Photo 7.)*

MIDDLEGROUND

For the larger evergreens, load the fan brush to a chiseled edge with a mixture of Prussian Blue, Alizarin Crimson and Midnight Black. Holding the brush vertically, touch the canvas to create the center line of each tree. Use just the corner of the brush to begin adding the small top branches. *(Photo 8.)* Working from side to side, as you move down each tree, apply more pressure to the brush, forcing the bristles to bend UPWARD and automatically the branches will become larger as you near the base of each tree. *(Photo 9.)*

Load the 2" brush with Titanium White and, holding the brush horizontally, use sweeping horizontal strokes to lay in the snow at the base of the middleground trees. *(Photo 10.)* By allowing the brush to pick up some of the dark tree color already on the canvas, shadows are automatically created in the snow. Concentrate on the lay-of-the-land.

Reload the 2" brush with the dark tree color (Prussian Blue-Alizarin Crimson-Midnight Black) and, holding the brush horizontally, pull down the reflections in the water. *(Photo 11.)* Brush lightly across for a water appearance. Use Titanium White on the fan brush *(Photo 12)* to add the sloping snow banks at the water's edge *(Photo 13)*.

Apply the snowy highlights to the evergreens with a mixture of Phthalo Blue, Titanium White and a small amount of Liquid White on the fan brush. *(Photo 14.)*

CABIN

Use the knife to remove paint from the canvas in the basic shape of the cabin. Load the long edge of the knife with Van Dyke Brown by pulling the paint out very flat on your palette and just cutting across. Paint the back edge of the roof, then pull down the front and side of the cabin. Use a marbled mixture of Dark Sienna and Titanium White to highlight the front of the cabin, using so little pressure that the paint "breaks". Use a darker Brown-White mixture to highlight the side of the cabin. Add boards and a door to the front of the cabin with Van Dyke Brown.

Add the snow-covered roof with Titanium White. Don't forget to add a bit of snow to the back edges of the roof. Shape the bottom edge of the cabin by removing the excess paint with a clean knife.

Load the fan brush with Titanium White and lay in the snow at the base of the cabin. *(Photo 15.)*

FOREGROUND

Working forward, continue to underpaint large evergreens with the dark tree color and the fan brush, then highlight with the Blue-White mixture.

The icicles hanging from the roof of the cabin are added with Liquid White on the liner brush. *(Photo 16.)*

The small trees and bushes in the foreground are underpainted with the dark tree color on the 1" brush. *(Photo 17.)*

To highlight the small trees and bushes, first dip the 1" brush into Liquid White (or paint thinner). Then, with the handle straight up, pull the brush (several times in one direction, to round one corner of the bristles) through Titanium White. With the rounded corner of the brush up, force the bristles to bend upward to highlight the individual trees and bushes. *(Photo 18.)* Concentrate on shape and form – try not to just "hit" at random.

Extend the snow from the base of the small trees and bushes into the foreground of the painting with Titanium White on the fan brush. *(Photo 19.)* Continue using Titanium White on the fan brush to swirl in the water's edge. *(Photo 20.)*

Use a mixture of Liquid White and a small amount of Phthalo Blue on the knife to cut in the indication of water lines and ripples. *(Photo 21.)*

FINISHING TOUCHES

Use very thin Van Dyke Brown on the liner brush to paint small sticks and twigs. (To load the liner brush, thin the Brown mixture to an ink-like consistency by first dipping the liner brush into paint thinner. Slowly turn the brush as you pull the bristles through the mixture, forcing them to a sharp point.) Apply very little pressure to the brush and turn and wiggle the brush to give the twigs a gnarled appearance. *(Photo 22.)*

Don't forget to sign your finished masterpiece! *(Photo 23.)*

Before the Snowfall

1. Paint the sky with criss-cross strokes . . .

2. . . . then add clouds with the 2" brush . . .

3. . . . and blend with the blender brush . . .

4. . . . to complete the sky.

5. Tap in leaf trees . . .

6. . . . and press in evergreens . . .

7. . . . to complete the subtle background trees.

Before the Snowfall

8. Use the fan brush . . .

9. . . . to paint more distinct evergreens.

10. Use the 2" brush to lay in snow . . .

11. . . . and to pull down reflections.

12. Use the fan brush to add sloping snow banks . . .

13. . . . to the water's edge.

14. Add snow to the evergreens with the fan brush.

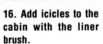

15. Progressional steps used to paint the cabin.

16. Add icicles to the cabin with the liner brush.

17. Underpaint small bushes . . .

18. . . . and highlight with the 1" brush.

19. Use the fan brush to add snow . . .

20. . . . and the frozen water's edge.

21. Cut in water lines with the knife . . .

22. . . . and add a tiny tree with the liner brush . . .

23. . . . and your masterpiece is complete.

BRIDGE TO AUTUMN

MATERIALS

2" Brush	Dark Sienna
#6 Fan Brush	Van Dyke Brown
#2 Script Liner Brush	Alizarin Crimson
Large Knife	Sap Green
Liquid White	Cadmium Yellow
Titanium White	Yellow Ochre
Prussian Blue	Indian Yellow
Midnight Black	Bright Red

Use the 2" brush to cover the entire canvas with a thin, even coat of Liquid White. With long horizontal and vertical strokes, work back and forth to ensure an even distribution of paint on the canvas. Do NOT allow the Liquid White to dry before you begin.

SKY

Load the 2" brush with a mixture of small amounts of Bright Red, Yellow Ochre and Cadmium Yellow. Starting at the top of the canvas and working downward, use criss-cross strokes to paint the sky. *(Photo 1.)*

BACKGROUND

Use the knife to make a Brown mixture on your palette with equal parts of Sap Green and Alizarin Crimson. Load the 2" brush by tapping the bristles of the 2" brush into this color. Holding the brush vertically, tap in the basic shapes of the background trees and bushes. *(Photo 2.)*

Add the background tree trunks using the Brown mixture and the liner brush. (To load the liner brush, thin the Brown mixture to an ink-like consistency by first dipping the liner brush into paint thinner. Slowly turn the brush as you pull the bristles through the mixtures, forcing them to a sharp point.) With very little pressure on the brush, shape the background trunks. *(Photo 3.)* By turning and twisting the brush, you can give the trunks a gnarled appearance. *(Photo 4.)*

Tap the bristles of the 2" brush into various mixtures of the Yellows, Sap Green and Bright Red. (A small amount of Liquid White may be added to thin the mixtures.) Using just the top corner of the brush *(Photo 5)*, tap downward to apply highlights to the background trees and bushes *(Photo 6)*.

MIDDLEGROUND

Load a clean, dry 2" brush with a mixture of the Brown color and Midnight Black. Hold the brush vertically *(Photo 7)* and, moving forward in the painting, block in the shapes of the middleground trees and bushes *(Photo 8)*. The point of the knife may be used to scratch in the indication of small trunks, sticks and twigs. Reload the 2" brush with the same dark undercolor and, holding the brush horizontally, pull straight down from the base of the trees and into the water. *(Photo 9.)* Brush lightly across for reflections.

Load the knife with a marbled mixture of Van Dyke Brown, Dark Sienna, Midnight Black and Titanium White. To load the knife, pull the mixture out very flat on your palette, hold the knife straight up and "cut" across the mixture to load the long edge of the blade with a small roll of paint. (Holding the knife straight up will force the small roll of paint to the very edge of the blade.) Hold the knife horizontally and add banks to the water's edge. *(Photo 10.)* Highlight the banks with a mixture of Yellow Ochre and Titanium White. *(Photo 11.)* Be careful not to over-do the highlights and use so little pressure that the paint "breaks". Use the fan brush to blend and diffuse the water's edge *(Photo 12)* with short upward strokes *(Photo 13)*.

Use a small roll of a mixture of Titanium White and a small amount of Prussian Blue on the knife to cut in the water lines and ripples. *(Photo 14.)*

COVERED BRIDGE

Load the knife with a small roll of the Brown color (Alizarin Crimson and Sap Green) and outline the covered bridge. Use Van Dyke Brown on the knife to pull down the roof and the front and side of the building.

Reload the knife with a marbled mixture of the Brown, Titanium White, Cadmium Yellow and Bright Red and touch in the indication of boards, using so little pressure that the paint "breaks". Separate the exposed areas at the base of the roof with Titanium White on the knife, then pull down the entrance with Van Dyke Brown. Highlight the roof with a marbled mixture of Titanium White and Midnight Black. Don't forget the back eaves. Use a mixture of the Brown and Titanium White on the knife to outline the entrance of the bridge.

Use a small roll of the Brown mixture on the knife and short, horizontal strokes to indicate a trail leading into the covered bridge.

The stones on the side of the building are made with the knife and Midnight Black; use Liquid White on the liner brush for the rails in the distance. Remove any excess paint from the base of the building with a clean knife. *(Photo 15.)*

Pull the color down from the base of the bridge with a clean, dry 2" brush, to create reflections. Brush lightly across for a watery appearance.

FOREGROUND

Load the 2" brush with the Brown mixture and Midnight Black to underpaint the foreground *(Photo 16)* and add small trees and bushes *(Photo 17)*.

Load the knife with a Gray mixture made from the Brown,

Titanium White and Midnight Black. Use horizontal strokes to highlight the trail, using so little pressure that the paint "breaks". For proper perspective, use progressively longer strokes as the trail extends into the foreground. *(Photo 18.)*

Highlight the bushes and soft grassy areas with the 2" brush and various mixtures of all of the Yellows, Bright Red and Sap Green. Proper loading of the brush is essential to creating this soft-grass effect. Load the 2" brush by holding it at a 45-degree angle and tapping the bristles into the various paint mixtures.

Allow the brush to "slide" slightly forward in the paint each time you tap, this assures that the very tips of the bristles are fully loaded with paint. Hold the brush horizontally and gently tap downward. Work in layers, carefully creating the lay-of-the-land. If you are also careful not to destroy all of the dark color already on the canvas, you can create grassy highlights that look almost like velvet. *(Photo 19.)*

Use the same highlight mixtures and just the corner of the 2" brush to highlight small foreground bushes. *(Photo 20.)*

FINISHING TOUCHES

Cut in final sticks and twigs with the point of the knife or use thinned Brown on the liner brush to complete your painting. Don't forget to sign your finished masterpiece! *(Photo 21.)*

Bridge to Autumn

1. Paint the sky with criss-cross strokes.

2. Tap in trees with the 2" brush . . .

3. . . . and add trunks with the liner brush . . .

4. . . . to underpaint the background trees.

5. Add highlights with the 2" brush . . .

6. . . . to complete the background trees.

7. Add small trees and bushes . . .

Bridge to Autumn

8. . . . to the base of the background trees.

9. Pull down reflections . . .

10. . . . then use the knife . . .

11. . . . to add banks to the water's edge.

12. Diffuse the water's edge . . .

13. . . . with short upward strokes.

14. Cut in water lines and ripples.

15. Progressional steps used to paint the covered bridge.

16. Use the 2" brush to pull down reflections . . .

17. . . . and to underpaint the foreground.

18. Use the knife to add the trail.

19. Highlight grassy areas . . .

20. . . . and foreground bushes . . .

21. . . . to complete your covered bridge painting.

TRAIL'S END

MATERIALS

2" Brush	Titanium White
#6 Filbert Brush	Phthalo Blue
#2 Script Liner Brush	Midnight Black
2" Blender Brush	Dark Sienna
Large Knife	Van Dyke Brown
Adhesive-Backed Plastic	Alizarin Crimson
Black Gesso	Sap Green
Liquid Clear	Yellow Ochre

Start by covering the entire canvas with a piece of adhesive-backed plastic (such as Con-Tact Paper) from which you have removed a center oval shape. (A 14 x 20 oval for an 18 x 24 canvas.)

Continue by using a foam applicator to apply a thin, even coat of Black Gesso to the entire oval and allow to DRY COMPLETELY. (Photo 1.)

When the Black Gesso is dry, use the 2" brush to completely cover the canvas with a VERY THIN coat of Liquid Clear. (It is important to stress that the Liquid Clear should be applied VERY, VERY sparingly and really scrubbed into the canvas! The Liquid Clear will not only ease with the application of the firmer paint, but will allow you to apply very little color, creating a glazed effect.) Do NOT allow the canvas to dry before you proceed. (Photo 2.)

SKY

Use the knife to make various Lavender sky mixtures on your palette using Alizarin Crimson, Phthalo Blue and Titanium White. (Adjust the value of the Lavender by using various amounts of Titanium White.)

Load the 2" brush by tapping the bristles into a light Lavender mixture. Starting at the top of the oval, use criss-cross strokes to begin painting the light areas in the sky. (Photo 3.) Without cleaning the brush, reload it with various mixtures of Phthalo Blue and Titanium White. Working down towards the horizon, continue painting the sky with criss-cross strokes.

Load a clean, dry 2" brush with a mixture of Titanium White and Yellow Ochre and use the corner of the brush to "spin-in" the bright portion of the sky at the very top of the oval.

Use the top corner of the 2" brush to tap in cloud shapes with various light mixtures. (Photo 4.)

Blend out the base of the clouds with circular strokes on the blender brush. (Photo 5.) Load the blender brush with the various sky mixtures and tap in the final cloud shapes in the sky. Again, blend out the base of the clouds. Use criss-cross strokes, then long, horizontal strokes to blend the entire sky area. (Photo 6.)

BACKGROUND

Use the knife to make a Brown mixture on your palette with equal parts of Alizarin Crimson and Sap Green. Load the 2" brush with this Brown color and use long, horizontal strokes to underpaint the lower portion of the canvas (below the horizon). With Brown still on the brush, tap in the basic tree and bush shapes in the background. (Photo 7.)

Add the background tree trunks using the Brown mixture and the liner brush. (To load the liner brush, thin the Brown mixture to an ink-like consistency by first dipping the liner brush into paint thinner. Slowly turn the brush as you pull the bristles through the mixture, forcing them to a sharp point.) Apply very little pressure to the brush, as you shape the trunks. (Photo 8.)

Load the 2" brush by tapping the top corner of the bristles into Yellow Ochre. Use just the top corner of the brush to highlight the large tree in the background. (Photo 9.) Concentrate on shape and form — try not to just "hit" at random. Highlight the smaller trees and bushes with mixtures of Yellow Ochre and Alizarin Crimson. (Photo 10.)

FOREGROUND

Load a clean, dry 2" brush with a mixture of Van Dyke Brown and Dark Sienna (small amounts of Midnight Black may also be used) and tap in the small foreground trees and bushes.

Load the knife with a small roll of a mixture of Brown, Titanium White and Yellow Ochre. To load the knife, pull the mixture out very flat on your palette, hold the knife straight up and "cut" across the mixture to load the long edge of the blade with a small roll of paint. (Holding the knife straight up will force the small roll of paint to the very edge of the blade.) Hold the knife horizontally *(Photo 11)* and use short, horizontal strokes to lay in the path *(Photo 12)*.

The large barren tree trunks in the foreground are shaped with Brown and the filbert brush. Just start at the top of each trunk and pull down to the base of the trunk. *(Photo 13.)* You can use short curved strokes to add "feet" to the base of the trees. Reload the filbert brush with a Brown-White mixture and just graze the left sides of the trunks to highlight. *(Photo 14.)*

Add the smaller limbs and branches to the trees with thinned Brown on the liner brush. *(Photo 15.)* Turn and wiggle the brush to give the branches a gnarled appearance. *(Photo 16.)*

Continue tapping in the small foreground tree and bush shapes with dark Brown on the 2" brush. *(Photo 17.)*

FENCE

To paint the fence, load the filbert brush with dark Brown, then pull one side of the bristles through a Brown-White mixture, to double-load the brush. With the light side of the brush on the left, and paying close attention to perspective, paint each fence post. By double-loading the brush, you can highlight and shadow each fence post with a single stroke. The rails of the fence are added with the light side of the brush facing up. *(Photo 18.)* The posts and rails can also be highlighted with the liner brush.

Use the corner of the 2" brush to highlight the foreground bushes with various mixtures of all of the Yellows and Alizarin Crimson. *(Photo 19.)*

FINISHING TOUCHES

Use thinned Brown mixtures on the liner brush to add tiny sticks and twigs. *(Photo 20.)* When you are satisfied with your painting *(Photo 21)* very carefully remove the Con-Tact Paper *(Photo 22)* to expose your oval masterpiece *(Photo 23)*!

Don't forget to sign your name with pride: Again, load the liner brush with thinned color of your choice. Sign just your initials, first name, last name or all of your names. Sign in the left corner, the right corner or one artist signs right in the middle of the canvas! The choice is yours. You might also consider including the date when you sign your painting. Whatever your choices, have fun, for hopefully with this painting you have truly experienced THE JOY OF PAINTING!

Trail's End

1. Paint the exposed oval with Black Gesso.

2. When dry, cover with Liquid Clear.

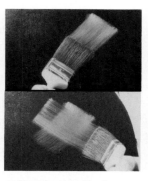
3. Paint the sky with criss-cross strokes . . .

4. . . . then tap in cloud shapes.

5. Use the soft blender brush . . .

6. . . . to blend the sky and clouds.

Trail's End

7. Underpaint background trees with the 2" brush . . .

8. . . . then add trunks with the liner brush.

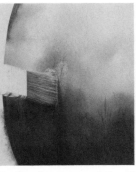

9. Use the corner of the 2" brush . . .

10. . . . to highlight the background trees.

11. Use the knife and horizontal strokes . . .

12. . . . to add the path.

13. Use the filbert brush to paint trunks . . .

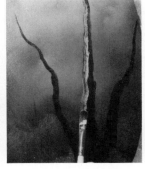

14. . . . and apply highlights.

15. Use thinned paint on the liner brush . . .

16. . . . to add small limbs and branches.

17. Tap in foreground foliage.

18. Paint the fence with the filbert brush . . .

19. . . . and highlight foreground foliage with the 2" brush.

20. Add tiny sticks and twigs . . .

21. . . . to complete the painting.

22. Carefully remove the Con-Tact Paper . . .

23. . . . and your oval masterpiece is complete.

IN THE MIDST OF WINTER

MATERIALS

2" Brush	Phthalo Blue
#6 Fan Brush	Prussian Blue
#2 Script Liner Brush	Midnight Black
Large Knife	Dark Sienna
Liquid White	Van Dyke Brown
Titanium White	Alizarin Crimson

Use the 2" brush to cover the entire canvas with a thin, even coat of Liquid White. With long horizontal and vertical strokes, work back and forth to ensure an even distribution of paint on the canvas. Do NOT allow the Liquid White to dry before you begin.

SKY

Load the 2" brush with a mixture of Midnight Black and a small amount of Prussian Blue. Starting at the top of the canvas and working downward, use criss-cross strokes to paint the sky, allowing some areas to remain quite light for the clouds.

Load a clean, dry 2" brush with a very small amount of Alizarin Crimson and use criss-cross strokes to add the Pink glow in the sky, just above the horizon.

Use a clean, dry 2" brush to blend the entire sky area with long, horizontal strokes.

Use the Midnight Black-Prussian Blue mixture and horizontal strokes on the 2" brush to underpaint the snow on the lower portion of the canvas. (Photo 1.)

BACKGROUND

To paint the background evergreens, load the fan brush to a chiseled edge with a mixture of Midnight Black, Prussian Blue, Alizarin Crimson and Titanium White. Holding the brush vertically, touch the canvas to create the center line of each tree. Use just the corner of the brush to begin adding the small top branches. Working from side to side, as you move down each tree, apply more pressure to the brush, forcing the bristles to bend UPWARD and automatically the branches will become larger as you near the base of each tree. (Photo 2.)

Use the 2" brush to firmly tap the base of the evergreens (Photo 3) to diffuse, creating the illusion of mist (Photo 4).

Load the 2" brush with Titanium White and, holding the brush horizontally, use sweeping horizontal strokes to lay in the background snow at the base of the evergreens. (Photo 5.) Pay close attention to the lay-of-the-land. (Photo 6.)

BARN

Use a clean knife to remove paint from the canvas in the basic shape of the barn and sheds. Load the long edge of the knife with a small roll of a mixture of Van Dyke Brown and Dark Sienna by pulling the paint out very flat on your palette and just cutting across. Touch in the back eaves of the roof, then pull down the front and side of the barn. Don't forget to indicate the underside of the large roof. Use the knife and a marbled mixture of Titanium White, Dark Sienna, Van Dyke Brown and a small amount of Alizarin Crimson to highlight the front of the barn. Use more Van Dyke Brown in the mixture for the darker side of the barn. Use pure Van Dyke Brown on the knife to indicate the boards. Pull down snow on the roofs (barn and sheds) with Titanium White. Don't forget to touch snow to the edges of the roofs. Add the door with Van Dyke Brown. Remove any excess paint from the base of the barn with a clean knife. (Photo 7.)

Use Titanium White on the 2" brush to add the snow at the base of the barn. (Photo 8.)

FOREGROUND

Working forward, add the larger evergreens with the fan brush and a mixture of Prussian Blue, Midnight Black, Alizarin Crimson and Van Dyke Brown. (Photo 9.) Apply the snowy highlights to the evergreen branches with a mixture of Liquid White, Titanium White and Phthalo Blue on the fan brush.

Load a clean fan brush with a dark Gray mixture made from Midnight Black, Prussian Blue and Titanium White. Holding the brush horizontally, use short horizontal strokes to lay in the path. For proper perspective, use progressively wider strokes as you work forward. (Photo 10.)

Load the fan brush with Titanium White and, holding the brush horizontally, use sweeping horizontal strokes to lay in the snow at the base of the large evergreens. *(Photo 11.)* (Notice that by allowing the brush to pick up some of the dark tree color, shadows are automatically created in the snow.)

Load the fan brush with the dark Gray mixture and, holding the brush horizontally, punch in the grassy areas in the foreground *(Photo 12)* then lift upward to indicate long grasses, sticks and twigs *(Photo 13)*.

Load a clean fan brush with a mixture of Van Dyke Brown and a small amount of Midnight Black. Holding the brush vertically, touch the canvas at the top of each birch tree and pull straight down to the base of the trunk. *(Photo 14.)* To highlight the right sides of the trunks, load the knife with a very small roll of Titanium White and use curved, short, horizontal strokes. *(Photo 15.)*

Add the smaller limbs and branches to the birch tree using a thin Brown mixture and the liner brush. (To load the liner brush, thin the Brown mixture to an ink-like consistency by first dipping the liner brush into paint thinner. Slowly turn the brush as you pull the bristles through the mixture, forcing them to a sharp point.) Apply very little pressure to the brush, as you shape the limbs and branches. Turn and twist the brush to give the limbs and branches a gnarled appearance. *(Photo 16.)*

FINISHING TOUCHES

Add the long grasses and tiny sticks and twigs to the foreground with thinned Brown on the liner brush *(Photo 17)* and your masterpiece is complete *(Photo 18)*.

Don't forget to sign your name with pride: Again, load the liner brush with thinned color on your choice. Sign just your initials, first name, last name or all of your names. Sign in the left corner, the right corner or one artist signs right in the middle of the canvas! The choice is yours. You might also consider including the date when you sign your painting. Whatever your choices, have fun, for hopefully with this painting you have truly experienced THE JOY OF PAINTING!

In the Midst of Winter

1. Paint the sky with criss-cross strokes and the water with horizontal strokes.

2. Use the fan brush to paint evergreens . . .

3. . . . then tap with the 2" brush . . .

4. . . . to create the illusion of mist.

5. Use horizontal strokes . . .

6. . . . to lay in the snow.

In the Midst of Winter

7. Progressional steps used to paint the barn.

8. Use the 2" brush to add snow to the base of the cabin.

9. Continue adding evergreens . . .

10. . . . and the path with the fan brush.

11. Add snow . . .

12. . . . and punch in grassy areas . . .

13. . . . along the edges of the path.

14. Shape trunks with the fan brush . . .

15. . . . and highlight with the knife.

16. Add branches . . .

17. . . . and long grasses with the liner brush . . .

18. . . . and your painting is ready for a signature!

WILDERNESS WAY

MATERIALS

2" Brush	Midnight Black
#6 Fan Brush	Dark Sienna
#2 Script Liner Brush	Van Dyke Brown
Large Knife	Alizarin Crimson
Black Gesso	Sap Green
Gray Gesso	Cadmium Yellow
Liquid Clear	Yellow Ochre
Titanium White	Indian Yellow
Phthalo Blue	Bright Red

Start by using Gray Gesso (highlight) and Black Gesso (shadow) on a foam applicator to paint the mountain and background shapes. The foreground tree shapes are made with Black Gesso and a natural sponge. Allow the gessos to DRY COMPLETELY before proceeding. (Photo 1.)

When the gessos are dry, use the 2" brush to completely cover the canvas with a VERY THIN coat of Liquid Clear. (It is important to stress that the Liquid Clear should be applied VERY, VERY sparingly and really scrubbed into the canvas! The Liquid Clear will not only ease with the application of the firmer paint, but will allow you to apply very little color, creating a glazed effect.)

SKY

Load the 2" brush with a small amount of Indian Yellow and, working upward from the horizon, begin painting the brilliant sky with criss-cross strokes. Without cleaning the brush, reload it with Yellow Ochre and use criss-cross strokes, just above the Indian Yellow. Still without cleaning the brush, reload it with a small amount of Bright Red (Alizarin Crimson may also be used) and continue painting the sky, still working upward with criss-cross strokes. (Photo 2.)

Use the knife to make a Lavender color on your palette with Alizarin Crimson and a small amount of Phthalo Blue. Reload the 2" brush with this color and continue using criss-cross strokes to paint the uppermost portion of the sky.

Clean and dry the bristles of the 2" brush and load it with a small amount of Titanium White. Paint the brightest area in the sky, working outward from the center of the horizon with criss-cross strokes. (Photo 3.) Blend the sky with long, horizontal strokes on the 2" brush.

BACKGROUND

Use the 2" brush and the Lavender mixture to underpaint the large leafy trees (Photo 4) and the entire lower portion of the canvas (Photo 5).

Load a clean, dry 2" brush with various mixtures of Sap Green, the Yellows and small amounts of Bright Red. Use just the corner of the brush to highlight the small background trees and bushes. (Photo 6.)

Continue using the 2" brush and the same Yellow highlight mixtures to highlight the soft grassy area at the base of the background trees and bushes. Load the 2" brush by holding it at a 45-degree angle and tapping the bristles into the various paint mixtures. Allow the brush to "slide" slightly forward in the paint each time you tap (this assures that the very tips of the bristles are fully loaded with paint). Hold the paint horizontally and gently tap downward. (Photo 7.) Work in layers, carefully creating the lay-of-the-land. If you are also careful not to destroy all of the dark color already on the canvas, you can create grassy highlights that look almost like velvet. (Photo 8.)

FOREGROUND

Load the 2" brush with the Lavender mixture and tap in the basic shapes of the remaining foreground trees. (Photo 9.)

Add the foreground tree trunks with the liner brush and a Gray mixture, made with Titanium White, Van Dyke Brown and Midnight Black. (To load the liner brush, thin the Gray mixture to an ink-like consistency by first dipping the liner brush into paint thinner. Slowly turn the brush as you pull the bristles through the mixture, forcing them to a sharp point.) Apply very little pressure to the brush, as you shape the trunks. (Photo 10.)

Highlight the leaf clusters of the foreground trees, bushes

and foliage with the Green-Yellow-Red highlight colors (small amounts of Phthalo Blue may also be used) on the corner of the 2" brush. *(Photo 11.)* Again, work in layers and concentrate on individual shapes and form. *(Photo 12.)*

The path is made with a mixture of Van Dyke Brown and Dark Sienna on the knife. Pull the mixture out very flat on your palette, hold the knife straight up and "cut" across the mixture to load the long edge of the blade with a small roll of paint. (Holding the knife straight up will force the small roll of paint to the very edge of the blade.) Hold the knife horizontally and use short, horizontal strokes to lay in the path. For proper perspective, use longer horizontal strokes as you extend the path into the very front of the painting. Highlight the path with a mixture of Titanium White, Van Dyke Brown, Dark Sienna and a small amount of Bright Red on the knife. Use so little pressure that the paint "breaks". *(Photo 13.)*

Continue highlighting the small trees, bushes and foliage in the foreground with Green-Yellow-Red on the 2" brush. *(Photo 14.)* Work in layers, carefully shaping individual limbs, branches and leaf clusters. Be very careful not to completely cover the dark undercolor. *(Photo 15.)*

Shape the large birch tree trunks with a small roll of dark Brown on the knife. *(Photo 16.)* Highlight the right sides of the trunks with a small roll of Titanium White on the knife and short, curved horizontal strokes. *(Photo 17.)* Add the smaller limbs and branches with very thin dark Brown on the liner brush. By turning and wiggling the brush, you can give your trunks a gnarled appearance. *(Photo 18.)*

FINISHING TOUCHES

Use a thinned Brown and White mixture on the liner brush to add final, small sticks and twigs in the foreground. Don't forget to sign your finished painting! *(Photo 19.)*

Wilderness Way

1. Use Black and Gray gesso to underpaint the picture.   **2. Paint the sky . . .**   **3. . . . and light source with criss-cross strokes.**   **4. Use the 2" brush . . .**   **5. . . . to underpaint the foreground leaf trees.**

Wilderness Way

6. Highlight background trees . . .

7. . . . and soft grassy areas . . .

8. . . . to complete the background.

9. Underpaint foreground trees . . .

10. . . . then add trunks with the liner brush.

11. Use the corner of the 2" brush . . .

12. . . . to highlight the foreground trees.

13. Paint the path with the knife . . .

14. . . . and add foliage with the 2" brush . . .

15. . . . to the foreground.

16. Shape the tree trunks . . .

17. . . . then apply the highlights with the knife.

18. Add branches with the liner brush . . .

19. . . . to complete the painting.

EVENING'S GLOW

MATERIALS

2" Brush	Dark Sienna
#6 Fan Brush	Van Dyke Brown
#3 Fan Brush	Alizarin Crimson
#2 Script Liner Brush	Sap Green
Large Knife	Cadmium Yellow
Liquid White	Yellow Ochre
Titanium White	Indian Yellow
Midnight Black	Bright Red

Use the 2" brush to cover the entire canvas with a thin, even coat of Liquid White. With long horizontal and vertical strokes, work back and forth to ensure an even distribution of paint on the canvas. Do NOT allow the Liquid White to dry before you begin.

SKY

Load the 2" brush with a very small amount of Indian Yellow to paint the glow in the center of the sky. Reload the brush with Cadmium Yellow and begin working outward from the center with criss-cross strokes. Reload the brush with Yellow Ochre and then Alizarin Crimson, always working outward with criss-cross strokes. Reload the 2" brush with a Brown mixture (made from equal parts of Alizarin Crimson and Sap Green) and continue outward, then use Van Dyke Brown and criss-cross strokes to paint the outside edges of the canvas in the sky area.

Lightly blend the sky with a clean, dry 2" brush, then use a small amount of Titanium White on the brush to brighten the center of the sky. (Photo 1.) Again, lightly blend the sky. You can add a sun to the center of the sky with a small amount of Titanium White on your fingertip. (Photo 2.) Blend the sun with very light criss-cross strokes and a clean, dry 2" brush. (Photo 3.)

BACKGROUND

Use various mixtures of the Brown, Titanium White and Indian Yellow on the 2" brush to tap in the distant hills. (Photo 4.) You can indicate tiny tree tops with very short upward strokes, carefully following the lay-of-the-land. (Photo 5.)

Add background trees with a mixture of Titanium White and the Brown mixture on the small fan brush. Hold the brush vertically and tap downward to paint just the impression of tiny evergreens. (Photo 6.) Use a clean, dry 2" brush to tap the base of the hills, then lift upward to create the illusion of mist. (Photo 7.) Use a mixture of Titanium White and Indian Yellow on the 2" brush to add the grassy area at the base of the trees. (Photo 8.)

This is a good time to underpaint the lower portion of the canvas with the Brown (Alizarin Crimson-Sap Green) mixture. Use the 2" brush and long, horizontal strokes.

Load the knife with a small roll of Titanium White to scrub in the water's edge (Photo 9) at the base of the distant hills (Photo 10).

Use a mixture of the Brown color and Midnight Black on the 2" brush to underpaint the foreground grassy area. Highlight the foreground with various mixtures of Sap Green and all of the Yellows on the 2" brush. Again, paying close attention to the lay-of-the-land (Photo 11) just tap downward to indicate soft grass in the foreground (Photo 12).

EVERGREENS

Load the small fan brush to a chiseled edge with a mixture of Van Dyke Brown, Alizarin Crimson and Midnight Black. Holding the brush vertically, touch the canvas to create the center line of each tree. Use just the corner of the brush to begin adding the small top branches. Working from side to side, as you move down each tree, apply more pressure to the brush, forcing the bristles to bend downward (Photo 13) and automatically the branches will become larger as you near the base of each tree (Photo 14).

Scratch in the indication of tree trunks with the point of the knife, then very lightly touch highlights to the evergreens with a mixture of the Brown, Bright Red and a very small amount of Titanium White on the fan brush.

CABIN

Use a clean knife to remove paint from the canvas in the basic shape of the cabin. Load the long edge of the knife with a small roll of a mixture of Van Dyke Brown and Dark Sienna by pulling the paint out very flat on your palette and just cutting across. Paying close attention to angles, paint the back edge, then the front of the roof. Pull down the front and then the side of the cabin. Use a mixture of Van Dyke Brown and Titanium White to highlight the front and side of the cabin, using so little pressure that the paint "breaks". Use less Titanium White in the mixture to highlight the darker side of the cabin.

Add the door to the cabin with Van Dyke Brown on the knife. Use a mixture of Bright Red, Titanium White and Dark Sienna on the knife to paint the roof. With the knife, remove excess paint to complete the shape of the base of the cabin. *(Photo 15.)*

Use Van Dyke Brown on the fan brush and short horizontal strokes to add the path in the foreground. Pay close attention to perspective; the path is much wider as it comes forward.

Highlight the path with a mixture of Van Dyke Brown and Titanium White on the fan brush. *(Photo 16.)*

Add the indication of tiny sticks and twigs *(Photo 17)* in the foreground *(Photo 18)* with thinned Brown on the liner brush.

Paint the large foreground tree trunks with a mixture of Van Dyke Brown and Midnight Black on the fan brush. *(Photo 19.)* Add limbs and branches to the trunks with thinned Brown on the liner brush. *(Photo 20.)* Highlight the trunks with a thin mixture of Midnight Black and Titanium White on the liner brush.

Use the 2" brush with the Sap Green and Yellows mixture to add soft grass to the base of the foreground trees.

FINISHING TOUCHES

Use thinned mixtures on the liner brush to add tiny sticks and twigs and most importantly, your signature! *(Photo 21.)*

Evening's Glow

1. Paint the sky with the 2" brush . . .

2. . . . then add sun with your finger tip . . .

3. . . . to complete the sky.

4. Tap downward with the 2" brush . . .

5. . . . to add the grassy hills.

6. Use the fan brush to paint tiny background evergreens . . .

7. . . . then firmly tap with the 2" brush . . .

Evening's Glow

8. . . . to create the illusion of mist.

9. With Liquid White on the knife . . .

10. . . . add water lines and ripples.

11. Work forward with grassy hills . . .

12. . . . then highlight with the 2" brush.

13. Use the fan brush . . .

14. . . . to add large foreground evergreens.

15. Progressional steps used to paint the cabin.

16. Add the foreground path with the fan brush.

17. With thinned paint on the liner brush . . .

18. . . . add small sticks and twigs.

19. Pull down the tree trunk with the fan brush . . .

20. . . . then use the liner brush to add limbs and branches . . .

21. . . . and your painting is complete.

FINAL GRACE

This is the painting seen at the beginning of each show, which was beautifully animated by the staff of WIPB-TV. It is one of the most challenging and rewarding paintings in the series.

MATERIALS

2" Brush	Cadmium Yellow
1" Brush	Bright Red
Large Knife	Prussian Blue
Liquid White	Sap Green
18 × 24 Canvas	Phthalo Blue
#6 Fan Brush	Phthalo Green
#2 Script Liner Brush	Titanium White
Alizarin Crimson	Van Dyke Brown

Cover the entire canvas with a thin, even coat of Liquid White using the 2" brush. Work the paint back and forth, up and down, in long horizontal and vertical strokes to cover the canvas evenly. Do not allow the Liquid White to dry before you begin.

SKY AND WATER:

With the large brush loaded with Phthalo Blue and Van Dyke Brown start your sky using criss-cross strokes. Work all the way across the top of the canvas, then downward in layers. Now add a little more Phthalo Blue and a touch of Phthalo Green. Make your water by holding the brush flat and pulling in horizontal strokes from the outside inward, leaving an area open. Use a clean, dry 2" brush to hypnotize the entire canvas. Clouds are a mixture of Prussian Blue, Van Dyke Brown and Alizarin Crimson applied with the top corner of the large brush. Lay in your basic cloud shapes using small, circular strokes. Highlight the clouds with Titanium White and a touch of Bright Red on the fan brush, using just the corner, in tight circular patterns. The top corner of the large brush is used to blend the bottom of the highlights into the darker area. Use long, upward circular strokes to "fluff" the cloud then hypnotize.

MOUNTAINS

The mountains are made with Prussian Blue, Van Dyke Brown and Alizarian Crimson for the base color. Load a small roll of paint on the knife and lay in the basic shape. Work on the most distant mountain first and totally complete it before you start the next one. Scrape off all excess paint and blend downward with the large brush. Highlights are Titanium White applied with the knife. Use a small roll of paint and follow the angles in your basic mountain shape. The shadows are Prussian Blue, Van Dyke Brown and Titanium White pulled in the opposite direction. Use the large brush vertically to tap the bottom of the mountain and create your mist. With the brush flat, lift upward following the angles in the mountain to remove tap marks and soften. The base color of your mountains should get darker as they get closer.

TREES AND BUSHES

The base color for all the trees and bushes is a mixture of equal parts of Prussian Blue, Van Dyke Brown and Sap Green. Indications of distant evergreens are made with the fan brush held vertically and tapped downward. The group area under the distant trees is made with the fan brush held horizontally and pushed into the canvas, moving slightly upward. Use the 2" brush held horizontally to touch just the very bottom of the distant trees and pull straight down to create reflections.

Highlights on the land area are made with the fan brush held horizontally loaded with Liquid White, Sap Green and Cadmium Yellow and pushed into the canvas bending the bristles upward. A small amount of Liquid White, with a touch of Van Dyke Brown, is used on the long edge of the knife to cut in waterlines. Larger evergreens are made with the fan brush held vertically and touched to the canvas to make the center of the tree. Turn the brush horizontally and use one corner to make branches, applying more pressure as you work down the tree. Highlights on these trees are

Liquid White, Cadmium Yellow and Sap Green applied the same way. Load the 2" brush rounding one corner and make your basic tree shapes by pushing into the canvas with the rounded corner up.

Grassy areas are made with the brush held horizontally and pushed into the canvas moving slightly upward. Highlights on leaf trees are a mixture of Liquid White, Cadmium Yellow, Sap Green, and Yellow Ochre. Load a 1" brush to round one corner and, with a rounded corner up, push in your highlights. Grassy areas in the foreground are made as before using the fan brush with Liquid White, Cadmium Yellow and Sap Green.

ROCKS AND STONES

Load a roll of Van Dyke Brown on the edge of the knife and lay in your basic shape. The highlights are a mixture of Van Dyke Brown, Titanium White and a little Prussian Blue. Apply the highlights with the knife using very little pressure allowing the paint to break.

FINISHING TOUCHES

The liner brush, loaded with Van Dyke Brown thinned with a light oil, is used to paint small trees, sticks and limbs. The point of the knife may be used to cut in sticks and twigs. A signature will complete your creation.

1. Initial cloud shapes made with the large brush.

2. Highlight the cloud shapes with the fan brush.

3. Blend together with the top corner of the 2" brush.

4. A roll of paint is used . . .

. . . to lay in the basic mountain shape.

5. First range of mountains completed.

6. Mist is created by tapping the bottom of the mountain.

7. Indication of distant evergreen trees made with the fan brush.

8. Allowing the tree indications to become smaller on one side will create distance.

9. Evergreen made with the fan brush.

10. Pull downward with the large brush to create reflections.

11. Loading the 1" brush . . .

. . . to make and highlight trees and bushes.

Welcome to the Joy of Painting Flowers!

Enjoy these beautiful bonus paintings by Annette Kowalski, lovely floral masterpieces not seen on TV. You can paint them yourself using the popular new Ross Floral Technique, even if you've never painted before!

MARINO'S MAGNOLIAS

by Annette Kowalski

MATERIALS

Bob Ross Brushes:
1" Landscape Brush
#2 Liner Brush
1/2" Floral Brush
Floral Filbert Brush

Bob Ross Supplies:
Liquid Opal
Floral Painting Medium
Odorless Thinner

**Bob Ross Soft Oil
Paints:**
Alizarin Crimson

Cadmium Orange
Cadmium Yellow Light
Flower Pink
Mauve
Sap Green
Titanium White
Turquoise
Ultramarine Blue

Other Supplies:
12" x 24" Canvas
Floral Painting Palette
Soft Paper Towels

One morning, much to my surprise, there appeared outside my large home-office window, a beautiful magnolia tree — in full bloom. It was Mother's Day and I had been presented with one of my favorite flowers — compliments of Marino, the most wonderful son-in-law in the world! I would like to dedicate this painting to him and share these majestic flowers with you.

BACKGROUND

Begin by using the 1" brush to cover the entire canvas with a thin, even coat of Liquid Opal. Without cleaning the brush, use criss-cross strokes to add mixtures of Ultramarine Blue, Turquoise, Mauve and Pink to the background.

With the filbert brush and Sap Green that has been thinned with Painting Medium, lightly sketch the large branch. *(See Progressional Step 1.)*

FOLIAGE

Continue by loosely sketching the placement of two, large magnolias with the filbert brush and Mauve which has been thinned with Painting Medium. Then, again use the 1" brush to underpaint foliage with various mixtures of Ultramarine Blue and Sap Green. *(See Progressional Step 2.)*

With the 1/2" brush, begin shaping the big, dark green leaves nearest the flowers with various mixtures of Ultramarine Blue and Sap Green. *(See Progressional Step 3.)*

UNDERPAINTING THE MAGNOLIAS

Use the 1/2" brush and Titanium White which has been thinned with Painting Medium to very loosely underpaint the two large magnolia blossoms. Allow the brush to pull in the background colors. *(See Progressional Step 4.)*

Use pure Titanium White on the filbert brush to define the four petals of the smaller flower. Add the dark center of the flower with a mixture of Ultramarine Blue and Mauve. *(See Progressional Step 5.)*

HIGHLIGHTING THE MAGNOLIAS

Load the 1/2" brush with Titanium White. Beginning at the outside edge of the petal, use a series of long, overlapping strokes (all directed towards the center of the flower) to shape and highlight the three large back petals of the flower.

Directing all strokes towards the base of the petal, add the three flipped-up petals in the front of the flower, still using Titanium White on the 1/2" brush. *(See Progressional Step 6.)*

Begin painting the large magnolia by using the 1/2" brush to add a dark mixture of Ultramarine Blue and Mauve to the center of the flower. With a clean, dry 1/2" brush, lightly blend the dark color out from the center of the flower. *(See Progressional Step 7.)*

Again, use the filbert brush and Titanium White to lightly sketch the six petals of the large magnolia. With Titanium White on the 1/2" brush and starting at the outside edge, highlight each of the six large petals with a series of overlapping strokes, all directed in towards the center of the flower. *(See Progressional Step 8.)*

Use the filbert brush with Titanium White to add a seventh, turned-up petal on the large magnolia. *(See Progressional Step 9.)*

The turned-up petal is also highlighted with Titanium White on the 1/2" brush and a series of overlapping strokes, all directed towards the base of the petal. Continue using Titanium White and the filbert brush to add the rolled edges to a few of the magnolia petals. *(See Progressional Step 10.)*

Also use the filbert brush to underpaint the large stamens in the center of each of the two flowers with mixtures of Alizarin Crimson, Sap Green and Cadmium Orange. Highlight with dots of Cadmium Yellow. With a mixture of Sap Green and Ultramarine Blue on the 1/2" brush, continue shaping the large branch.

BUDS

Use Titanium White, which has been thinned with painting medium, and the filbert brush to loosely sketch the two large magnolia buds. *(See Progressional Step 11.)*

Use the 1/2" brush and Titanium White to paint the bud petals. Again, start at the outside edge of each petal and direct all strokes to the base of the bud.

FINISHING TOUCHES

Magnolia leaves often have a rust-colored underside. Highlight a few of the leaves with the 1/2" brush and various mixtures of Alizarin Crimson, Cadmium Orange and Cadmium Yellow.

Use the liner brush and various mixtures which have been thinned to a water-like consistency with Painting Medium, to add tendrils, final details and your signature. *(See Progressional Step 12.)*

Marino's Magnolias

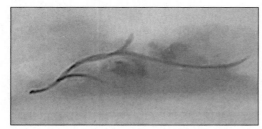

1. With the 1" brush, cover the entire canvas with a thin coat of Liquid Opal. Add mixtures of Blue, Turquoise, Mauve and Pink to the background. Then, use the filbert brush with Green that has been thinned with Painting Medium to lightly sketch the large branch.

2. Loosely sketch the placement of two, large magnolias with the filbert brush and thinned Mauve, then use the 1" brush to underpaint foliage with various mixtures of Blue and Green.

3. Add leaves with the 1/2" brush and various mixtures of Blue and Green.

Marino's Magnolias

4. Underpaint the two flowers with thinned Titanium White and the 1/2" brush, allowing the brush to pull in the background colors.

5. Use White on the filbert brush to define four petals of the smaller flower, then add a mixture of Blue and Mauve to the center of the flower.

6. With White on the 1/2" brush, use a series of long, overlapping strokes (all directed toward the center of the flower) to shape the three large back petals of the flower. Directing all strokes toward the base of the petal, add the three large flipped up petals in the front of the flower, still using White on the 1/2"brush.

7. Use the 1/2" brush to add a dark mixture of Blue and Mauve to the center of the large magnolia.

8. Use white on the 1/2" brush to paint each of the six large petals with a series of overlapping strokes, all directed in toward the center of the flower.

9. Sketch a seventh, turned-up petal on the large magnolia . . .

10. . . . then paint the turned-up petal with a series of overlapping strokes, all directed toward the base of the petal. Use White on the filbert brush to add the rolled edges to a few of the magnolia petals.

11. Continue using the filbert to underpaint large stamens in the center of each of the two flowers with mixtures of Alizarin Crimson, Green and Orange. Highlight with dots of Yellow. Use a mixture of Green and Blue with the 1/2" brush to add the large branch, then use thinned White on the filbert to loosely sketch the two large buds.

12. Again, use the 1/2" brush and White to paint the bud petals. Highlight the leaves with mixtures of Alizarin Crimson, Orange and Yellow. Use the liner brush to add tendrils and your signature.

MIDNIGHT ROSES

by Annette Kowalski

MATERIALS

Bob Ross Brushes:
1" Landscape Brush
#2 Liner Brush
1/2" Floral Brush
Small Round Floral Brush

Bob Ross Supplies:
Floral Painting Medium
Odorless Thinner

Bob Ross Soft Oil Paints:
Alizarin Crimson
Black

Cadmium Red Light
Cadmium Yellow
Flower Pink
Mauve
Sap Green
Titanium White
Turquoise
Ultramarine Blue

Other Supplies:
18" x 24" Canvas
Floral Painting Palette
Soft Paper Towels

To me, painting flowers is just a fantasy, like painting jewels in the moonlight. I love flowers on a black background, and these midnight roses simply sparkle against the mystical darkness.

BACKGROUND

Begin by using the small round brush with a very thin mixture of Floral Painting Medium and Alizarin Crimson to lightly sketch the placement of the large roses and rose bud.

With the 1" brush and loose criss-cross strokes, add the dark background with various mixtures of Painting Medium, Alizarin Crimson and Black. Add a small amount of Cadmium Red Light to the lightest area and a very small amount of Turquoise and Mauve to the shadow areas of the background.

Use the 1/2" brush and loose criss-cross strokes to begin underpainting the foliage with various mixtures of Sap Green and Ultramarine Blue, thinning the paint with Floral Painting Medium as necessary. *(See Progressional Step 1.)*

UNDERPAINTING THE ROSES

Underpaint the Yellow rose with the 1/2" brush and a thin mixture of Painting Medium and Cadmium Yellow Light blended with a small amount of Sap Green. Use long, loose, flowing strokes, allowing the brush to pull in the rich background colors, creating the shadowed areas of the rose. *(See Progressional Step 2.)*

The deep center of the Yellow rose is added with a very small amount of dry (no Painting Medium) Alizarin Crimson, then blended out in the direction the rose is facing. *(See Progressional Step 3.)*

Underpaint the White rose with a thin mixture of Titanium White and Black, again allowing the background colors to blend with the rose. Again, try not to make tight, little balls — use long, loose, flowing strokes. The center of the White rose is added with a mixture of Alizarin Crimson and Cadmium Yellow Light. *(See Progressional Step 4.)*

Underpaint the half-open rose with various mixtures of Flower Pink and Cadmium Yellow Light. The shadowed areas are added with Alizarin Crimson. *(See Progressional Step 5.)*

The Red rose is underpainted with Alizarin Crimson. The light center is added with a very small amount of Cadmium Red Light. *(See Progressional Step 6.)*

HIGHLIGHTING THE ROSES

You may find it helpful to first loosely sketch each rose petal with thinned Titanium White and the small round floral brush. Highlight the White rose petals by loading the 1/2" brush to a chiseled edge with Titanium White. To define and highlight each of the White rose petals, start at the outside edge of the petal and direct a series of overlapping strokes in towards the center of the flower. Keep the strokes loose and flowing and again, allow the brush to pull in the surrounding colors, creating the illusion of transparency. *(See Progressional Step 7.)*

Continue by highlighting the Yellow rose with the 1/2" brush and a mixture of Cadmium Yellow and Titanium White. The half-open rose is highlighted with Flower Pink, Titanium White and Cadmium Yellow Light. Use a very small amount of Cadmium Red Light to add subtle highlights to the Red rose. *(See Progressional Step 8.)*

FINISHING TOUCHES

Use the small round brush with thinned Alizarin Crimson to add stamens to the center of the roses. Highlight the leaves with the 1/2" brush and various mixtures of Cadmium Yellow Light, Sap Green, Mauve, Turquoise and Titanium White. Shape tiny rose buds with the 1/2" brush. With the liner brush, use very thin mixtures to add stems, twigs, tiny details and most importantly, your signature. Happy Painting! *(See Progressional Step 9.)*

Midnight Roses

1. Use the small round brush to lightly sketch the roses. With the 1" brush, add the background with various mixtures of Alizarin Crimson and Black. Add small amounts of Cadmium Red Light, Turquoise and Mauve. Paint leaves with a mixture of Sap Green and Ultramarine Blue.

2. Underpaint the Yellow rose with the 1/2" brush and a thin mixture of Painting Medium and Cadmium Yellow Light blended with a small amount of Sap Green.

3. The deep center of the rose is added with a very small amount of Alizarin Crimson, then blended out in the direction the rose is facing.

Midnight Roses

4. Underpaint the White rose with a thin mixture of Titanium White and Black, again allowing the background colors to blend with the rose. The center of the rose is added with a mixture of Alizarin Crimson and Cadmium Yellow Light.

5. Underpaint the half-open rose with various mixtures of Flower Pink and Cadmium Yellow Light. The shadowed areas are Alizarin Crimson.

6. The Red rose is underpainted with Alizarin Crimson. Add the light center with Cadmium Red Light.

7. Load the 1/2" brush to a chiseled edge with Titanium White. To define and highlight each of the White rose petals, start at the outside edge of the petal and direct a series of overlapping strokes in towards the center of the flower.

8. Highlight the Yellow rose with a mixture of Cadmium Yellow Light and Titanium White and the half-open rose with Flower Pink, Titanium White and Cadmium Yellow Light. Use Cadmium Red Light to add subtle highlights to the Red rose.

9. Use Alizarin Crimson to add stamens to the center of the roses, then highlight the leaves with Cadmium Yellow Light. Add tiny rose buds, stems and twigs. Use the liner brush with a very thin mixture of Painting Medium and the color of your choice to sign your Happy Painting!

TROPICAL FANTASY

by Annette Kowalski

MATERIALS

Bob Ross Brushes:
1" Landscape Brush
#2 Liner Brush
3/4" Floral Brush
1/2" Floral Brush
Floral Filbert Brush
Small Round Floral Brush

Bob Ross Supplies:
Liquid Opal
Floral Painting Medium
Odorless Thinner

Bob Ross Soft Oil Paints:
Alizarin Crimson
Cadmium Red Light
Cadmium Yellow
Mauve
Sap Green
Titanium White
Turquoise
Ultramarine Blue

Other Supplies:
18" x 24" Canvas
Floral Painting Palette
Soft Paper Towels

The hibiscus is a large, dramatic flower that grows in many colors. Try painting this Tropical Fantasy in Yellow, Orange, Pink or White.

BACKGROUND

Start by using a very thin mixture of Painting Medium and Mauve on the small round brush to loosely sketch the flower and foliage placement on your canvas. Allowing the flower to remain dry and unpainted, use the 1" landscape brush to cover the background with a thin, even coat of Liquid Opal. (See Progressional Step1.)

Continue using the 1" brush and loose criss-cross strokes to underpaint the foliage with various mixtures of Sap Green, Ultramarine Blue and a small amount of Turquoise. (See Progressional Step 2.)

Starting at the top of the canvas and working downward, use the 1/2" and 3/4" brushes to add long, tapered leaves with mixtures of Sap Green, Ultramarine Blue, Turquoise, Mauve and Titanium White.

To paint tapered leaves, begin by loading the brush to a chiseled edge. Start at the base of the leaf with the chiseled edge of the brush and paint a fine line or stem. Turn the brush to its flat side to paint the length of the leaf, then return the brush to its chiseled edge to paint the long tapered end of the leaf. Paint single large tapered leaves or clusters of small tapered leaves.

Add basic leaves with various mixtures of Painting Medium, Sap Green, Ultramarine Blue, Mauve and Turquoise and Titanium White. Start by sketching the leaf with the small round brush. Use the 1/2" brush or the 3/4" brush and loose, criss-cross strokes to paint the center of the leaf. Reload the brush to a chiseled edge and angle a series of overlapping strokes from the outside edge of the leaf in towards the center of the leaf. Complete one side of the leaf, then repeat for the second side of the leaf. (See Progressional Step 3.)

UNDERPAINTING THE FLOWER

Use a very thin mixture of Painting Medium and Mauve with the 1/2" brush to loosely underpaint the flower. Try not to paint a perfect, hard circle. Work quickly, keeping your strokes loose and flowing, creating an uneven shape with soft, ruffled edges. *(This step is very important to this technique!) (See Progressional Step 4.)*

When you are satisfied with your flower shape, clean and dry the brush with a soft paper towel and reload it with dry (no Medium) Alizarin Crimson to indicate the placement of five hibiscus petals. *(See Progressional Step 5.)*

Continue by placing a mixture of Alizarin Crimson and Cadmium Red Light in the center of the flower. *(See Progressional Step 6.)*

Again, clean the brush with a soft paper towel and use it to fan the dark color out in the direction that the flower is facing. *(See Progressional Step 7.)*

HIGHLIGHTING THE FLOWER

Load a clean, dry 1/2" brush with a mixture of a small amount of Painting Medium and Titanium White. The bristles of the brush must be carefully groomed and very smooth! Highlight the flower, one petal at a time. Place the carefully loaded brush at the outer edge of the first petal, just *outside* the sketch. Apply pressure and slowly stroke in towards the center of the flower, releasing pressure as you near the dark flower center. Reloading the brush as necessary, continue by fanning a series of overlapping strokes around each of the four lower petals, being very careful to keep the outside edges of each petal loose and ruffly. *(See Progressional Step 8.)*

Use the 1/2" brush with Titanium White to establish the base of the fifth petal with a single, curved stroke. *(See Progressional Step 9.)*

Highlight the fifth, turned-up petal with the 1/2" brush and a series of overlapping strokes. *(See Progressional Step 10.)*

STAMEN

Use the filbert brush with thinned Alizarin Crimson to paint a long stamen in the center of the flower. Then use the liner brush with thinned Alizarin Crimson to add tiny stems and dots on the end of the stamen. *(See Progressional Step 11.)* Highlight the stamen with the small round brush and a mixture of Cadmium Yellow and Titanium White.

FINISHING TOUCHES

Use the 1/2" brush to add additional highlights and ruffles to the flower, then use the liner brush to paint tendrils, stems and your signature. *(See Progressional Step 12.)*

Tropical Fantasy

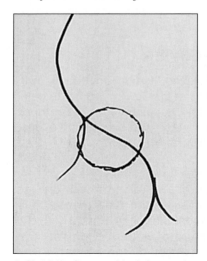

1. Sketch the flower and leaf placement.

2. Add Liquid Opal to background and underpaint the foliage.

3. Add long, tapered leaves and basic leaves to the background.

4. Underpaint the flower with thinned Mauve.

Tropical Fantasy

5. Indicate the placement of the five hibiscus petals.

6. Add Alizarin Crimson to the center of the flower . . .

7. . . . then blend the color out from the center.

8. Highlight the four large lower petals.

9. Establish the base of the fifth petal . . .

10. . . . before highlighting the fifth, turned-back petal.

11. Use the filbert brush to paint the long stamen.

12. Additional highlights and ruffles can be added before signing your painting.

POT O' POSIES

by Annette Kowalski

Annette Kowalski

Flowers are a passionate form of delicate natural beauty; painting them is the most requested "new technique" by Bob Ross fanatics. Now Annette Kowalski's thirty-year love affair with floral painting comes alive in the new Ross Floral Painting Technique.

The artist is publishing a new Ross Floral book containing more paintings like "Pot o' Posies". And like Bob's "Joy of" method, the easy format promises to lead painters quite naturally into florals (with startling results), even if it's a first painting.

MATERIALS

1" Brush	Soft Alizarin Crimson
2" Soft Blender Brush	Soft Sap Green
1/2" Soft Flat Brush	Soft Mauve
Soft Filbert Brush	Soft Orange
#2 Script Liner Brush	Soft Pink
Painting Medium	Soft Red
Odorless Paint Thinner	Soft Light Red
12x24 Canvas	Soft Turquoise
Black Gesso	Soft Yellow
Soft Black	Soft White
Soft Ultra Blue	

Start by using a foam applicator to apply Black Gesso to the entire canvas and allow to DRY COMPLETELY. When the Black Gesso is dry, use the 1" brush to completely cover the canvas with a VERY THIN coat of Painting Medium.

With a very small amount of Alizarin Crimson on the filbert brush, begin by loosely sketching the hanging pot containing two slightly oval, flower shapes. *(Photo 1.)*

Load the 1" brush by tapping the bristles into a very small amount of Red. Use loose criss-cross strokes to apply just a suggestion of color to the background above the flowers and below the pot. Blend lightly with the soft blender brush.

CLAY POT

Load the 1/2" brush with a very dark Brown mixture made from equal parts of Alizarin Crimson and Sap Green and use loose criss-cross strokes to paint the darkest area of the clay pot. *(Photo 2.)* The light in this painting is coming from the right, so the left side, the bottom and a small portion of the right side of the pot should be very dark.

Reload the 1/2" brush with a mixture of Red and Orange and again use loose criss-cross strokes to add the middle value of the pot. *(Photo 3.)* Clean the brush with a soft paper towel and apply Yellow to the center lightest area of the pot. *(Photo 4.)* Clean the 1/2" brush and use criss-cross strokes to lightly blend one value into the other. Lightly blend the clay pot with the 1" brush *(Photo 5)* then add the reflected light on the left side with a mixture of Turquoise and Mauve on the 1/2" brush *(Photo 6).*

UNDERPAINTING

Use Sap Green and Ultra Blue on the 1/2" brush and loose criss-cross strokes to underpaint the foliage areas. *(Photo 7.)*

Carefully shape the lip of the pot with the Red-Orange mixture and highlight with Yellow. *(Photo 8.)*

With a very small amount of Alizarin Crimson on the 1/2" brush, very loosely underpaint the two flower shapes. This underpainting should be very thin; if necessary, add a small amount of Medium or paint thinner when loading the brush. *(Photo 9.)*

LEAVES

When painting leaves or flowers it is important to always load your brush to a chiseled edge; carefully smoothing the paint into the bristles. Load the ½" brush with a mixture of Sap Green and Ultra Blue. Carefully shape a few leaves, right over the underpainting. Paint each leaf with a series of strokes which start at the outside edge of each leaf and angle back towards the base (stem end) of the leaf. *(Photo 10.)* The leaves should be very dark at this point. Place a few leaves under the flowers, a couple above the flowers and several cascading down the right side of the painting. Again, avoid covering the lip of the pot; we need it to attach our hanging cord! *(Photo 11.)*

Touch a few highlights to the edges of the leaves with a mixture of Turquoise and Mauve, on the dark shadowed side of the pot. *(Photo 12.)* Use a mixture of Yellow and Sap Green to highlight some of the leaves on the right side of the pot.

FLOWERS

Use the ½" brush to add the deep shadowed areas of the flower-centers with a mixture of Ultra Blue, Alizarin Crimson and Mauve, extending the color out from the center in the direction that the flower is facing. Also add some of this dark shadow color to the area just below the cup of each flower. *(Photo 13.)*

Load a clean ½" brush by carefully smoothing Red into the bristles. Starting at the outside edge of each petal, and directing each stroke towards the center of the flower, make a series of long, smooth strokes to shape each petal. *(Photo 14.)* Vary the length of the strokes, keeping the edges of the petals ruffly. *(Photo 15.)* Carefully shape each of the two flowers and use the blender brush to very lightly smooth out any harsh areas of paint. *(Photo 16.)*

Additional highlights can be added to the edges of a few of the petals with Light Red.

CORDS

Use Black to paint the three cords from which the clay pot is suspended. Add a little knot under the lip of the pot, then carefully curve the cord around the contour of the pot. Paint a large knot at the base of the pot and underpaint the tassel. *(Photo 17.)*

BUDS

Underpaint the buds with very loose strokes using a mixture of Medium and Alizarin Crimson on the ½" brush. *(Photo 18.)* Add the dark centers with Mauve. Again, shape the petals with Red and highlight with a small amount of Light Red. *(Photo 19.)*

Highlight the cord with tiny curved strokes using a mixture of Brown, Orange and White on the filbert brush. *(Photo 20.)*

Use the filbert brush to tap dark dots in the center of the posies with Black and Mauve. Use the chiseled edge of the flat brush to pull out individual, long stamens. Add dots of Pink and Yellow to highlight the stamens. *(Photo 21.)*

DAISIES

Use a mixture of Pink and White on the filbert brush to add the daisies. *(Photo 22.)* Add the centers with dots of Alizarin Crimson.

FINISHING TOUCHES

Add long flowing strings to the tassel with Painting Medium, Brown, Orange and White on the liner brush. *(Photo 23.)*

Use Sap Green and Yellow on the filbert brush to wrap a leaf around one of the top cords. *(Photo 24.)* Use the liner brush to add the most important final detail, your signature! *(Photo 25.)*

Pot O' Posies

1. Loosely sketch the clay pot and flowers.

2. Add the dark value to the pot . . .

3. . . . then add the middle value . . .

4. . . . and finally the light value.

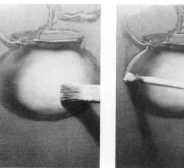
5. Blend the pot with the 1" brush . . .

6. . . . before adding the reflected light.

7. Use the flat brush to underpaint foliage.

Pot O' Posies

     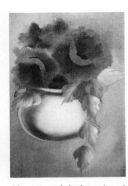

8. Add the rim of the pot . . .

9. . . . then underpaint the flowers.

10. Use the soft flat brush . . .

11. . . . to carefully shape the leaves.

12. Add highlights to the leaves . . .

13. . . . and dark centers to the flowers.

14. Make long smooth strokes . . .

15. . . . to paint the flower petals . . .

16. . . . then blend lightly with the blender brush.

17. Use the filbert brush to begin painting the cords.

18. Underpaint the buds with loose strokes . . .

19. . . . then add dark centers and highlight the petals.

20. Use the filbert brush to highlight the cords . . .

21. . . . and the stamens . . .

22. . . . and to add the daisies.

23. Paint the long flowing cords with the liner brush . . .

24. . . . then wrap a leaf around the cord . . .

25. . . . to complete your Pot O' Posies!

HYDRANGEAS IN TALAVERA

by Annette Kowalski

MATERIALS

Bob Ross Brushes:
1" Brush
#2 Liner Brush
1/2" Floral Brush
Floral Filbert Brush

Optional Bob Ross Brushes:
2" Soft Blender Brush

Bob Ross Supplies:
Black Gesso
Gray Gesso
White Gesso
Floral Painting Medium
Odorless Thinner

Bob Ross Soft Oil Paints:
Alizarin Crimson
Black
Cadmium Yellow Light
Floral Pink
Mauve
Sap Green
Titanium White
Turquoise
Ultramarine Blue

Other Supplies:
18" x 24" Canvas
Foam Applicator

This painting is dedicated to all of my Mexican friends. Many years ago, while visiting Mexico, we painted hydrangeas in Mexican pottery which is called Talavera. This book would not be complete without including that painting.

To begin this painting, you must first underpaint the Mexican pot with a small foam applicator and three values of gesso. The light source in the painting is on the right side. Paint the left side of the pot, the bottom of the post and the top of the pot with a dark value made from a mixture of Gray and Black Gesso. The middle value of the pot is painted with Gray Gesso. The lightest area of the pot is painted with a mixture of Gray and White Gesso. Blend lightly to merge the values. Allow the gesso to dry completely before proceeding. *(See Progressional Step 1.)*

When the gesso is dry, use the filbert brush and a very thin mixture of Painting Medium and Ultramarine Blue to loosely sketch the flower placement.

BACKGROUND

To paint the background, use the 1" brush and criss-cross strokes. Use a mixture of Painting Medium, Ultramarine Blue, Sap Green and Black on the left side of the pot and below the pot. Working up the right side of the canvas, use less Black in the mixture. Continuing across the top of the canvas, add Titanium White to the mixture to paint the upper left side of the background. Add a small amount of light, sneaking out from behind the right side of the pot with a mixture of Cadmium Yellow and Titanium White. Use a clean, dry 1" brush or the 2" soft blender brush to lightly blend the entire background.

Use the 1/2" brush to "paint" the gessoed pot with a very small amount of Painting Medium.

UNDERPAINTING FOLIAGE

Add the indication of dark foliage areas between the flowers with the 1/2" brush and a mixture of Sap Green and Ultramarine Blue. *(See Progressional Step 2.)*

It may be helpful at this stage to lightly sketch the placement of individual leaves with the filbert brush and a very thin mixture of painting medium and Sap Green. Use the 1/2" brush and various mixtures of Sap Green and Ultramarine Blue to underpaint the leaves.

UNDERPAINTING THE FLOWERS

Underpaint the flowers with the 1/2" brush and loose criss-cross strokes. Use various mixtures of Titanium White with Ultramarine Blue, Turquoise and Mauve and Alizarin Crimson which have all been thinned with Painting Medium. Vary the mixtures, allowing your brush to pull in some of the surrounding foliage colors; these flowers can sometimes be quite Green. *(See Progressional Step 3.)*

To complete the foliage, paint individual leaves by reloading the 1/2" brush with a mixture of Sap Green and Ultramarine Blue, grooming the bristles until they are very smooth. Starting at the base of each leaf, angle the first stroke from the outside edge back towards the stem and center of the leaf. Reload the brush to a chiseled edge, and working towards the tip of the leaf, continue angling a series of overlapping strokes until you have completed one side of the leaf. Try to keep the edges of the leaf uneven by varying the length of your strokes.

Again, reload the brush to a chiseled edge. Starting at the base of the leaf, and working towards the tip, repeat for the second side of the leaf. Use the chiseled edge of the brush to "cut" in the center vein, from the base of the leaf to the tip.

Highlight some of the leaves by overpainting with a dry mixture of Mauve and Titanium White.

HIGHLIGHTING THE FLOWERS

Hydrangeas are big ball-shaped clusters of tiny florets, each consisting of four petals. As with any round object, they are painted with light, medium and dark values. Create these values by adjusting the amount of White used in the various mixtures. When painting cluster flowers, most of the petals are just suggested; the lighter petals are more distinct.

Use the filbert brush and various mixtures of Titanium White, Ultramarine Blue, Turquoise and Mauve to highlight the hydrangeas by painting groupings of a few individual petals. As you work into the dark area of the flowers, paint just the indication of petals. If desired, you can blend these dark areas with the 2" soft blender brush.

FINISHING THE POT

Now comes the fun part! Use the liner brush with a very thin mixture of Painting Medium and Ultramarine Blue to add the design to the pot.

FINISHING TOUCHES

Add small florets to the base of the pot with the various flower mixtures and again, highlight individual petals with Titanium White and the filbert brush.

Add stems and twigs with thinned foliage color on liner brush. The small filler leaves are pressed onto the canvas with the 1/2" brush and mixtures of Sap Green and Ultramarine Blue and Titanium White and Mauve. Add tiny centers to some of the florets with thinned Yellow on the filbert or liner brush. *(See Progressional Step 4.)*

Hydrangeas in Talavera

1. Start by using the foam applicator to underpaint the pot with three values of Gray Gesso. Blend lightly. Allow the Gesso to dry completely before proceeding.

2. Paint the background with a mixture of Sap Green, Ultramarine Blue and Black. Add Titanium White to the upper left corner and a mixture of Cadmium Yellow and Titanium White on the lower right side of the pot. Block in the dark foliage areas between the flowers with mixtures of Sap Green and Ultramarine Blue.

3. Underpaint the leaves with a mixture of Sap Green and Ultramarine Blue. Underpaint the flowers with thin mixtures of Titanium White, Ultramarine Blue, Turquoise and Mauve.

4. Use the 3/4" brush and Sap Green, Ultramarine Blue, Mauve and Titanium White to complete the leaves. Highlight the flowers with the filbert brush and Titanium White blended with the various flower mixtures. Use the liner brush to paint the design on the pot with thinned Ultramarine Blue, and to add stems and twigs with foliage color. Add the tiny flower centers with thinned Yellow and Alizarin Crimson on the filbert brush.

BOB ROSS AMARYLLIS IN A DUTCH POT

by Annette Kowalski

MATERIALS

Bob Ross Brushes:
1" Brush
#2 Liner Brush
1/2" Floral Brush

Bob Ross Soft Oil Paints:
Alizarin Crimson
Cadmium Red Medium
Cadmium Orange
Cadmium Yellow
Sap Green
Titanium White
Turquoise
Ultramarine Blue

Bob Ross Supplies:
Black Gesso

Gray Gesso
White Gesso
Painting Medium
Odorless Thinner

Other Supplies:
12" x 24" Canvas
Foam Applicator
Water Paint Brushes
Masking Tape
Floral Painting Palette
Soft Paper Towels

Optional:
Krylon Spray Paint
(Turquoise)
Dressmaker's Tracing Paper
(White)

You'll have fun painting the little Delft pot that holds this lovely Bob Ross Amaryllis in the window. This is traditional earthenware originating in Delft, Holland and is almost always done in blue and white with tiny windmills, houses and other Dutch scenery. While you're painting his memorial flower, remember that Bob Ross has signed each petal with his signature brush and red paint. Enjoy the "Bob Ross Amaryllis in a Dutch Pot!"

CANVAS PREPARATION

Start by using a foam applicator to coat the entire canvas with a thin, even coat of Black Gesso and allow to dry completely. Apply strips of masking tape to the dry canvas to create a 2"

border and diamond-shaped window panes. (Optional: At this time you can spray the canvas very lightly with Krylon Turquoise spray paint.) *(See Progressional Step 1.)*

When the canvas is dry, carefully remove the masking tape. Loosely sketch the amaryllis with White Gesso and a small water-paint brush. Or, use dressmaker's tracing paper to transfer the design onto your prepared canvas. *(See Progressional Step 2.)*

Continue using water-paint brushes to underpaint the blossoms and the pot with shades of White and Gray Gessoes. Use Black Gesso to add the stem and Delft design on the pot. Allow the canvas to DRY COMPLETELY. *(See Progressional Step 3.)*

BACKGROUND

Use the 1" brush to cover the entire canvas with a very, very thin coat of Painting Medium. With various thin mixtures of Painting Medium, Ultramarine Blue, Sap Green, Turquoise and Titanium White, continue using the 1" brush to add the background colors. (Optional: Droplets of paint thinner sprayed on the background will create a mottled, glass effect.) *(See Progressional Step 4.)*

FLOWERS

Use the 1/2" brush to overpaint the amaryllis blossoms with Titanium White and Painting Medium. Add the shadowed areas with mixtures of Ultramarine Blue and Sap Green and very small amounts of Turquoise. Blend lightly with a clean, dry 1/2" brush.

Add the stem (and optional leaves) with the 1/2" brush and a mixture of Painting Medium, Sap Green and Ultramarine Blue. Add a small amount of Titanium White near the base of the stem.

The bulb at the base of the stem is a Dark Brown mixture made from equal portions of Alizarin Crimson and Sap Green.

DELFT POT

Use a very thin mixture of Ultramarine Blue and Painting Medium on the 1/2" brush to glaze (overpaint) the pot. Add a single highlight to the pot with dry Titanium White on the 1/2" brush. *(See Progressional Step 5.)*

HIGHLIGHTS

With a very clean, dry 1/2" brush, add final highlights to each petal with pure Titanium White, directing each stroke from the outside edge of the petal in towards the center of the flower.

Highlight the stem (and optional leaves) with the 1/2" brush and Cadmium Yellow. Highlight the bulb with Cadmium Orange.

Use very thin mixtures of Sap Green and Titanium White on the liner brush to add the stamens. The tips of the stamens are dots of Cadmium Orange.

With Cadmium Orange on the 1/2" brush, apply highlights to the bulb at the base of the flower.

FINISHING TOUCHES

Use a very, very thin mixture of Painting Medium and Cadmium Red on the liner brush to outline each petal.

Bob signed each petal, now your painting is ready for your signature! Again, use very thinned color on the liner brush. (Don't forget to add a tiny bird!) *(See Progressional Step 6.)*

Bob Ross Amaryllis in a Dutch Pot

1. Paint the entire canvas with Black Gesso and allow to dry completely. Apply masking tape then spray lightly with Turquoise spray paint.

2. Remove the masking tape and use white transfer paper to sketch the Amaryllis, the pot and the Delft design on the pot.

3. Use various shades of Black, White and Gray Gesso to underpaint the flower and pot. Paint the Delft design on the pot with Black Gesso and dry completely.

4. Add the background with Painting Medium, Green, Blue, Turquoise and White.

Bob Ross Amaryllis in a Dutch Pot

5. Overpaint the flower with shades of White, Blue, Green and Turquoise. The stem is a mixture of Green and Blue. Glaze the pot with a very thin mixture of Blue and Painting Medium.

6. Edge the petals with Red. Add stamens and other final highlights and details and your painting is ready for a signature.

BOB ROSS PRODUCTIONS

**Proudly Presents
The Bob Ross Art-Video Series**

PAINTING FOR EVERYONE

Shown below are some of the colorful art projects available on video cassette. These professionally-produced instructional videos feature outstanding artists, including Bob Ross and Dorothy Dent, teaching you to paint, easily and quickly, with detailed step-by-step directions and demonstrations. Each modestly-priced one-hour tape is packed with close-up detail and leads you to the completion of a beautiful painting in a variety of styles and methods.

New titles are continually being added. Ask for our FREE Color Brochure showing all of the projects available in the Bob Ross Art-Video Series and information on how to obtain further savings when purchasing combination videos.

**BR-01
"Peace Offerings of Summer"**

**BR-02
"Winter Glory"**

**BR-03
"Grandeur of Summer"**

**BR-04
"Autumn Stream"**

**BR-05
"Winter Harmony"**

**BR-06
"Winter Nocturne"
(black canvas)**

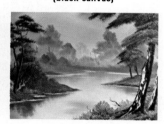

**BR-07
"Seascape with Lighthouse"**

**BR-08
"Times Past"**

**BR-09
"Summer Reflections"**

In addition to the nine Bob Ross videos above, there has been added this exciting new workshop tape.

NEW!!! YOUR PRIVATE CLASSROOM WITH BOB ROSS!!!

Presented in Bob Ross' own warm and patient style, this 3-hour video workshop graphically answers all of the questions you've been asking about the "wet-on-wet" technique. Bob covers, in great detail, the basics of Skies, Mountains, Trees, Water, Reflections, etc. In the final segment of this video, Bob helps you "assemble" all of the component parts into a finished painting. In the process, he anticipates the problems which you are most likely to encounter and provides you with clear, understandable solutions. An absolute "must have" video.

**BRW-001
"Bob Ross Workshop"**